WALKING THE LAKE DISTRICT FELLS

WASDALE

THE SCAFELLS, GREAT GABLE, PILLAR

MARK RICHARDS

CICERONE

Second edition 2019
ISBN: 978 1 78631 031 6

Originally published as Lakeland Fellranger, 2011
ISBN: 978 1 85284 544 5

Printed in China on behalf of Latitude Press Ltd
A catalogue record for this book is available from the British Library.
All photographs are by the author unless otherwise stated.
All artwork is by the author.

Maps are reproduced with permission from HARVEY Maps, www.harveymaps.co.uk

Updates to this Guide

While every effort is made by our authors to ensure the accuracy of guidebooks as they go to print, changes can occur during the lifetime of an edition. Any updates that we know of for this guide will be on the Cicerone website (www.cicerone.co.uk/1031/updates), so please check before planning your trip. We also advise that you check information about such things as transport, accommodation and shops locally. Even rights of way can be altered over time. We are always grateful for information about any discrepancies between a guidebook and the facts on the ground, sent by email to updates@cicerone.co.uk or by post to Cicerone, Juniper House, Murley Moss, Oxenholme Road, Kendal, LA9 7RL.

Register your book: To sign up to receive free updates, special offers and GPX files where available, register your book at www.cicerone.co.uk.

Front cover: Great Gable from Haystacks

Title page: Pinnacles on Lingmell

CONTENTS

Great Gable from Kirk Fell

Key to route maps and topos

Route on a defined path

Route on an intermittent or undefined path

12 **Starting point**

4 **Route number** (on topos)

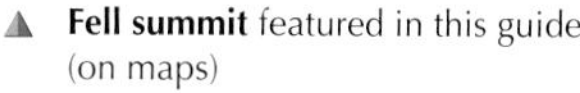

Fell summit featured in this guide (on maps)

Fell summit featured in this guide (on maps)

3 **Route number** (on maps)

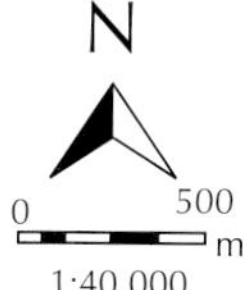

Harvey map legend

Lake, small tarn, pond

River, footbridge

Wide stream

Narrow stream

Peat hags

Marshy ground

Contours change from brown to grey where the ground is predominantly rocky outcrops, small crags and other bare rock.

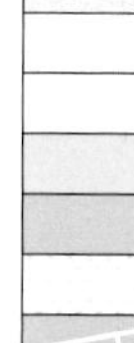
Improved pasture

Rough pasture

Fell or moorland

Open forest or woodland

Dense forest or woodland

Felled or new plantation

Forest ride or firebreak

Settlement

Boundary, maintained

Boundary, remains

On moorland, walls, ruined walls and fences are shown. For farmland, only the outer boundary wall or fence is shown.

Contour (15m interval)

Index contour (75m interval)

Auxiliary contour

Scree, spoil heap

Boulder field

Scattered rock and boulders

Predominantly rocky ground

Major crag, large boulder

O.S. trig pillar, large cairn

Spot height (from air survey)

Dual carriageway

Main road (fenced)

Minor road (unfenced)

Track or forest road

Footpath or old track

Intermittent path

Long distance path

Powerline, pipeline

Building, ruin or sheepfold, shaft

The representation of a road, track or footpath is no evidence of the existence of a right of way.

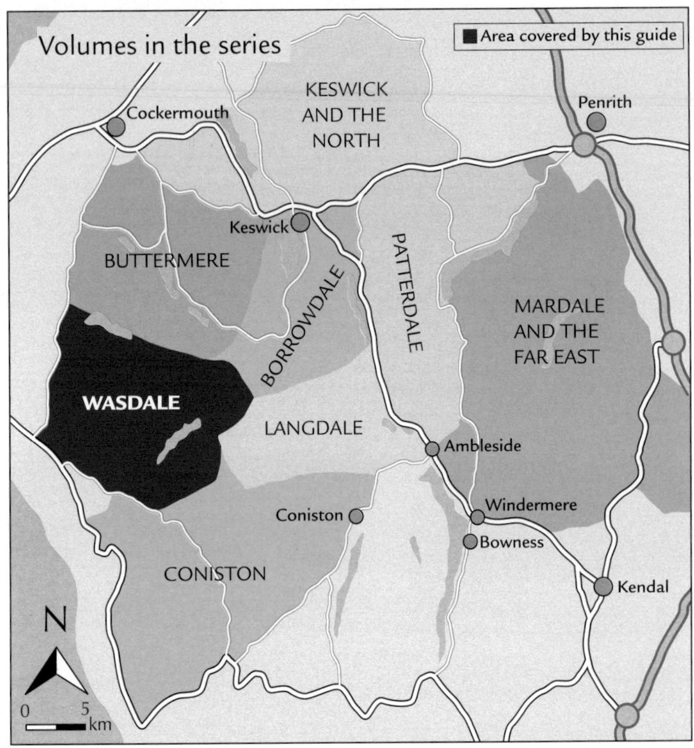
Volumes in the series
Area covered by this guide
Cockermouth
KESWICK AND THE NORTH
Penrith
Keswick
BUTTERMERE
BORROWDALE
PATTERDALE
MARDALE AND THE FAR EAST
WASDALE
LANGDALE
Ambleside
Windermere
Coniston
Bowness
CONISTON
Kendal
N
0
5
km

Stone circle on Eskdale Moor (photo: Andrew Leaney)

Styhead Tarn from Windy Gap

STARTING POINTS

Location			GR NY...	Access	Ascents described from here
1	Wasdale Head Village Green	lots of rough parking (but fills up in season)	186 085	FP	Great End, Great Gable, Kirk Fell, Lingmell, Pillar, Red Pike, Scafell Pike, Scoat Fell, Yewbarrow
2	Wasdale Head	NT car park	183 075	NT	Great How, Illgill Head, Lingmell, Scafell, Scafell Pike
3	Overbeck Bridge	small car park on N of road	168 068	FP	Red Pike, Yewbarrow
4	Netherbeck Bridge	small off-road parking area on N of road	162 065	FP	Haycock, Red Pike, Scoat Fell, Seatallan
5	Goat Gill	small off-road parking areas on both sides	157 061	FP	Middle Fell
6	Greendale	large off-road parking area on E edge of village	144 056	FP	Buckbarrow, Middle Fell, Seatallan
7	Nether Wasdale (Forest Bridge)	small car park at Cinderdale Bridge	128 038	FP	Whin Rigg
8	Nether Wasdale	kerbside parking in the village	125 041	FP	Buckbarrow
9	Harrow Head	small off-road parking area on N of road	127 055	FP	Buckbarrow, Haycock, Seatallan
10	Blengdale Forest	roadside parking just S of the forest entrance	085 053	FP	Caw Fell
11	Coldfell Gate	small off-road parking area on E of road	055 101	FP	Caw Fell, Iron Crag, Lank Rigg
12	Blakeley	handful of rough roadside spaces	067 130	FP	Lank Rigg
13	Scaly Moss	small off-road parking area on W of road	061 137	FP	Crag Fell, Grike, Iron Crag
14	Scarny Brow	small off-road parking area on E of road	062 144	FP	Crag Fell, Grike, Iron Crag
15	Bleach Green	large car park	085 154	FP	Caw Fell, Crag Fell, Grike, Iron Crag
16	Bowness Knott	large car park	109 154	FP	Caw Fell, Haycock, Iron Crag, Pillar, Scoat Fell, Steeple

Location			GR NY...	Access	Ascents described from here
17	Black Sail Hut	walk/bike-in youth hostel at the head of Ennerdale	195 124	F	Great Gable, Kirk Fell, Pillar
18	Gatesgarth	bus stop, small private car park	195 150	PP, B	Great Gable, Pillar
19	Honister Pass	bus stop and large car park just E of the Slate Mine	225 135	NT, B	Great Gable
20	Seathwaite	large layby, before Seathwaite Farm, head of Borrowdale	235 123	FP	Great End, Great Gable, Scafell Pike
21	Old Dungeon Ghyll	NT car park, head of Great Langdale	286 061	NT, B	Scafell Pike
22	Brotherilkeld	layby at the foot of Hardknott Pass	210 012	FP	Scafell, Scafell Pike
23	Wha House	small car park N of Wha House Farm	200 009	FP	Scafell, Scafell Pike, Slight Side
24	Woolpack Inn	large car park on road side of pub	190 010	FP	Great How, Slight Side
25	Dalegarth Station	large station car park	173 007	FP	Eskdale Moor, Great How, Illgill Head, Scafell, Slight Side
26	Eskdale Green	marked roadside parking spaces by Giggle Alley wood	142 002	FP	Eskdale Moor, Whin Rigg
27	Miterdale Forest	small off-road parking area, E of Santon Bridge	146 012	FP	Eskdale Moor, Illgill Head
28	Santon Bridge	small tarmac car park on N of road	122 013	FP	Whin Rigg

FP – free parking

PP – pay parking

NT – National Trust (free to members)

B – on a bus route (in season)

F – only accessible by foot or bike

The Scafells from Bowfell

↑ *The upper Over Beck valley*

INTRODUCTION

Valley bases

The three valleys that are the focus of this guidebook – Ennerdale, Wasdale and Eskdale – all run roughly west from the Lake District watershed towards the west coast of Cumbria. The most northerly, Ennerdale, points towards the faded Georgian town of Whitehaven, Wasdale towards the seaside village of Seascale just south of Sellafield nuclear power station and Eskdale to the Roman fort at Ravenglass. All are surrounded by fine mountain scenery, naturally, but otherwise they could not be more different.

Ennerdale is a long deep valley decked with conifers. There is no vehicular access above Ennerdale Water. Ascents this way are therefore challenging, demanding careful planning of your time. The mountains of Wasdale are emblematic of the rugged drama of the National Park and the valley's narrow access roads are all too quickly congested. Eskdale is an enchantingly green crag-rimmed valley whose minor road threads through and over the fells by Ulpha and the daunting Hardknott Pass into the Duddon. From this valley the Scafells are ever more enigmatically seen and remotely climbed.

Facilities

The majority of walkers visiting these fine valleys base themselves as close to the walks as they can – and, as long as you have a car, there are plenty of accessible hotels, B&Bs or self-catering cottages, as well as hostels and camp sites, scattered around. (The Visit Cumbria website (www.visitcumbria.com, click Accommodation) seems to have the best database or you could just use a search engine.)

'Wild' Ennerdale naturally has very little in the valley itself. Unless you want hostel accommodation, including the famous pedestrian access-only Black Sail Hut youth hostel, Ennerdale Bridge and Lamplugh are the places to look. Gosforth is a busy little holiday village not far from Wasdale and there are also several options at Nether Wasdale and Santon Bridge. The Wasdale Head Inn is the iconic pub that offers (B&B and self-catering) accommodation right under Yewbarrow, at the head of the valley, next to one of the camp sites. Eskdale, by contrast, having no lake to get in the way and a road running right through it, boasts accommodation the length of the valley from The Woolpack at the foot of Hardknott Pass to facilities at Eskdale Green – and no fewer than four pubs at the time of writing!

Getting around

Buses are as rare as chicken's teeth in this area and those that do exist are of no use for fell ascents. The Cumbrian Coast Line, when combined with La'al Ratty (a seasonal narrow-gauge line from Ravenglass to Dalegarth), gives a useful means in the summer season to steam up Eskdale. A reminder about Ennerdale – if you plan to stay at Black Sail Hut you can use the Honister Rambler bus from Keswick alighting at Gatesgarth Farm at the foot of Buttermere and skip over Scarth Gap. Also, the Borrowdale Rambler 79 bus service turns at Seatoller (giving access to Seatoller) and is useful for long Scafell Pike ascents, via Sty Head and Esk Hause.

A fork of popular paths on Scafell Pike

Parking is not to be taken for granted anywhere in the National Park. Always allow time to find an alternative parking place, if not to switch to a different plan for your day or just set out directly from your door – perfectly possible if you find accommodation within any of the three valleys. Also take care always to park safely and only in laybys and car parks, not on the side of the narrow country roads. Depending on where you are basing yourself, consider joining the National Trust (www.nationaltrust.org.uk) in order to use their several car parks for free. Consult the Starting Points table to find out where they, and other parking places, are.

Fix the Fells

The Fellranger series has always highlighted the hugely important work of the Fix the Fells project in repairing the most seriously damaged fell paths. The mighty challenge has been a great learning curve and the more recent work, including complex guttering, is quite superb. It ensures a flat foot-fall where possible, easy to use in ascent and descent, and excess water escapes efficiently minimising future damage.

The original National Trust and National Park Authority partnership came into being in 2001 and expanded with the arrival of Natural England, with additional financial support from the Friends of the Lake District and now the Lake District Foundation (www.lakedistrictfoundation.org). But, and it's a big but, the whole endeavour needs to raise £500,000 a year to function. This enormous figure is necessary to keep pace with the challenges caused by the joint tyranny of boots and brutal weather. The dedicated and highly skilled team, including volunteers, deserve our sincerest gratitude for making our hill paths secure and sympathetic to their setting. It is a task without end, including pre-emptive repair to stop paths from washing out in the first place.

Mindful that a metre of path costs upwards of £200 there is every good reason to cultivate the involvement of fellwalkers in a cause that must be dear to our hearts… indeed our soles! Please make a beeline for www.fixthefells.co.uk to make a donation, however modest. Your commitment will, to quote John Muir, 'make the mountains glad'.

Using this guide

Unlike other guidebooks which show a single or limited number of routes up the Lakeland fells, the purpose of the Fellranger series has always been to offer the independent fellwalker the full range of approaches and paths available and invite them to combine them to create their own unique experiences. A valuable by-product of this approach has been to spread effects of walkers' footfall more evenly over the path network.

Corridor Route above Piers Gill

This guide is divided into two parts: 'Fells' describes ascents up each of the 25 fells covered by this volume, arranged in alphabetical order. 'Ridge Routes' describes a small selection of popular routes linking these summits.

Fells

In the first part, each fell chapter begins with an information panel outlining the character of the fell and potential starting points (numbered in blue on the guide overview map and the accompanying 1:40,000 HARVEY fell map, and listed – with grid refs – in Starting Points in the introduction). The panel also suggests neighbouring fells to tackle at the same time, including any classic ridge routes. The 'fell-friendly route' – one which has been reinforced by the National Park or is less vulnerable to erosion – is also identified for those particularly keen to minimise their environmental impact.

After a fuller introduction to the fell, summarising the main approaches and expanding on its unique character and features, come the route descriptions. Paths on the fell are divided into numbered sections. Ascent routes are grouped according to starting point and described as combinations of (the red-numbered) path sections. The opportunities for exploration are endless. For each ascent route, the ascent and distance involved are given, along with a walking time that should be achievable in most conditions by a reasonably fit group of walkers keen to soak up the views rather than just tick off the summit. (Over time you will be able to gauge your own likely timings against these figures.) To avoid appearance of impossibly precise accuracy, in the route information distance has been rounded to the nearest 0.1km (and ¼ mile) and ascent/descent to the nearest 5m (and 5ft). Please note that conversions can only therefore be approximate.

In many instances a topo diagram is provided, alongside the main fell map, to help with visualisation and route planning. When features shown on the maps or diagrams appear in the route descriptions for the first time (or the most significant time for navigational purposes), they are highlighted in **bold**, to help you trace the routes as easily as possible.

As a good guide should also be a revelation, panoramas are provided for a small number of key summits and panoramas for every fell in this guide can be downloaded free from www.cicerone.co.uk (see 'Additional online resources' below). These name the principal fells and key features in the direction of view.

Advice is also given at the end of each fell chapter on routes to neighbouring fells and safe lines of descent should the weather close in. In fell-walking, as in any mountain activity, retreat is often the greater part of valour.

The Ennerdale Fence

A feature you will quickly become familiar with in the Wasdale area is the Ennerdale Fence. This aged ridge marker stretches from west of Iron Crag to the summit of Scoat Fell and a footpath follows along it on one side or the other. Although it is universally known as a 'Fence', it is a wall for most of its length and only rarely patched with fencing.

Ridge routes

The second part of this guide describes some classic ridge routes in the Wasdale area. Beginning with an information panel giving the start and finish points, the summits included and a very brief overview, each ridge route is described step by step, from start to finish, with the summits and other features that appear on the accompanying map highlighted in bold in the text to help you orientate yourself with the HARVEY route map provided. Some final suggestions are included after the main routes for expeditions which you can piece together yourself from the comprehensive route descriptions in 'Fells'.

Appendices

For more information about facilities and services in the Lake District, some useful phone numbers and websites are listed in Appendix A. Appendix B offers a glossary to help newcomers decode the language of the fells as well as explanations of some of the most intriguing place names that you might come across in this area. Appendix C is a comprehensive list of all the fells included in this 8-volume series to help you decide which volume you need to buy next!

Safety and access

Always take a map and compass with you – make a habit of regularly looking at your map and take pride in learning how yo take bearings from it. In mist this will be a time-, and potentially a life-, saver. The map can enhance your day by showing additional landscape features and setting your walk in its wider context. That said, beware of the green dashed lines on Ordnance Survey maps. They are public rights of way but no guarantee of an actual route on the ground. There are many anomalies, such as the green line striking up the side of Iron Crag by Long Sike and then leading straight off over the edge of the crag, only to be used if you have the gear for flying. Take care to study the maps and diagrams provided carefully and plan your route according to your own capabilities and the prevailing conditions.

I beseech you not to rely solely on your mobile phone or other electronic device for navigation. Local mountain rescue teams report that this is increasingly the main factor in the incidents they attend.

Hand-gate beneath Dropping Crag, Yewbarrow, framing Gosforth Crag, Red Pike

Please note that Scafell Pike, although perennially popular and on occasion crowded, is not to be undertaken lightly or in poor weather conditions by any route. The Wasdale Mountain Rescue Team is called to the fell far too often searching for

Great Gable from Lingmell Col

inexperienced, ill-informed, ill-equipped and frequently ill-tempered walkers. Do not, on any account, attempt to connect Scafell with Scafell Pike across Mickledore by Broad Stand. Lord's Rake is also extremely dangerous.

The author has taken care to follow time-honoured routes, and keep within bounds of access, yet access and rights of way can change and are not guaranteed. Any updates that we know of to the routes in this guide will be made available on the Cicerone website, www.cicerone.co.uk/1031/updates, and we are always grateful for information about discrepancies between a guidebook and the facts on the ground, sent by email to updates@cicerone.co.uk or by post to Cicerone Press, Juniper House, Murley Moss, Oxenholme Road, Kendal, Cumbria LA9 7RL.

Additional online resources

Summit panoramas for all of the fells in this volume can be downloaded for free from the guide page on Cicerone website (www.cicerone.co.uk/1031). You will also find a ticklist of the summits in the Walking the Lake District Fells series here, should you wish to keep a log of your ascents. For further information about the series, visit www.cicerone.co.uk/fellranger.

1 BUCKBARROW 430M/1411FT

Climb it from	Nether Wasdale **8**, Harrow Head **9** or Greendale **6**
Character	Striking craggy scarp forming the southern rim of Seatallan
Fell-friendly route	4
Summit grid ref	NY 136 061
Link it with	Seatallan

Visitors to Wasdale driving directly from Gosforth get their first impression of this amazing valley when they clap their eyes on the craggy facade of Buckbarrow, dead ahead, after crossing the cattle grid short of Harrow Head. The glacial forces that scoured the Wasdale Screes have replicated their effects here in microcosm.

Climbing this little hill can bring all the pleasure of scaling the mightiest of fells. You will love it most of all for the wide Wasdale valley view, the Screes and the Scafells – particularly stunning towards the latter part of the day when the sun's rays illuminate the facing fellsides in golden light. It is also the perfect partner to neighbouring Seatallan – no ascent of the latter is truly complete without visiting this little top.

The peak is commonly climbed from the open road running along its base either above Gill (4), Buckbarrow Farm (5) or the hamlet of Greendale (6). Yet

↑ *Buckbarrow from Harrow Head*

the connoisseur will derive much pleasure from starting and ending their walk at the tiny community of Nether Wasdale (also known as Strands), fashioning a circular walk that clambers over the fell-top via any of these popular start points. The lead-in and concluding pastures and woods (1, 2 or 3) make a lovely contrast, complementing the craggy scarp.

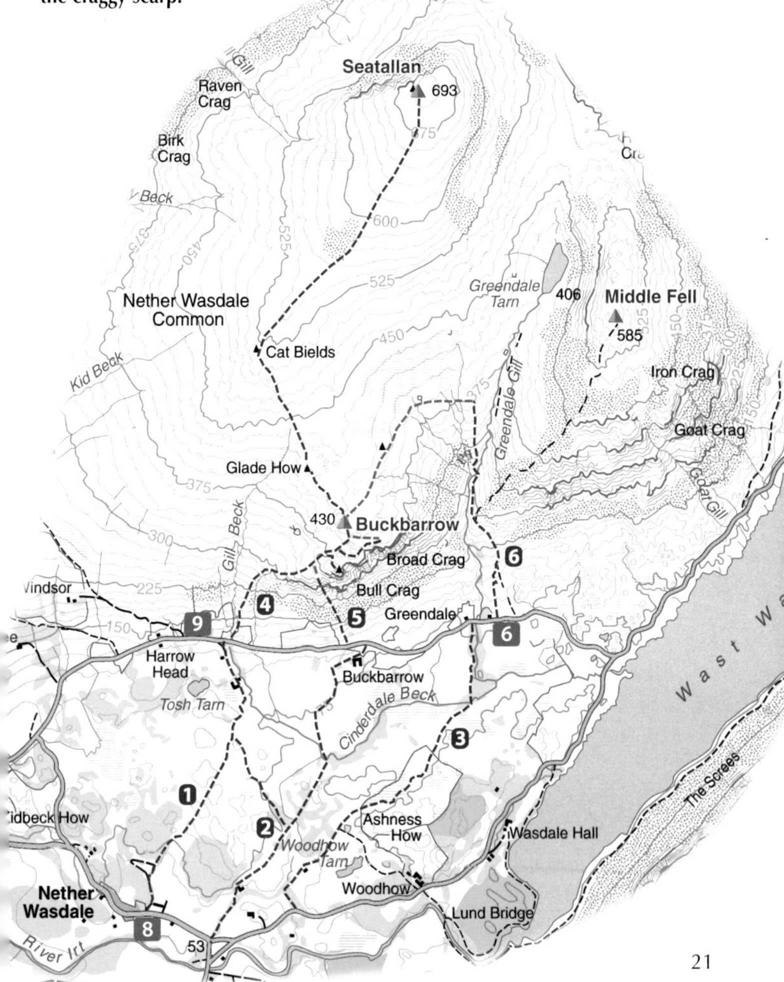

Ascent from Nether Wasdale 8

Three different routes lead across the fields from the Nether Wasdale area to the road underneath Buckbarrow from where the ascents proper begin. Route 1 is the most direct.

Via Gill Farm → *1.6km/1 mile* ↑*325m/1065ft* ⏲*35min*

1 Follow the footpath leading from the vicinity of the maypole, passing the tiny parish church of St Michael and All Angels and community hall, and leading through the yard of Kirkstile Farm en route to the holiday park camping field. The footpath is waymarked through fields to the lane leading past **Gill Farm**.

Via Buckbarrow Farm → *1.6km/1 mile* ↑*320m/1050ft* ⏲*25min*

2 Leave the road immediately beyond Cinderdale Bridge, following the lane to and through Mill Place and then the gated bridleway wending on towards Scale Bridge. At the wall-stile and gate just short of Scale Bridge, you can follow the bridleway to the left which links to the previous footpath (**1**) at the start of the walled lane to Gill. Alternatively, it is possible to cross the narrow meadow straight ahead via the gated Scale Bridge, heading on by green lanes and field-edges to **Buckbarrow Farm**, a retiring National Trust farmstead.

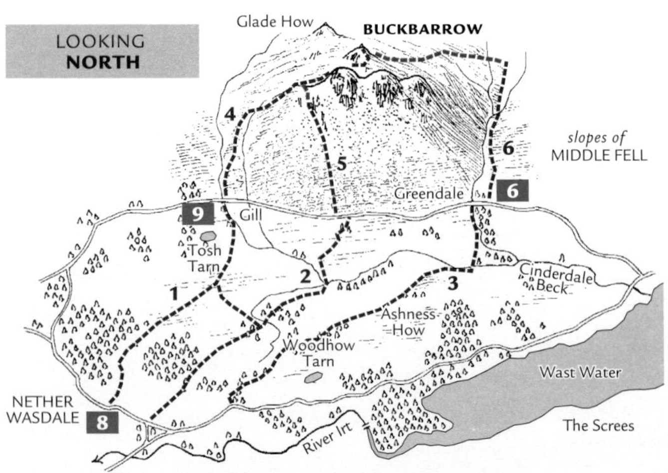

Via Ashness How →*2.4km/1½ miles* ↑*320m/1050ft* ⏲*35min*

3 Leave the minor road 0.4km (¼ mile) from the village, after the lane to Murt. A gated bridle-lane leads left, passes a derelict cottage and heads on as an open way by **Ashness How** and Roan Wood to arrive at the valley road by the bridge at **Greendale**.

Ascent from Harrow Head 9

Two contrasting ways up to the summit from the road, the first on paths and the second steeply up loose scree for those with an excess of zeal!

Via Gill Beck →*1.6km/1 mile* ↑*325m/1065ft* ⏲*40min*

Summit cairn, looking to Whin Rigg

4 Leave the road above the lane from **Gill Farm**, with **Gill Beck** left and a wall right (with 'children playing' notice on wall), and soon meet the remnants of a small sheepfold. The stony path fends off the bracken beside the beck and then drifts easily right, gaining ground to ford a tiny gill, and follows the obvious rib onto the ridge. The path forks with the prospect of a great wall of rock ahead (do not try to clamber up this unless you are a competent climber). Keep left, easing round the left-hand end of the rock band. Notice the unusual three-compartment sheepfold in the hollow down to the left, with rounded walls and gather wings. The regular path to the summit heads on up to the notch, and passes a marsh before gaining the summit up to the left.

Direct →*1.2km/¾ mile* ↑*330m/1085ft* ⏲*45min*

Definitely not a route for descent

5 Some 30m E of the wall-end a path breaks off the open road into the bracken and goes straight up the slope, heading for the pale stripe of scree. Avoid actually treading in the very loose material, for all it is easier said than

These two walled structures were built as grand seats by Greendale resident and famous fell-runner Joss Naylor

done. A natural line can be followed to the head of the open gully, left of the cliff and a narrow gully, then go over the brow to join the regular path (**4**) from **Gill**.

Ascent from Greendale 6

Via Greendale Gill →*2.8km/1¾ miles* ↑*355m/1165ft* ⌚*55min*

A longer, and partially pathless, approach.

6 Directly east of the hamlet of Greendale paths run N from the open road, cutting a swathe through the bracken and climbing into the **Greendale Gill** gorge. Brush past gorse and above a holly to reach an obvious ford. Head up the ridge (N), with a fine view of a narrow waterfall over to the left. After some 200m of ascent trend left, fording minor gills, and pass an old sheepfold. From this point take a gentle rising line SW, passing the slender cairn built in honour of Queen Elizabeth the Queen Mother (1900-2002) by the Lakeland fell-running legend Joss Naylor, an inhabitant of Greendale. Keep the same line over the damp fellside to claim the high point of Buckbarrow.

The summit

The summit is a bold knuckle of rock set well back from the edge and surmounted by a small cairn. Most visitors will seek the greater scenic merits of the scarp edge, with the course of commonly trod paths marked on the map. The cairned prow above **Bull Crag** is a notable spot to venture to. Pecked into the rock on its southern face is a white dated and initialled memorial.

Safe descents

Avoid the southern edge and stick to the tried and tested path trending SW down by Gill Beck (**4**), avoiding all obstacles, or head NE across damp slopes (**6**), passing the tall cairn and contouring via tiny gill fords to swing S down a ridge into the Greendale Gill valley.

Ridge route

Seatallan →*3.2km/2miles* ↓*25m/80ft* ↑*280m/920ft* ◷ *1hr 15min*
A continuing path leads NW via the little cairned knoll of Glade How. The path winds over the odd damp patch and rises to the skyline to a further distinctive cairn at Cat Bields. From here turn NE and pass unhindered along the grassy ridge-top direct to the summit.

Buckbarrow from Woodhow

2 CAW FELL 697M/2287FT

Climb it from	Blengdale Forest **10**, Coldfell Gate **11**, Bleach Green **15** or Bowness Knott **16**
Character	Ridge-end rising above the upper Bleng and forming the western end of the southern skyline of Ennerdale
Fell-friendly route	4
Summit grid ref	NY 132 110
Link it with	Haycock or Iron Crag

The impressive westward march of the ridge defining Ennerdale's southern skyline, springing from Great Gable and running over Kirk Fell, Pillar, Scoat Fell and Haycock, comes to a definite halt upon Caw Fell. This bulky end-piece is a stone-strewn plateau with broken north-facing cliffs. Two lower ridges break from this plateau – that to the south merges into Stockdale Moor above lonesome Blengdale, while that to the north continues the high ground over Iron Crag to terminate upon Crag Fell and Grike.

The ascent is normally part of a greater fellwalking endeavour, with Haycock the primary objective. Nonetheless, the fell occupies a fine position and commands really handsome views north across Ennerdale, down Silver Cove and, particularly late in the day, west towards the Isle of Man.

↑ *Caw Fell from the Ennerdale Fence on Iron Crag*

For an exclusive and largely pathless adventure from the Gosforth direction, park in Blengdale Forest and combine Routes 1 and 2, returning via the Mountain Pinfold and Scalderskew. On another day approach on clear ridge paths from the Ennerdale direction to traverse Crag Fell and Iron Crag on the way up and return along the shores of ever-wilder Ennerdale Water (Routes 4 and 5).

Ascent from Blengdale Forest 10 *off map SW*

These routes entail a long march in and thus a long march out, but they both make most enjoyable, largely pathless, adventures if you have the time to do them.

Direct →*8.8km/5½ miles* ↑*620m/2035ft* ⌚*3hr 20min*

1 Walk up the valley, crossing the river bridge at Blengdale Lodge, where you bear left along the footpath by the barrier to enter **Blengdale Forest**. Flood damage is causing the path to be realigned. The ensuing valley path is dominated by mature sky-high log-pole pines. Watch for the path-fork some 40m after a footpath waymark post on the right. Here go left down to Bleng Tongue Bridge, a wooden footbridge spanning the **River Bleng**. Beyond, bear left and right upon the ramped roadway, a grass-covered metalled track which

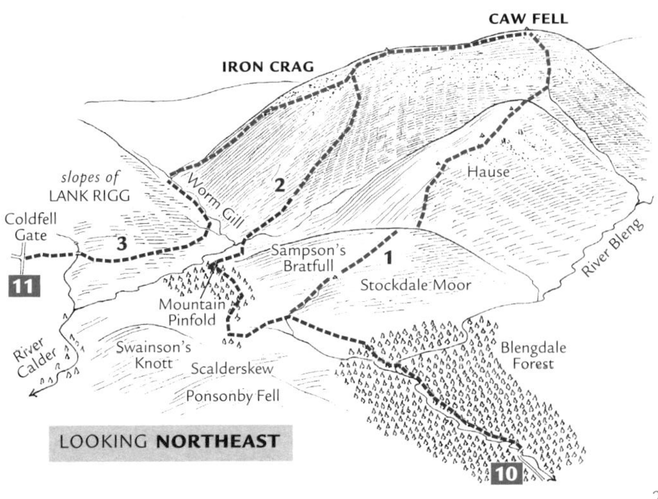

Caw Fell above Stockdale Head

winds uphill to reconnect with the farm access track, still within the forestry. Head forward along the straight track to a cattle grid and entry onto the open moor.

Between the open track and the dry ridge of **Hause** leading to the summit of Caw Fell lies a tract of damp fell known as **Stockdale Moor**. The route best embarks upon the moor where the farm track swings left (NY 092 075) heading for the farm enclosure cattle grid. There is no hint of a path. Follow the shallow gill draining the moor gently up the moor to find the rush-enveloped pile of stones (29 metres by 14 metres) dignified by the name **Sampson's Bratfull**. This linear cairn, along with the diverse array of cairns and shy stone alignments on this section of moor, are of Celtic origin. They suggest that this west-facing hill was the scene of a considerable pastoral farming community some 2000 to 3000 years ago.

After a quick rock-step the moor levels, with a modern cairn adaptation of an ancient cairn the highest point after a tiny fenced bog. Tussocks make for difficult walking en route ENE to the shallow saddle. Sheep paths converge and the grassy ridge rises easily, with a small wind-shelter an early feature. Follow the easily rising ridge, pathless, as it leads NE, and backward views draw the eyes seaward to the Isle of Man. Stonier ground yields more cairn building and two high points sporting linear cairns near the southern edge. Each provides fine views to Seatallan and the wild bowl of Stockdale Head. After passing the fourth ridge cairn the grassy slope soon

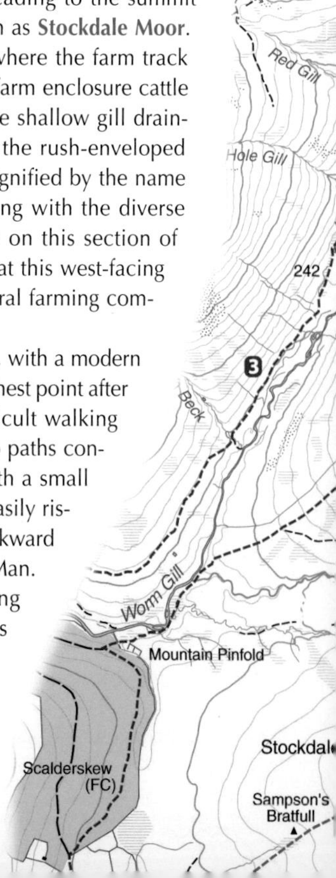

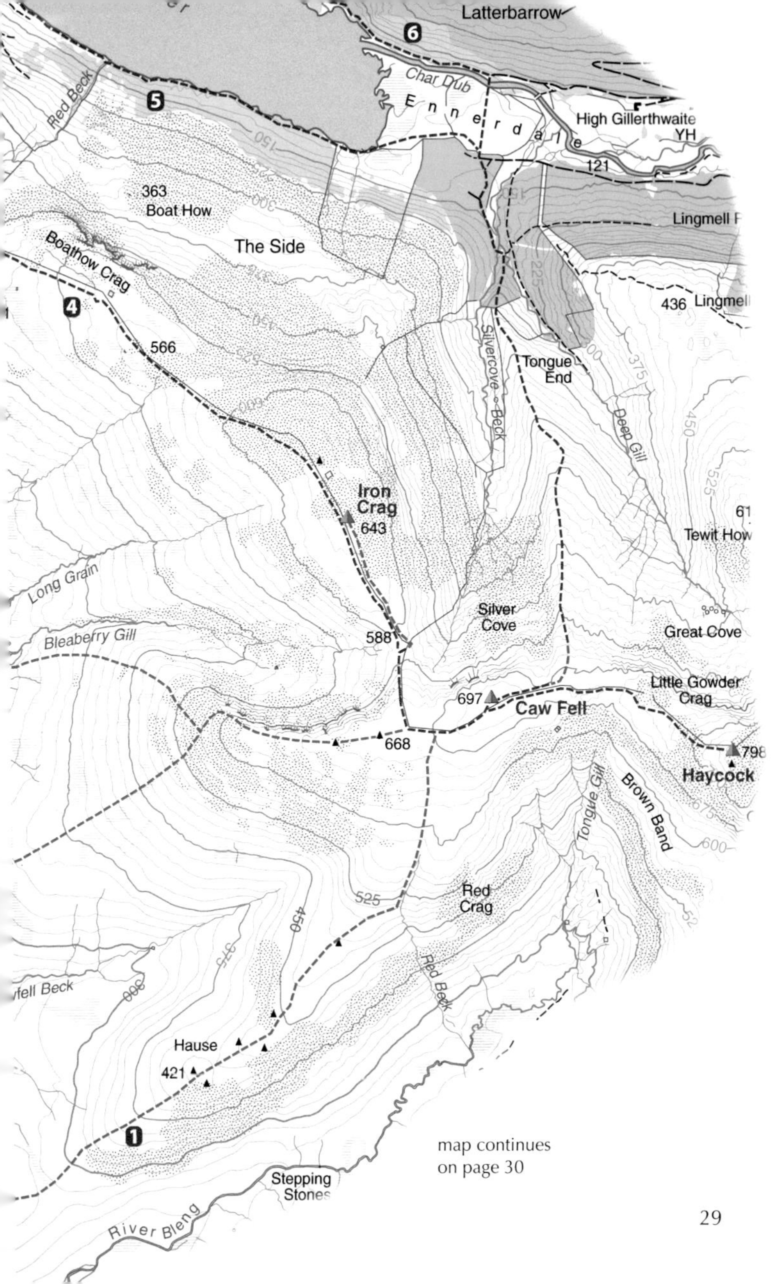

map continues on page 30

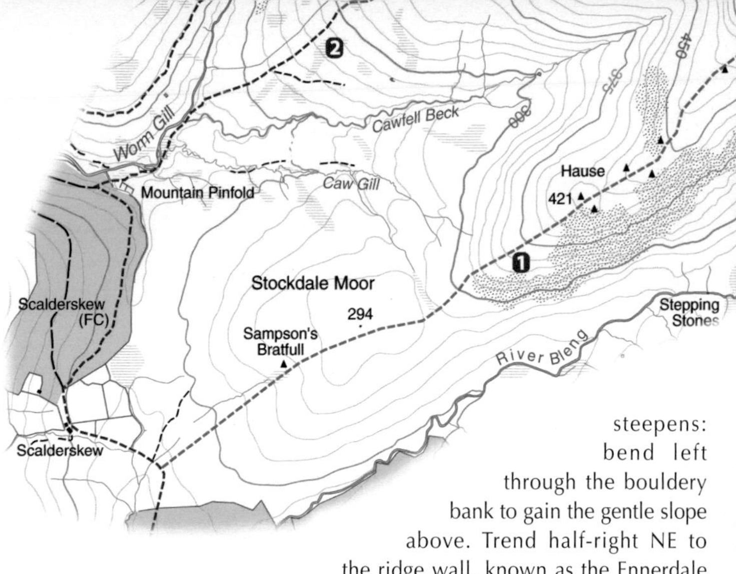

steepens: bend left through the bouldery bank to gain the gentle slope above. Trend half-right NE to the ridge wall, known as the Ennerdale Fence. Follow this right until a complete section of wall is reached, where you slip through the last tumbled wall-gap to the fence-stile and reach the summit.

Via Scalderskew → *10.5km/6½ miles* ↑*635m/2085ft* ◷*3hr 40min*

2 Where **1** heads NE across Stockdale Moor, follow the track to **Scalderskew Farm** and continue along the ensuing lane to a gate into the Forestry Commission's Scalderskew. Keep to the open track and seek a gate which exits down at the northeast corner, from where you ford a minor gill and follow on with the green track passing the **Mountain Pinfold** (a collection point for the various flocks that formerly ran on the open common, rare in Lakeland). The track dwindles beside **Caw Gill** ford, where you head N alongside **Worm Gill** to a sheepfold then bear NNE, then NE, onto the plain fell. A faint path follows along just to the south of a seasonal beck and then peters out leaving you to stride on in the same direction towards the steeper contours. The upper slopes are laced with boulders, easily circumvented or enjoyed. Pass the ridge-end cairn and advance by a shelter-cairn along the flat plateau to the sharp corner of the Ennerdale Fence. Either cross the secreted fence-stile or follow on with the wall to your left to find a similar fence-stile near the crest of the fell. Cross this to reach the summit cairn.

Mountain pinfold beside Worm Gill

Ascent from Coldfell Gate **11** *off map W*

Direct → *10km/6¼ miles* ↑*550m/1805ft* ⌚*4hr*

No less remote than the first two routes, but more efficient, this one follows a clear track to the foot of the fell near the headstream of Worm Gill – which will seem every bit a river if you contemplate fording it!

3 Follow the track E into the valley, passing a barrier, and on down through the gated pens to cross the gated footbridge over the **River Calder**. Keep forward on the green-way, forking left at the obvious split in the way and heading over Tongue How, passing to the left of a massive ring enclosure of unknown antiquity. Escaping the rushes for a while the level bridle-track then resumes a course through damp rushes to decline a little (ignore the inferior bridle fork right). Swinging naturally round the curve of the southern slopes of **Lank Rigg**, the track heads NE to arrive at the water extraction compounds known as the Intake Works.

Pass the enclosures, including the sheepfold, seeking a convenient fording place over the southern-flowing feeder gill and then the combined waters of **Long Grain** and **Bleaberry Gill**. Bleaberry Gill has washed down a good deal of ridge-bank debris, so the next steps are awkward, but once you are on the high right-hand bank proper a sheep track gives a sure route on up the fell. Take a good look at the upper western slopes of Caw Fell from low down, and notice a distinct right-slanting gap through the boulder slope, which is key to a comfortable ascent. As the higher ground is attained aim slightly left to follow the burgeoning edge overlooking the northern combe and facing towards the blank slopes of **Iron Crag**. A prominent cairn heralds the plateau. Pass on by a shelter-cairn to meet the sharp-left bend of the Ennerdale Fence, and head on E to the summit.

Ascent from Bleach Green 15 *off map NW*

Via Crag Fell and Iron Crag →*8.8km/5½ miles* ↑*620m/2035ft* 🕒*3hr 45min*

A steady climb along a clear track with constantly improving views.

4 Step back over the access cattle grid and follow the roadway left, forking right past Bleach Green Cottage by a hand-gate at a second cattle grid. Take the open track towards Crag Farm. As the track bears right go straight on, with the garden fence left, to an integrated wall step-stile and hand-gate. On joining the track beneath the forestry turn right, following the track until the wall on the right ends. Here switch acutely left up into the forestry (no sign) on a definite green path. This path climbs steadily to a stile/gate onto the open fell and shortly comes above the craggy ravine of Ben Gill, with an impressive view down upon the outflow of the lake. From a simple ford the path leads on up the scarp edge of Revelin Crag, shaking free of the right-hand fence, then there is a simple climb to the top of **Crag Fell**. On gaining the upper slope, follow the edge and gain the finest views down on Cragfell Pinnacles and over the expanse of **Ennerdale Water**. Head SSE from the summit and a clear path leads down to a fence-stile at the edge of conifers and enters a heather clearing. The path advances to the forest track by a cairn. Go left and quickly right (S) down the ride, which is damp underfoot. Tread gingerly across the stake raft set in place for a shepherd's quad-bike. Bear left and cross the fence-stile and follow the handsomely constructed rising wall (Ennerdale Fence). At the

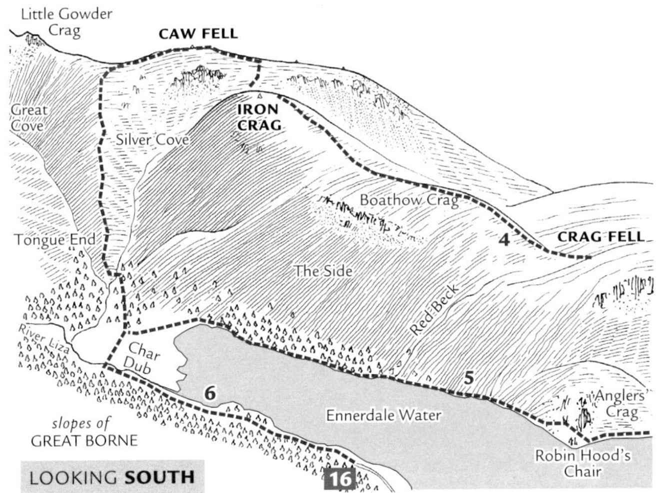

third gate in the wall go through onto **Iron Crag**. Keep beside the continuing Ennerdale Fence wall through the saddle at the head of **Silver Cove** and **Bleaberry Gill**. Head on S, up onto the plateau beside the fence-strengthened wall and turn E along the wall to the summit.

Via the lakeshore path and Tongue End →*8.4km/5¼ miles* ↑*600m/1970ft* ◷*3hr 45min*

The Coast to Coast path along the south shore of Ennerdale Water leads to a stiff heathery climb to the summit.

5 Follow the popular path leading to and beyond the outflow of **Ennerdale Water**. After the kissing-gate in the wall the path runs on beside the shore to mount the rock slab at **Robin Hood's Chair**, beneath the striking headland of **Anglers' Crag**. Maintain company with the shore path via hand-gates. The path negotiates tree roots and pitched boulders to reach the meadow at the lake-head and advances to enter the lane from Irish Bridge. Bear right to pass through a double-gate entering open mature forestry. From here you may encounter placid Galloway cattle, brought in as an alternative to tight-grazing

Looking towards Haycock from the summit (photo: Anne Bowskill)

fell sheep to encourage a diversity of flora to flourish. Follow the track directly ahead, coming alongside Woundell Beck, and after an awkward bank pass the confluence of **Deep Gill** and **Silvercove Beck** to cross the footbridge. Ascend the felled ridge to a fence-stile, and from there follow the path. Engulfed in mature heather it can be a tough pull. The upper ridge beyond the heather has a few modest outcrops, which are easily passed to reach a prominent cairn on the ridge, where you turn right with the wall to the summit cairn.

From Bowness Knott 16 *off map NW*

Via Tongue End →*7.6km/4¾ miles* ↑*580m/1900ft* ⏲*3hr 40min*

A similar route to Route 5 but this time along the north shore of the lake.

6 Follow the forest road (casual traffic debarred). This descends and runs attractively alongside the lake then beside the inflowing **River Liza**, here called **Char Dub**, a reference to the native fish. Turn right and cross the flood-adapted concrete bridge, known as Irish Bridge. The ensuing lane leads to a double-gate entering the forest to join Route **5**.

The summit

Striding happily alongside the Ennerdale Fence you could easily miss the summit cairn, some 30m north of the wall and accessed by a stile in the fence. Here attention is naturally drawn to the view over Silver Cove and the great heather declivity of the Side, falling from Iron Crag.

Safe descents

Follow the Ennerdale Fence for safest descent over Iron Crag and down through the plantations for either Bleach Green (**4**) or Kinniside stone circle. Do not think of finding a direct route due north of the summit... there are cliffs! The north ridge running down to Tongue End (**5**) is safe, although the heather makes for tough going. To south and west the only hazard is fording Worm Gill.

Ridge routes

Haycock →*1.6km/1 mile* ↓*35m/115ft* ↑*140m/460ft* 🕒*1hr*
Follow the Ennerdale Fence wall E, interrupted only by Little Gowder Crag, where the ridge path skirts to the right.

Iron Crag →*1.6km/1 mile* ↓*110m/360ft* ↑*55m/180ft* 🕒*45min*
Follow the Ennerdale Fence wall W (**4**), turning N down to the saddle, where you'll find a wall-stile lurking in the corner by the fence-junction. Cross it and follow the wall up to the first cairn on the brow.

3 CRAG FELL 523M/1716FT

Climb it from	Bleach Green **15**, Scaly Moss **13** or Scarny Brow **14**
Character	Attention-seeking craggy fell overbearing Ennerdale Water
Fell-friendly route	6
Summit grid ref	NY 097 144
Link it with	Grike, Iron Crag or Lank Rigg

Many Lakeland lakes have one fell with a particularly strong presence and Ennerdale Water has Crag Fell. Viewed from the north, across the lake, the heather and craggy facade lend a gracious dignity to the setting. To the west the fell unites with Grike to form the headwaters of the Calder and from both the north and west the central promontory of Anglers' Crag captivates the eye.

The curtain of rock higher up the fellside, known as Cragfell Pinnacles, provides a particularly fine outward viewing point across the lake, and an intriguing line of ascent from Anglers' Crag. There is also evidence of iron mining high on the eastern flank of the fell – workings active during the latter half of the 19th century, now reclaimed by nature. The spoil and mine entrance, enveloped in heather, are interesting to discover.

↑ *Crag Fell from Bowness*

Ambitious walkers will see the fell as the start point for the handsome long-striding ridge walk to Haycock, via Iron Crag and Caw Fell. The primary routes (1–5) all head up from Bleach Green and offer views of Ennerdale Water all day long however you put your day together. Come from the fell road to the west for a gradual valley ascent rewarded by a stunning view at the summit (6–8).

Ascent from Bleach Green 15

The two most direct lines of ascent (Routes 1 and 2) focus on Ben Gill without entering the ravine itself while Route 3 heads off to take in the view from the saddle above Anglers' Crag.

Via Revelin Crag →*3.2km/2 miles* ↑*410m/1345ft* 🕒*1hr 25min*

1 Step back over the access cattle grid and follow the roadway left, forking right past Bleach Green Cottage by a hand-gate at a second cattle grid. Advance along the open track towards **Crag Farm**. As the track bears right go straight on, with the garden fence left, to an integrated wall step-stile and hand-gate. On joining the track beneath the forestry turn right, following the track until the wall on the right ends. Here switch acutely left up into the forestry (no sign) on a definite green path. This path climbs steadily to a stile/gate onto the open fell, quickly to be joined by Route **2** entering steeply stage left. The heather-fringed path comes above the craggy ravine of **Ben Gill**, with

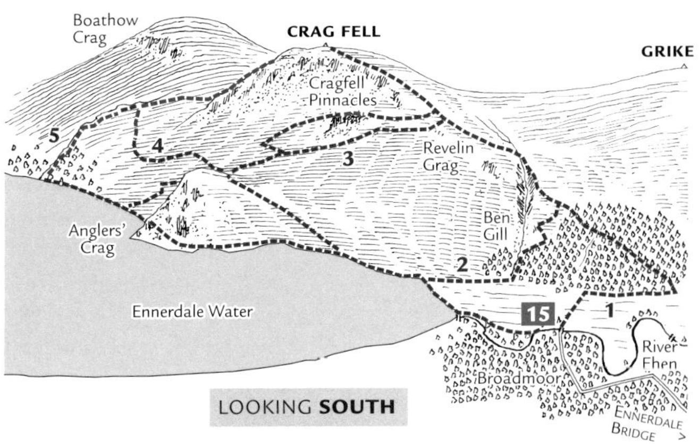

an impressive view down upon the outflow of the lake. From a simple ford the path leads on up the scarp edge of **Revelin Crag**, shaking free of the right-hand fence, then there is a simple climb to the fell-top. When you reach the upper slope, follow the edge for the finest views down on Cragfell Pinnacles and over the expanse of Ennerdale Water.

2 Leave the enclosed car park by the hand-gate and follow the primary path to the outflow of **Ennerdale Water**, passing the outflow (weir). Continue with the grand long view of Ennerdale ahead to go through a kissing-gate (with NT sign 'Anglers' Crag'). Turn sharp right and follow the wall back W, passing under the conifers to ford **Ben Gill** and immediately bear off the footpath, clambering beside the fence to the right of the stony gill. At the fence-top go up right with the obvious path which, in turn, switches left and then right to meet up with the direct path coming up from the plantation. Go left with Route **1**.

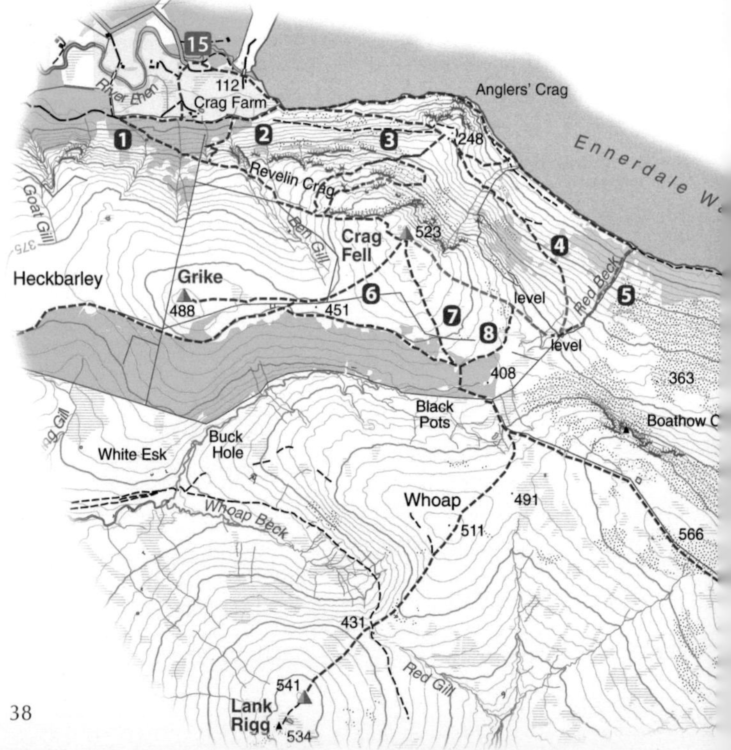

Via Anglers' Crag and Cragfell Pinnacles →*4.1km/2½ miles* ↑*425m/1395ft* *1hr 40min*

3 Follow the path, which leads on by the outflow (weir) of **Ennerdale Water** to a kissing-gate (with NT sign 'Anglers' Crag'). This path runs along the stony shore of the lake. Watch for the rising path after some 300m, and climb with it to the grassy saddle at the top of the **Anglers' Crag** promontory. Precisely in the saddle, branch up right on the obvious path, with two options at this point. Either keep with the steady trod, mounting well below the **Cragfell Pinnacles** outcropping as the path comes over a rocky rim and draws round the fellside to unite with the **Revelin Crag** path from Ben Gill (**1**). Alternatively, for the more intimate view of this peculiar curtain of rock, watch for an acute left turn by a small cairn. A less than obvious path contours through the bracken before climbing immediately left of the fans of scree. Above, the path veers right with the natural rake to come close behind the curtain of rock in a confused area of slipped rock and boulders. The path is equally confused here. Tread cautiously over and down by the wall of rock, continuing to cross the rocky rim a little higher than the lower route, naturally sweeping round to meet the Revelin Crag edge path and follow it to the summit.

Ennerdale Water outflow weir

Via the miners' path →*4.8km/3 miles* ↑*425m/1395ft* *1hr 55min*

The miners' path to and from the iron-ore levels at the head of Red Beck, now seldom used, leads over the saddle of the Anglers' Crag promontory.

4 Follow Route **3** up to the saddle. Cross it and, 100m after, take care to avoid breaking left with the more popular path. The miners' path contours to an adapted wall-stile, beyond a

Anglers' Crag

gill ford. Notice the section of iron tram-track. The path declines to avoid small outcrops, then curves up the slope southward, becoming less distinct and fording **Red Beck** to reach the wall-stile. Angle half-right over the old iron-mine spoil and traverse the heather without the benefit of a path – the remains of a miners' bothy can be found and a further iron-mine level. Climb directly from the mine-level, pathless, and from the rank heather to the grassy banks to the summit.

Via the lakeshore path →*4.8km/3 miles* ↑*425m/1395ft* ⏲*1hr 55min*

Stay with the lakeshore path as far as the foot of Red Beck for a bit of hands-on action and great views up to the head of the valley.

5 The lakeshore path can also be followed to the foot of Red Beck. Either cross the saddle with Route **4** and then follow the initially zig-zagging path down to the lakeshore path, or take lakeshore path all the way from the gate, scrambling up over the obstacle of Robin Hood's Chair, beneath **Anglers' Crag**. The path rounds this impressive rock headland, inevitably bringing hands into action, to be joined by the path coming down from the saddle and going through a wall-base kissing-gate. The path weaves on with the shore enjoying lovely views up the lake towards Pillar and Steeple and across the lake to Bowness Knott, backed by Great Borne. After coming into a fringe of native oak arrive at the ford of **Red Beck**, short of a wall hand-gate.

Do not go through. Instead, bear up tight by the wall, climbing steeply, soon with a fence left, but then – for the greater part – a wall. On emerging from the woodland keep by the wall, although at one point Red Beck bites into its base requiring walkers to skip right and left to get back to the wall-side. Rise to a wall-stile to meet and continue on with Route **4**.

Ascent from Scaly Moss 13 or Scarny Brow 14
both off map W

A long, gradual ascent can be made from the road on Kinniside Common, using the forest tracks, with a couple of variants to choose from for the final climb.

Via Heckbarley forest track →*4.5km/2¾ miles or* →*5.2km/3¼ miles* ↑*330m/1085ft* ⏲ *1hr 35min or* ⏲ *1hr 50min*

6 From Scaly Moss, south of the Kinniside stone circle, a bridleway is signposted off the open road. Follow this green track into the part-cleared forestry, via a hand-gate situated above a large boundary marker, the Great Stone of Blakeley. Alternatively, start at the '**Heckbarley**' forest entrance adjacent to the common-access cattle grid at Scarny Brow. This forestry track winds up to a junction with the more direct bridleway. Heading E, keep with the forest-edge track, passing the mast. A matter of 200m after the mast compound find a gate in the fence on the left. Go through, cross the subsequent fence-stile and follow the open fell path rising NE to the summit.

7 Continue with the forest track, and after a section where conifers encroach on both sides, pass out of the trees to the left. A cairn marks the crossing point of the ridge path. Here you can switch back left with this path, rising to a fence-stile and continuing NNW to the summit.

8 If in a more exploratory mood, continue E from the crossing point with the forest ride, with Starling Dodd framed ahead. Pass out of the trees from the forest ride and follow the path down through a hand-gate and follow the dwindling path through the

Western stack of Cragfell Pinnacles

Looking north to Knock Murton from the summit (photo: Andrew Leaney)

heather to reach the upper iron-ore mine-level. Here the path runs out. Turn left with Route **4** to climb pathless to the summit.

The summit

The summit cairn surmounts one of several grassy knolls, with a small hollow to the north. The eastward view into Ennerdale is stupendous. The better northern viewpoint is to be found by skirting left round the hollow to reach the brink, looking down on Cragfell Pinnacles and the broad expanse of Ennerdale Water, with Great Borne on the far side.

Safe descents

All dangers lurk to the north. So either retreat W down the Revelin Crag edge (**1**) for Bleach Green car park or join the forest track (**6**) for the Kinniside Common road.

Ridge routes

Grike →*1.6km/1 mile* ↓*80m/260ft* ↑*45m/150ft 1hr*
Leave the summit due SW. A clear path wends down to a fence-stile. Now with a fence (left) guiding over damp ground rise past the mast enclosure to reach the summit cairn.

Iron Crag →*4.5km/2¾ miles* ↓*115m/375ft* ↑*235m/770ft* 🕒*1hr 35min*
Head SSE, and a clear path leads down to a fence-stile at the edge of conifers and enters a heather clearing. The path advances to the forest track by a cairn. Go left and quickly right (S) down the ride, which is damp underfoot. Cross the stake raft carefully. Bear left and cross the fence-stile and follow the handsome rising wall. At the third gate in the wall go through. The cairn close by is not the actual summit, that lies further S beyond the fenced enclosure.

Lank Rigg →*3.2km/2 miles* ↓*210m/690ft* ↑*230m/755ft* 🕒*1hr 15min*
Follow the route to Iron Crag but branch from the Ennerdale Fence with the quad-bike track, on the early rise up the wet moor. Cross SW over the plateau top of Whoap, easily declining to the small depression at the head of Whoap Beck, and climb straight on up to the OS pillar.

Crag Fell across Ennerdale Water

4 ESKDALE MOOR 337M/1105FT

Climb it from	Dalegarth Station **25**, Miterdale Forest **27** or Eskdale Green **26**
Character	Tract of fascinating moorland between Miterdale and Eskdale, with tarns and ancient relics
Fell-friendly route	2
Summit grid ref	NY 177 035

The long shank of Eskdale Moor runs southwest from Burnmoor Tarn to be chiselled to a point above Eskdale Green by Miterdale. In its upper reaches, this shy valley is itself quite unique, being more akin to the narrow mountain limestone valleys characteristic of the Derbyshire Dales and the Yorkshire Three Peaks.

This triangular wedge is the perfect place to explore when all the old favourite fell-tops are blanketed in mist, even if it brings to mind Wainwright's image of an old-timer trudging up the foothills from the cover of *Outlying Fells*. **Only a fraction of the happy travellers to Boot venture up to explore it and its Bronze Age antiquities – a cluster of stone circles and cairns on Brat's Moss – or the placid waters of Burnmoor Tarn or, at its tip, the excellent minor viewpoint, Fell End, looking out over the Irish Sea.**

↑ *Great Bank and Miterdale Forest from Fell End*

Three contrasting routes lead up from the village (1–3) any of which could be linked with those heading up Miterdale or over Fell End from further west (4–7) to offer a long and largely solitary day out, with ample opportunities for refreshment at the end.

Ascent from Dalegarth Station 25

Route 1 overshoots the fell initially to visit Burnmoor Tarn and Lodge, Route 2 visits some ancient peat huts as well as the stone circles further up the fell and Route 3 takes in Blea Tarn after a stiff climb.

Via Burnmoor Tarn →*5km/3 miles* ↑*290m/950ft* 🕒*1hr 40min*

1 Follow the brief village street through to cross the single-arch bridge and reach the charming Eskdale Mill. From the gate a track leads up the slope of Boot Bank. Soon after passing through this first gate watch for the fork in the way. The bridleway to Wasdale Head bears half-right via a sequence of enclosure gates rising gently above the **Whillan Beck** valley to **Burnmoor Tarn**, a little over 3km distant. After gazing across the tarn to the flank of Illgill Head, turn to admire Scafell and the bold escarpment of Great How. At the outflow (the plank footbridge marked Bulatt Bridge on maps has washed away), switch back to follow the green track slanting onto the shoulder of Eskdale Moor.

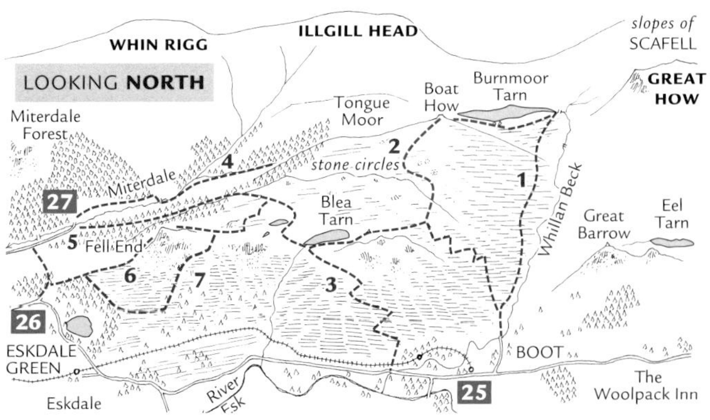

Here, you can visit the environs of **Burnmoor Lodge** from where a confident trod sets out across the shoulder of **Boat How** from the top of the brow. To reach the summit, take a faint path (uncairned, unfortunately), bearing off half-right from the main green track at its highest point, into the tough moor grass. As you brush your boots through the prairie towards Boat How the upturned hull shape is unmistakable.

Via Brat's Moss *→2.2km/1½ miles ↑340m/1115ft ◷1hr 20min*

2 Where Route **1** branches right keep to the track with the wall to the right rising to the group of six derelict 18th-century **peat huts**, built for storing and preparing peat cut on Miterdale Moss for winter fuel. The path forks in their midst. The cairned left-hand way leads unerringly gently onto **Bleatarn Hill** and **Blea Tarn**. The right-hand branch leads to **Brat's Moss**. Watch out for three 3000-year old stone circles (the first a double ring) on the left as you walk. How much water has sluggishly drained from this moor in their time – enough to fill the Irish Sea? The plain track curves northeast but the narrow ridge route takes a slightly more westerly line via a cairn. Two further circles of lesser moment on Low Longrigg can be visited but following the ridge path makes for more comfortable walking. Passing a low wall, clamber up a shallow slope and advance to the broken bank of **Boat How**, with a tiny fold in its lap.

Via the Beckfoot zig-zags and Blea Tarn *→3.5km/2¼ miles ↑450m/1480ft ◷2hr 10min*

3 From **Beckfoot Station** cross the railway to a gate. Find the footpath winding up the bracken bank. A slow plod does the trick and the view down upon Boot and across the broader Eskdale valley is worth every bead of sweat. On reaching **Blea Tarn**, turn right along the shore to ascend an unusual rocky dry valley to a prodigious cairn. The path winds on, nicely cairned (using old walling as a source), passing a fenced mine shaft – take care! At this point either continue

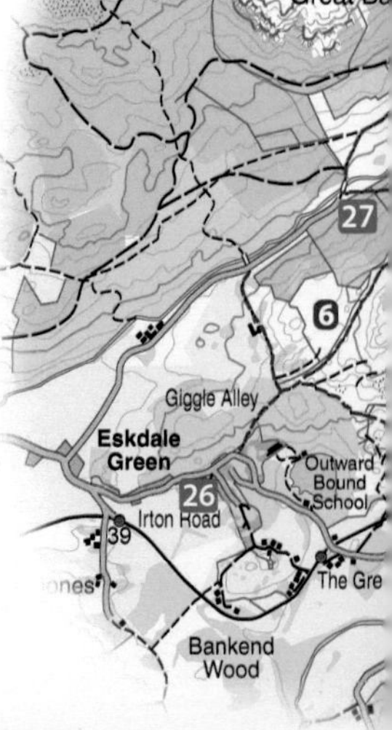

down to the peat houses, or contour with sheep trods, directly to the Bronze Age stone circles, joining Route **2**.

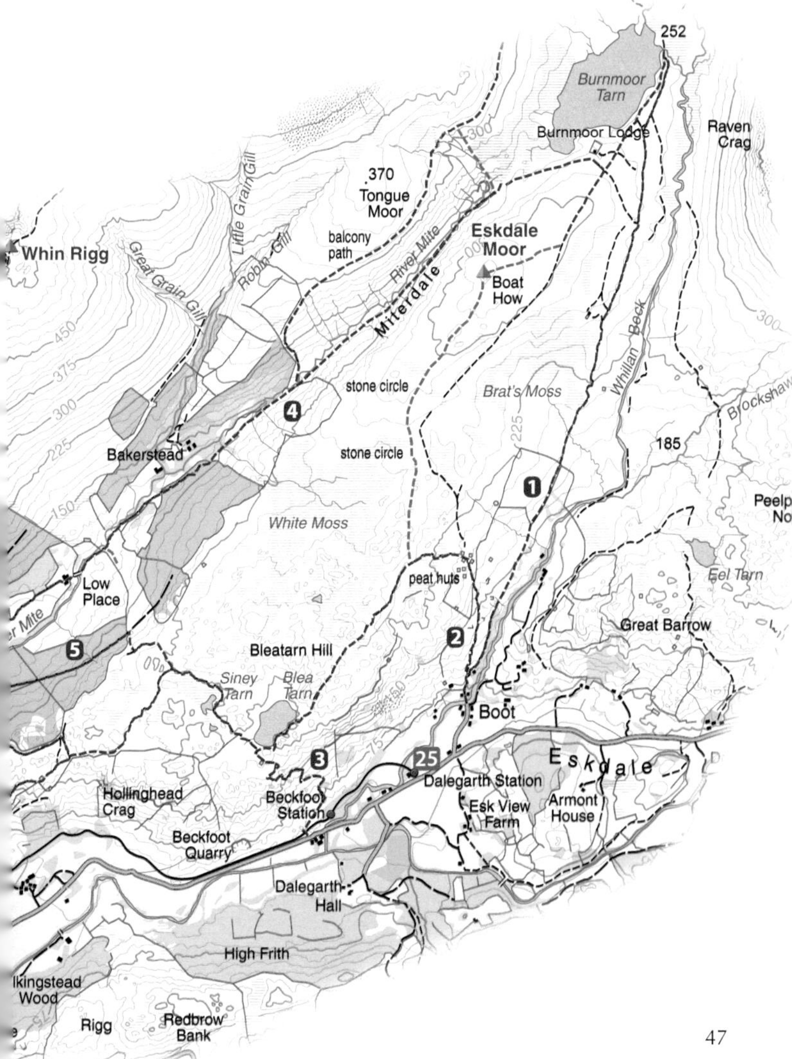

Scafell from Boat How

Ascent from Miterdale Forest 27

The Miterdale Forest picnic area and open space car park provides the ideal starting point for a quiet exploration of Miterdale and Eskdale Moor.

Via Miterdale and Burnmoor Tarn →*6.7km/4 miles* ↑*270m/885ft* ⏲*2hr 20min*

The longer option follows the Miterdale valley with a view of Scafell all the way up the dale.

4 Leave the open space crossing the broad bridge and follow the farm-track to **Low Place**. Pass between the farmhouse and the traditional barn, go right via the gate, curving round left with the wall. Notice the farmer's wooden board in Cumbrian dialect set into the wall, prompted by frequent requests for directions from walkers: 'HOD REET FUR ESHDEL'. Twenty metres after the ford cross the footbridge lurking in the bushes. Follow the rough open track leading through a gateway and then a gate into a lane. Ignore the greenway left to **Bakerstead** outdoor pursuits centre. Instead advance on a path to a stile at the corner of the plantation. The path next fords a gill, crossing a marshy patch, then continues up the valley with conifers up to the left. At a ladder-stile and gate by a sheep handling pen the open but very narrow upper section of the dale is entered.

There are two options at this point: the natural valley route or the higher, drier balcony path. The natural valley path keeps down by the south bank, though there is some trace of a path on the immediate north bank. In summer the mid-section of the river runs in subterranean silence, reminiscent of a White Peak valley.

The amphitheatre at the valley head is a curious feature. Either enter to explore and climb out on the south side, or bypass just prior. From the north a picturesque waterfall spills into the rocky combe. Ignore the continuing path. **Boat How** can be reached more sedately by bearing half-right bound for **Burnmoor Lodge**, to switch back onto the brow, or make an abrupt turn sharp right up the steep bank, crossing sheep trods for a direct approach.

Via Siney and Blea Tarns →*5.2km/3¼ miles* ↑*275m/900ft* ⌚*2hr 45min*

The shorter route takes in no fewer than three tarns before heading to the summit.

5 To visit Siney and Blea Tarns, ahead of the main mass of the fell, take the forest track directly from the picnic site and cross the stile right of the broad forest gate. Gently rising to exit at a gate, ignore the advancing track connecting to the next block of forestry. Go immediately up right, on the footpath coming south from **Low Place**, quickly reaching the moorland. Bear left on a pronounced path and watch for the right fork which leads to a further fork, right for **Fell End**, left to **Siney Tarn**. Skirt the broad marsh, which eventually reveals the tarns. Either go straight on, or skirt half-right by Siney and Blind Tarns, to reach **Blea Tarn** and cross the outflow to join Route **3**.

Blea Tarn (photo: Andrew Leaney)

Ascent from Eskdale Green 26

The best paths up from here start along Giggle Alley, diverging to take different routes round Fell End and reconvening to head towards Siney Tarn.

Via Fell End →*6.5km/4 miles* ↑*275m/900ft* ⏲*2hr 45min*

6 Giggle Alley is the more efficient approach, rising directly from the village street in Eskdale Green. At the top of the wooded lane branch right into the narrow path leading to a hand-gate. Here either hold to the left-hand wall, skirting under the craggy brow of **Fell End** (worth clambering to the top for a superb view) or **7** slip down to the cross-paths, bearing left via gates, climbing through the undergrowth and outcrops to a fence to rejoin the main path. Wind on eastward, skirting Sineytarn Moss, and link up with the path from Miterdale Forest (**5**) leading to **Blea Tarn**.

Boat How – the distinctive summit outcrop

The summit

There being many Bronze Age monuments in the vicinity, you might assume from afar that the distinctive summit (Boat How) is man-made but close at hand the outcropping bedrock is clear to see! A single stone marks the top.

Safe descents

There are no hidden hazards in descent and no opportunities for ridge routes.

5 GREAT END 907M/2976FT

Climb it from	Seathwaite **20** or Wasdale Green **1**
Character	A commanding viewpoint, above a forbidding northern rim of crags, the best place to survey upper Borrowdale
Fell-friendly route	2
Summit grid ref	NY 227 084
Link it with	Esk Pike or Scafell Pike
Part of	The Roof of England

Whether viewed from Wasdale Head or Borrowdale, Great End is clearly the abrupt conclusion of the high plateau, linking naturally to the southwest to Broad Crag and Ill Crag. From Sprinkling Tarn, its shadow-darkened north face, etched with gullies and renowned for its winter ice climbs, is seen to perfection.

Worthy objective though it is, for fellwalkers as much as climbers, if you stand at the brink of this sumptuous north-facing cliff to enjoy the uninhibited views you will most likely be alone with your elation. And despite its outward ferocity, there are wonderful ways to discover Great End, up dramatic ravines and over ancient packhorse routes or perhaps following in the footsteps of thirsty travellers heading over from Borrowdale to partake of a pint at the Wasdale Head Inn and stumble back in the dark?

↑ *Great End from Sprinkling Tarn*

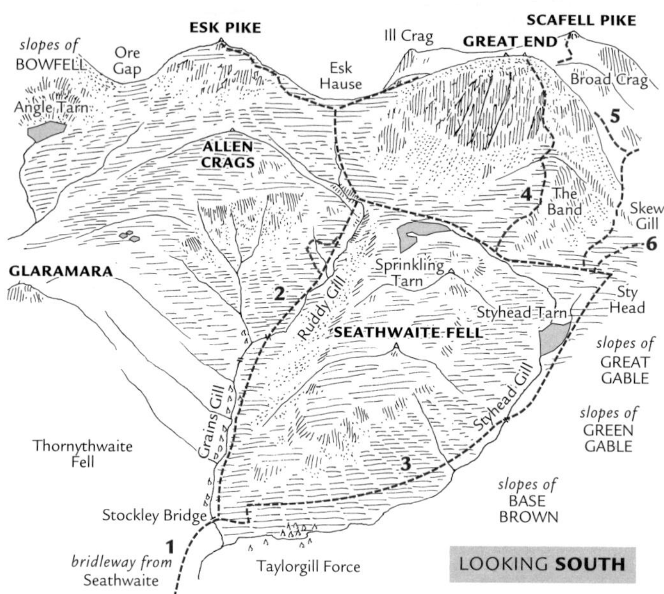

The fell is often added to expeditions from Great Langdale, conveniently bolted onto the journeys to and from Scafell Pike. The primary lines up to Styhead Pass and Sprinkling Tarn, however, are a gradual out-and-back up Lingmell Beck from Wasdale (6) and the two packhorse routes (1–3) from Borrowdale. There you can choose from three contrasting lines to the summit.

Ascent from Seathwaite **20** *off map N*

The lynch-pin for ascents from Borrowdale is Stockley Bridge.

1 The valley track leads from the farm, via gates, to this elegant single-span packhorse bridge, constructed stoutly on bare rocks, where **Grains Gill** forces through a modest but quite beautiful ravine, especially exciting when the gill is in spate. The gate on the west side is the point where two dale routes divide.

Via Grains Gill →*4.7km/3 miles* ↑*790m/2590ft* ⏲*3hr 45min*

Without question, this is the easiest route to the top.

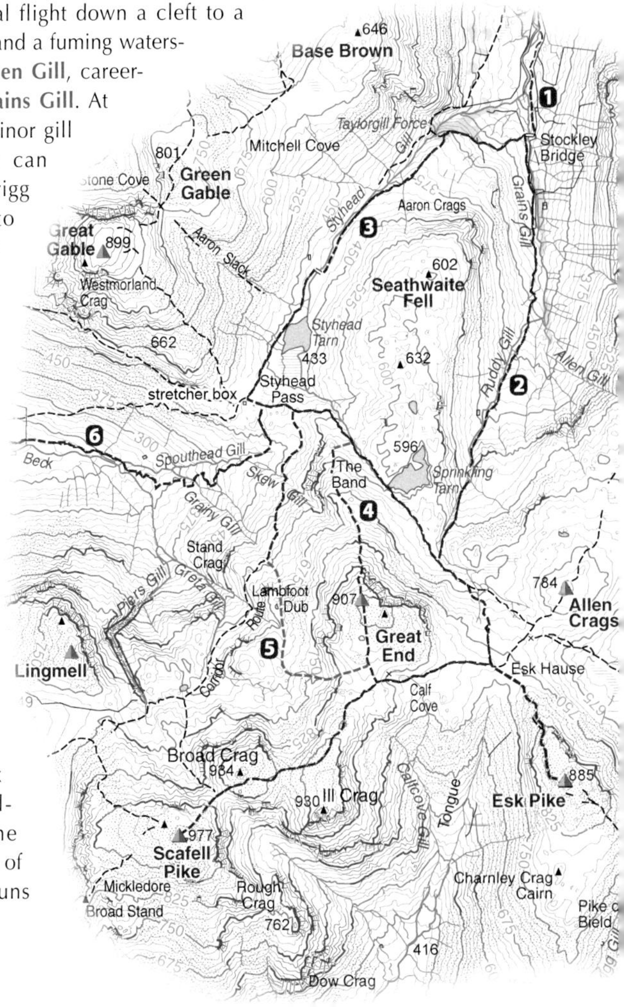

2 This path has become the high-road to Esk Hause thanks to intensive pitching works. It crosses a footbridge as **Ruddy Gill** makes its final flight down a cleft to a secretive fall and a fuming waters-meet with **Allen Gill**, careering on as **Grains Gill**. At the second minor gill crossing you can drift up the rigg half-left onto the prominent shelf. This is the older packhorse route and makes an interesting soft staircase alternative to the hard pitching. If you do, then skirt the marshy ground on the shelf to the west side and link back to the modern trail. The upper section of Ruddy Gill runs through a deep ravine with some trees managing to grow unhindered by the Herdwicks!

Ford the gill to join the path ascending from **Sprinkling Tarn**, taking the right-hand fork to reach **Esk Hause** above the cross-wall shelter. Leading into the shallow combe of **Calf Cove**, a ceaseless flow of walkers ensures a clear path with a superfluity of cairns to boot. As the ground eases above this damp hollow, branch right heading north up the broad semi-pasture ridge to the summit, thereby completely side-stepping the boulder-infested east slope.

Via Styhead Pass →*5.5km/3½ miles* ↑*800m/2625ft* ⌚*3hr 25min*

The setting of this ancient route is a stirring one and the popular rocky path is unmistakable.

Stockley Bridge

3 The path winds up from the gate beyond **Stockley Bridge**, via a rock-step to a gate in the intake wall below Black Waugh, a broad, ice-smoothed grim-looking rock-face. The path continues, gradually easing in gradient though not necessarily in its roughness. Cross a foot-bridge and walk forward to glance by the western shore of **Styhead Tarn** – a popular high-level camp site. Arrive at the Mountain Rescue stretcher box at **Styhead Pass**, a natural rendezvous point. Go left, setting course for **Esk Hause**. The path, never in doubt, crosses the outflow of **Sprinkling Tarn**. Cross a low saddle to join Route **2** by Ruddy Gill.

Via the Band →*5.5km/3½ miles* ↑*800m/2625ft* ⌚*3hr 30min*

This ridge is nowhere near as intimidating a climb as might be thought at first sight.

4 Leave the route to **Esk Hause**, when you reach outcrops on the slopes of Seathwaite Fell to the left and after a stretch of pitching. Climb to a small col, as a grassy trod winds on up the ridge. The impressive Spouthead scarp close to the right gives magnificent views to **Lingmell**. A shallow gully marks the top of **Skew Gill**, a point of further divide. The direct, mild scramble continues upward with a certain inevitable vagueness. Never fear, there is a simple line which draws up to a gully providing a fine view to Cust's Gully, identified by its huge chockstone. This gully, itself a demanding scramble, is not recommended, so it's best to give it a miss unless you have the necessary climbing skills. Instead tackle the final stretch of bouldery slope to reach the top. Make a point of skirting the cliff edge to see the top of Cust's and Central Gullies and the dramatic fell arena below.

Via Lambfoot Dub →*4.5km/2¾ miles* ↑*805m/2640ft* ⌚*3hr 40min*

This route starts with the busy Corridor Route but slips away, off-path, to find the tranquil Lambfoot Dub and a quiet western approach to the summit.

5 Set off from the **Styhead Pass** stretcher box, heading up the Esk Hause path onto the first rise to branch right, to cross the vestige of a short wall, dip and contour to the mouth of the **Skew Gill** ravine. At Skew Gill, frequently a dry jumble of stones, mount the opposing slope and climb on, slipping through a short rock cutting. The pitched staircase is clear ahead. When you spot a round-headed knoll high above, branch off the **Corridor Route**. Clamber up the predominantly grassy slope, slipping behind the knoll to find **Lambfoot Dub**.

Lambfoot Dub

The view from the top of Central Gully

The pool is surprisingly clear and deep, a lovely spot to rest alone, blissfully gazing across to Great Gable, well above the chattering trekkers on the Corridor Route. Traverse into the nameless combe behind Round How, joining the headstream of **Greta Gill** which curves up left to its source at the natural weakness in the scarp. This gives steep, but simple, access to the saddle above and thereby the summit up to the left (north).

Ascent from Wasdale Green 1 *off map W*

Via Styhead Pass →*5km/3 miles* ↑*830m/2725ft* ◷*3hr 30min*

Great End captivates the attention on the walk up Lingmell Beck from Burnthwaite, the high, rugged skyline a tempting call to arms – or to legs!

6 Leave the car park and follow the lane to Burnthwaite. Pass to the left of the farm buildings to a gate. Keep right. The obvious way heads on between varying walls, via a gate, to cross a footbridge spanning Gable Beck. Soon you face a choice of routes to Sty Head, both equally sound. The standard route sticks religiously to the rising path which passes through a hand-gate before reaching scree. The smart route lies up the valley. (Alternatively take the scree on the way up and return along the valley for a little variety.) Either bear off as bracken begins to encroach or wait a further hundred metres to find a clear path slanting down to the hand-gate near the foot of a wall. Keep alongside **Lingmell Beck**, fording the stream just after the confluence with **Piers Gill**. A clear green trail winds up the rigg, then fords a gill to the left. Slant across the next rigg to ford **Spouthead Gill**, then zig-zag up to **Styhead Pass**.

The summit

Two tops of almost identical height vie for pre-eminence. The northwest cairn is further forward and so it better commands the northern prospect, although the Langdale Pikes and Lingmoor Fell are hidden from view from here.

Safe descents

Walk S to the depression, a little over a quarter of a mile distant, to meet up with the path from Scafell Pike. Switch sharp left in the company of this popular trail (**2**) descending Calf Cove to Esk Hause. **Do not** walk south from this point. Find the cross-wall. It is only a short stride NE to Allen Crags hause – the 'false' Esk Hause – from here. Crossing the saddle E–W, a regular path leads to safety: E to Angle Tarn and Rossett Gill for Great Langdale and W for Ruddy Gill (**2**) and Borrowdale, or further to Styhead Pass for Wasdale Head (**6**).

Ridge routes

Esk Pike →*2km/1¼ miles* ↓*160m/525ft* ↑*125m/410ft* 🕒*30min*
Descend S to the depression, with minimal hindrance from rocks or boulders. Join the path from Scafell Pike switching left, E. Descend Calf Cove following the line of cairns to Esk Hause. Cross straight over, mounting the well-marked path up the NW ridge.

Scafell Pike →*2.5km/1½ miles* ↓*100m/330ft* ↑*185m/605ft* 🕒*40min*
Descend S to the depression to join the path emerging from Calf Cove. Continue SW, soon encountering an awkward and unavoidable section of boulders. The ridge narrows, succeeded by a mild interval of gravelly trail slipping into the dip between Ill Crag and Broad Crag, and then, over the east shoulder of the latter, boulder-hopping resumes with a vengeance! Descend to Broadcrag Col and climb the facing narrow, greatly hammered ridge, loose stones in abundance. Eventually matters ease and the walled summit stand hoves into view. The best shelters from the wind are to be found on the east side, over to the left as you reach the plateau.

6 GREAT GABLE 899M/2949FT

Climb it from	Seathwaite **20**, Honister Pass **19**, Gatesgarth **18**, Black Sail Hut **17** or Wasdale Green **1**
Character	Tumultuously craggy, an iconic peak pivotal to Wasdale, Ennerdale and Borrowdale
Fell-friendly route	1 and 4
Summit grid ref	NY 211 104
Link it with	Green Gable or Kirk Fell
Part of	The Upper Ennerdale Round

Great Gable is everything we desire of a mountain – a domed cathedral. From around the compass its good looks are quite distinct. Stand on Great End overlooking Sty Head and view the long Breast Route climbing to the near square-cut top. Stand on Lingmell and be thrilled by the illusion of vertical cliffs and scree on the Great Napes. But for many it is the composition from Wast Water, framed by Yewbarrow and Lingmell, that is most iconic and the emblem of the National Park.

Great Gable ranks as one of the most popular climbs in the district, alongside Helvellyn and Scafell Pike – the kind of hill that draws you back time after time.

↑ *Great Gable from Wasdale Head – the classic view*

Central to its appeal is the Great Napes, a majestic mass of buttresses that draw up to a crest linking to the base of Westmorland Crags on the southern lip of the summit. Fellwalkers venture around it and scramblers visit such amazing features as Napes Needle, Sphinx Rock and Sphinx Ridge above it, out of Little Hell Gate.

The South Traverse from Sty Head to Beck Head is a really fine high-level fell walk, especially when combined with the North Traverse under Gable Crag to make up the Gable Girdle (14). Whether from Buttermere (7), Borrowdale (1–5) or Wasdale (10–13) Great Gable is a serious day out, with lots of variants to choose from. Shorter approaches start from Honister Pass (6) or Black Sail Hut youth hostel (8–9).

Ascent from Seathwaite 20

Via Stockley Bridge, Aaron Slack and Sty Head →*6.8km/4¼ miles* ↑*780m/2560ft* ⏲*4hr*

Stick to Routes 1 and 4 for a straightforward ascent, or start on Route 2 to take in a stretch of scrambling and finish on Route 3 to lose the crowds.

1 Walk straight on through the farm and follow the track via gates to cross **Stockley Bridge**. Keep with the main part-pitched path through two subsequent gates and, higher up, a footbridge, after a particularly stony beck-side passage.

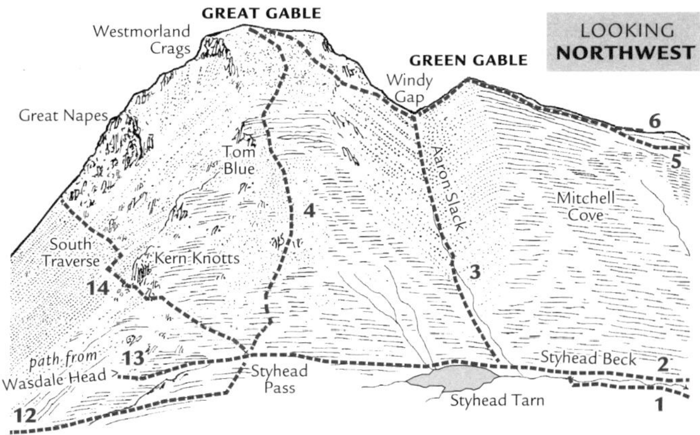

2 The footbridge can also be reached by following the footpath running under the flanks of **Base Brown**. Turn right through the barn opposite Seathwaite farmhouse and cross the footbridge over the Derwent. Then turn left through a gate and follow the footpath upstream. The path drifts up from the stony river via a kissing-gate with stony passages unavoidable. Cross a ladder-stile beside a sheep-creep and pine, passing below an old fold and wall and by large boulders, with Hind Crag prominent across the valley shielding the western flanks of Glaramara. The path draws towards **Taylorgill Force** and mounts rocks to a hand-gate tight by a cliff, after which more earnest scrambling ensues, simple stuff when dry and reminiscent of a minor Jack's Rake. Fear not – the journey soon eases, and the path scoops on with handsome views of the graceful waterfall. (Steer well clear of the stony gully up to the right. It is not a means of ascent – notice the huge boulders resting at the 'Y' fork constriction above the broad lower screes and the even narrower rift in the cliff adjacent.) Continue up **Styhead Gill** and past the footbridge.

3 Approaching **Styhead Tarn** a ford marks the point of departure of the improved path up **Aaron Slack**, which rises and fords the gill to complete the ascent to **Windy Gap** on looser scree, there joining the ridge route from **Green Gable** en route to the summit.

4 Pass on by **Styhead Tarn** to reach **Styhead Pass**, a veritable Piccadilly Circus of fell paths, the stretcher box a stark reminder of the latent perils of these mountains. From this point it is a 410m/1345ft climb to the summit. Embark upon the traditional tourist or Breast Route, which turns abruptly right (due NW), abundantly cairned. Higher, solid pitching has given stability to the path where it negotiates scree close under **Tom Blue**. There is almost no scope to lose the path which leads directly to the summit.

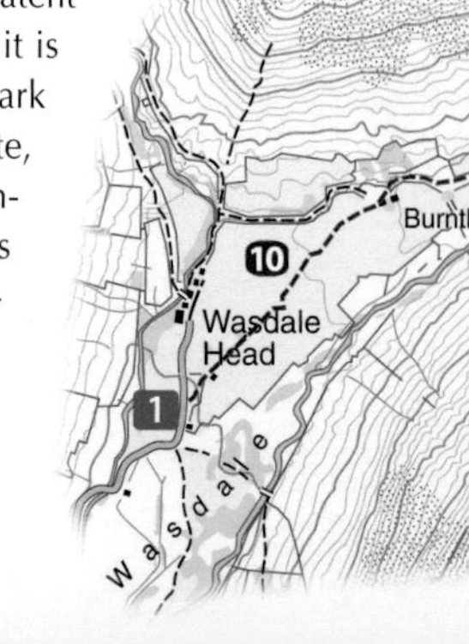

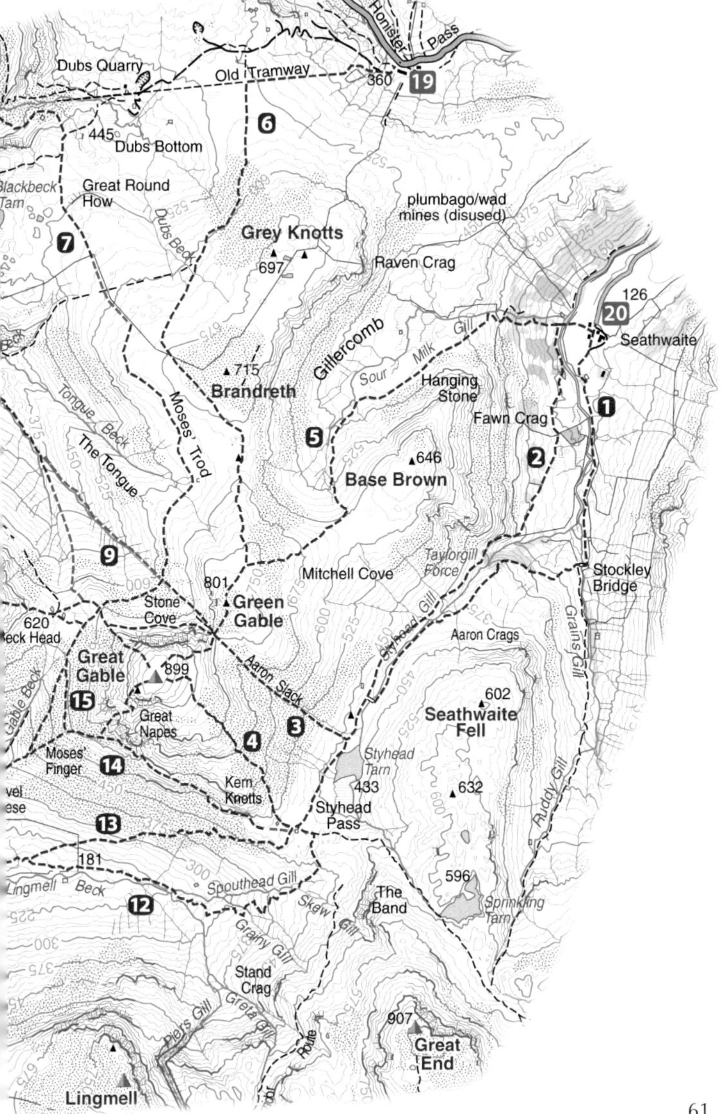
Honister Pass
Dubs Quarry
Old Tramway
360
19
6
445
Dubs Bottom
Blackbeck Tarn
Great Round How
Dubs Beck
plumbago/wad mines (disused)
Grey Knotts
697
Raven Crag
7
126
20
Seathwaite
Gillercomb
Sour Milk Gill
715
Brandreth
Hanging Stone
Fawn Crag
1
Moses' Trod
Tongue Beck
The Tongue
5
646
Base Brown
2
9
Taylorgill Force
Stockley Bridge
Mitchell Cove
801
Stone Cove
Green Gable
620
Beck Head
Styhead Gill
Aaron Crags
Grains Gill
Great Gable
899
Aaron Slack
Gable Beck
15
602
Seathwaite Fell
Great Napes
4
3
Moses' Finger
14
Styhead Tarn
433
632
Kern Knotts
Styhead Pass
Ruddy Gill
13
181
Spouthead Gill
596
Lingmell Beck
12
The Band
Skew Gill
Sprinkling Tarn
Grainy Gill
Stand Crag
Piers Gill
Greta Gill
907
Great End
Lingmell

Via Gillercomb →*4.5km/2¾ miles* ↑*825m/2705ft* ◷*3hr 45min*

This popular route sets about earnest climbing from the start.

5 Turn right through the barn opposite Seathwaite farmhouse and cross the footbridge over the Derwent. At once the path gets to grips with a pitched ascent of **Sour Milk Gill**. Entering **Gillercomb**, the part-pitched path sweeps S up the western slopes of **Base Brown**, climbing to the ridge heading for **Green Gable**, latterly in harmony with the regular path from Honister. The quick, loose descent to **Windy Gap** cairn is succeeded by a steady climb on a clear path that has one short rocky section en route to the stony summit plateau.

Ascent from Honister Pass 19

Direct →*4.8km/3 miles* ↑*595m/1950ft* ◷*3hr 30min*

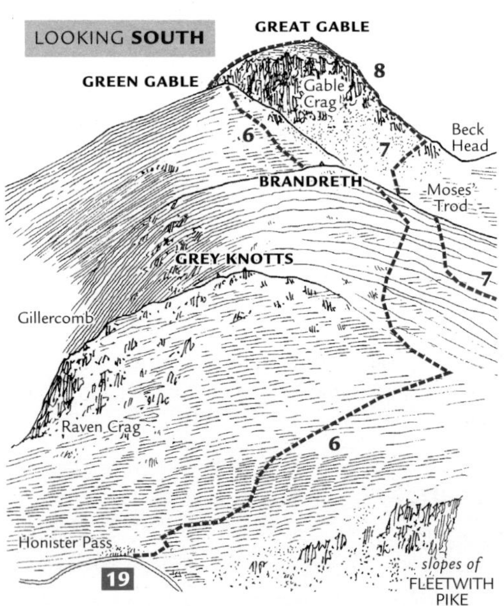

The shorter winter months make this a particularly attractive option, with its lofty start and more gradual, if less exciting, approach via Green Gable.

6 From the car park begin with the quarry track, stepping up left on the realigned pitched path which soon reconnects with the **Old Tramway**. A few remnant sleepers are evident underfoot as you draw near to the ruined site of Drum House on the brow of the hill. Turn left and follow the chain of cairns on a worn path, making easy progress across the flanks of **Grey Knotts**. Where the path forks keep left, and after crossing a fence-stile advance to the tarn-jewelled depression of Gillercomb Head. The path holds to a southerly course, climbing up onto **Green Gable**. Pause awhile and admire the impressive view of Gable Crag from the wind-shelter, then head on S into the narrow defile of **Windy Gap** – invariably true to its name. From the cairn continue, now curving up on a SW course and navigating up a minor rocky scramble to reach the rock-strewn summit dome.

Ascent from Gatesgarth **18** *off map NW*

Via Warnscale and Moses' Trod →*6.4km/4 miles* ↑*855m/2805ft* ⌚*4hr 15min*

Climb up from the Buttermere valley on a steady gradient.

7 Follow the regular open track into the Warnscale valley, branch right to cross the broad footbridge and make your way up the old miners' path below the northern cliffs of **Haystacks** to Warnscale Head (bothy), working up to the brow left of Green Crag. Turn right with the popular path (as to Haystacks), but turn left at the next junction, ascending S to the right of **Great Round How** to meet and cross a fence by a stile. Bear up left with the fence. The next fence-stile marks the crossing of the course of the Coast to Coast Walk. Ignore this, and continue up to the next fence-stile where an evident path breaks right – this is **Moses' Trod**. Follow this path above Brin Crag, round the head of **Tongue Beck** and along the upper slopes of **Green Gable** on a contouring course. The track drifts into the aptly named **Stone Cove** and crosses below the dark shadow of Gable Crag, mounting to a shoulder, where it is joined by the North Traverse. Great Gable's northwest ridge ensues, requiring minor rock-hopping and scrambling to the top.

Ascent from Black Sail Hut **17**

From the youth hostel at the head of Ennerdale you have two, occasionally rough and pathless but pretty direct, ways to choose from.

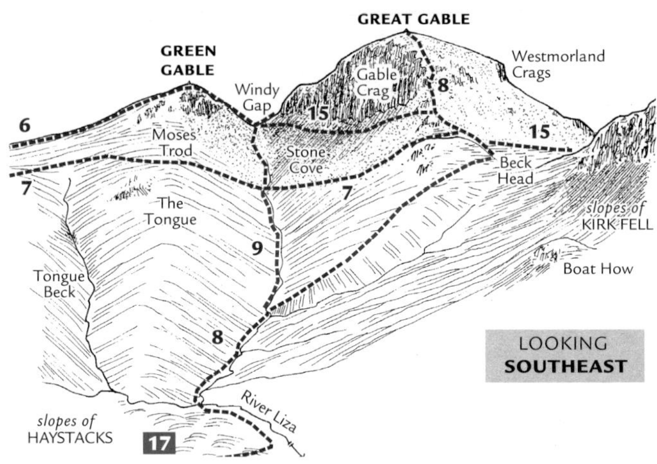

Via Beck Head and Stone Cove →*3.7km/2¼ miles* ↑*795m/2610ft* ⏲*3hr*

8 From Black Sail Hut stride SE down the bank path towards the Liza footbridge. Short of the bridge a path contours left along the foot of the moraine. Ford **Loft Beck** close to its confluence with the newly born **River Liza**. Keep company with the north bank of the Liza on a modest path. At the first significant waters-meet, ford the beck and clamber up the steep bank onto the grassy ridge heading SSE. Typically the path inevitably fades in the long grass. Aim to the right of the prominent outcropping towards the top to reach the broad saddle of **Beck Head**. Turn left and follow the clear, if loose, path onto the northwest ridge and to the summit.

9 Keep with the irregular path tussling up beside the confined Liza gill. This crosses the well-marked **Moses' Trod** and continues into **Stone Cove**. The higher path is subject to wear and is loose underfoot. Reaching the large cairn in **Windy Gap** bear right (joining Route **5**) to complete the ascent.

Ascent from Wasdale Green 1

The lane leading up to the valley head (Route 10) is the starting point for a handful of contrasting approaches. Route 11, if you choose to take in the scree scramble that is Little Hell Gate, is the most direct approach to the fell.

Via Gavel Neese and Beck Head →*4.1km/2½ miles* ↑*825m/2705ft* 🕒*3hr 30min*

10 Follow the lane leading NE from Wasdale Green by Lingmell House. Pass St Olaf's, a charming little place of worship sheltering amid yews and tombstones. The lane weaves through the irregular stone-walled enclosure of the dale floor, the excess of beck-stone that once was spread across the meadows accumulated in tidy piles and broad-girth wall sections. The lane enters the environs of **Burnthwaite Farm**. Angle left, passing through a gate into an irregular walled drove-way that leads on by a hand-gate to reach the footbridge spanning **Gable Beck** and join Route **11** or **12**.

11 You can confront the fell right away by climbing **Gavel Neese**, climbing either to Beck Head or onto the South Traverse. Step up left, climbing steadily via a hand-gate, with intermittent stone pitching. The large waterfall

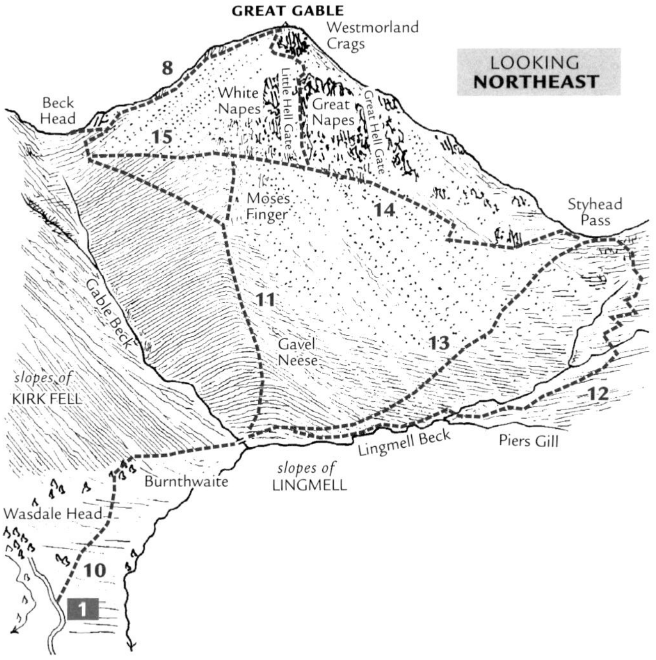

Looking past Sphinx Rock (R) towards Kirk Fell (photo: Ron Kenyon)

in **Gable Beck**, seen from Burnthwaite, is inconveniently obscured from the path. Ignore the first branch path, which moves into the upper confines of Gable Beck. Continue until the turf gives way to loose rock.

Here you have two options. Bear left and climb under the considerable scree spilling from the upper portion of **White Napes** to reach **Beck Head**. From the broad saddle, between Kirk Fell and Gable, the path then holds to the right-hand slope, rising to mount by the northwest ridge (with Route **7**). The second option is to continue up from Gavel Neese to pass the stump of rock known as **Moses' Finger**. The going can be mitigated by keeping to turf patches. The ascent lands you on the lateral section of the South Traverse path, with the option of trending left to Beck Head or contouring right to encounter Little Hell Gate (both on Route **15**). This tidal flow of scree can be ascended, but there will be many a faltering step on the loose stone. The actual rock-squeeze 'gate' comes quite high up, from where you can trend left or right onto easier ground before angling left to round Westmorland Crags and reach the summit. The confident scrambler will see that it is possible to step from just below the throttle point onto the Sphinx Ridge to the right. **Do so only with due caution** – the upper section is quite sensational, placing you right on the 'nape', a grassy ridge leading up to the base of **Westmorland Crags**.

Via Styhead Pass →*6.4km/4 miles* ↑*830m/2725ft* ⏲*3hr 45min*

The more pleasant option of these two, and by far the less trafficked, is the Pony Route (12).

12 From the **Gable Beck** footbridge follow on with the level bridle-path. As the main path becomes challenged by bracken and starts to ascend, break right when you choose to, following the dale-floor wall/fence adjacent to **Lingmell Beck**. Pass through a wall-gate and advance over progressively stonier ground to a ford, some 100m beyond the confluence of **Piers** and **Spouthead Gills**. The old bridle-path is largely evident as a green trod, with some pitching winding up the mid-ridge in harmony with Spouthead Gill. This fords **Grainy Gill**, then **Skew Gill**, as it climbs over grass to the skyline brow of **Styhead Pass**.

13 Most walkers stick resolutely to the bee-line path to **Styhead Pass**, largely because they are unaware of the old route, but there is a penalty. The path, working up the scree-clad southern slopes of Gable, is excessively worn and so there is much pitching to cope with on the rise to Sty Head. At the stretcher box you can join the Breast Route (Route **4**).

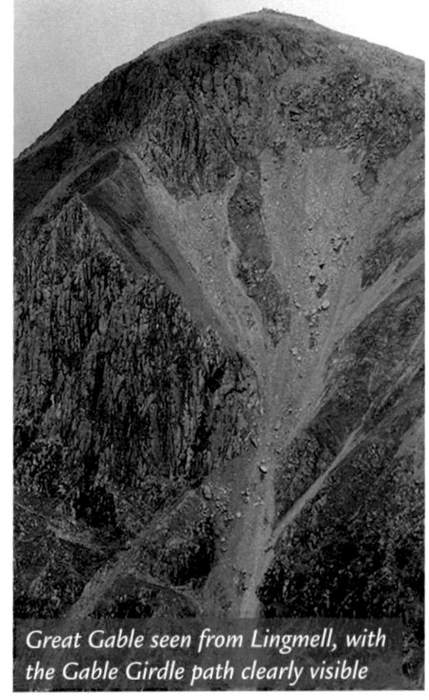
Great Gable seen from Lingmell, with the Gable Girdle path clearly visible

The Gable Girdle →*4.8km/3 miles* ⏲*2hr 10min*

Whether you arrive from Borrowdale (Routes 1 and 2) or Wasdale (Routes 12 and 13), the South Traverse is a real treasure to find and follow. The route is especially fine if linked to the North Traverse bound for Windy Gap. The whole tour undulates between the 460m and 760m contour lines.

14 From the stretcher box the first objective is **Kern Knotts**. The path begins without much evidence on the ground. Aim due W and a path becomes evident on rising to the brow. This trends towards Kern Knotts, but watch for the awkward rock-step down. Where the path forks, keep left below the crag, rounding the massive boulders, then come up below the face upon a clearer path. This path has one exaggerated zig-zag before contouring. (Watch for a cave with a fresh spring just above the path – to be appreciated on a hot day.) Anticipation mounts as the path nears Great Hell Gate, with **Great Napes** towering awesomely ahead. Fear not, the path works over the loose scree and keeps to a firm footing thereafter.

Climbers have made their own scrambling paths up from the traverse, notably a way to gain Napes Needle. Walkers with a definite head for heights can ascend Needle Gully and reach the tiny platform called the Dress Circle, up the final cleft. From this spot you can admire, and perhaps converse with, climbers tackling the famous pinnacle climb. Good scramblers can 'thread the needle' by squeezing through the gap behind Napes Needle. The author traversed west from the Dress Circle – a delicate move – and afterwards descended a steep cleft at the foot of Eagle's Nest Gully before clambering up to the Sphinx Rock. You need both a calm day and a calm head for such antics. You can move over the ridge immediately below the rock to enter Little Hell Gate. The South Traverse, on the other hand, avoids all the tricky stuff, but still provides handsome views up to these remarkable rock features. Little Hell Gate can be climbed to reach the summit (see Route **11**).

15 The South Traverse continues across Great Hell Gate, running under **White Napes** and stepping over boulders along the scree-strewn western flank of the fell to merge onto the grassy saddle of **Beck Head**. Keep up right, climbing to a shoulder where Moses' Trod skips down into Stone Cove. Ignore this, keep up right and climb to the next definite step, before the real onset of rocks upon the northwest ridge. A small cairn indicates the point of departure of the North Traverse. This angles down to run directly beneath Gable Crag. The path completes its mission at last at the large cairn in the tight depression of **Windy Gap**. (The full girdle then descends **Aaron Slack** to regain **Styhead Pass**.)

The summit

The highest point is a small outcrop given special grace by the Fell & Rock Climbing Club plaque dedicated in 1924. It bears a roll of honour to those members who lost their lives during the Great War. The spectacular view from the summit is completed by the views from two others on the edge of the plateau. From the brink cairn above Westmorland Crags to the southwest Scafell and Lingmell are superbly displayed, but the crème de la crème is Wasdale. There is a jigsaw of fields, beyond The Screes and Wast Water, within which the golden light of late afternoon can shimmer, or it may be seen glinting on the distant Irish Sea and Isle of Man. A fine outlook also awaits anyone who wanders to the brink of Gable Crag on the northern edge of the summit plateau, overlooking the upper realms of Ennerdale.

The new summit plaque

Safe descents

From the summit there are three directions to choose from. To the NW is a path (**8**) leading down the rocky ridge to Beck Head, convenient for Ennerdale, and by Gable Beck, Wasdale (**11**). To the NE a well-cairned trail leads down by a short rock-step into Windy Gap (**3**), from where you can descend Aaron Slack for Borrowdale, or climb over Green Gable for Honister (**6**) or Gillercomb (**5**). Finally, to the SE – the Breast Route sweeps in from the E to descend predominantly SE to Sty Head (**4**) for Borrowdale and Wasdale.

Ridge routes

Green Gable →*0.8km/½ mile* ↓*150m/490ft* ↑*50m/165ft* 🕒*30min*
Cairns guide NE and ensure a secure course is held, via one short rock-step, on the descent into Windy Gap. Climb the worn trail directly NNE to the summit.

Kirk Fell →*2.4km/1½ miles* ↓*280m/920ft* ↑*180m/590ft* 🕒*50min*
Head NW, descending the rocky ridge to Beck Head. Pass between the two tarns and follow the old fence on a clear path climbing W to the east top. Go straight over and cross the depression cradling Kirkfell Tarns, then rise to the main summit.

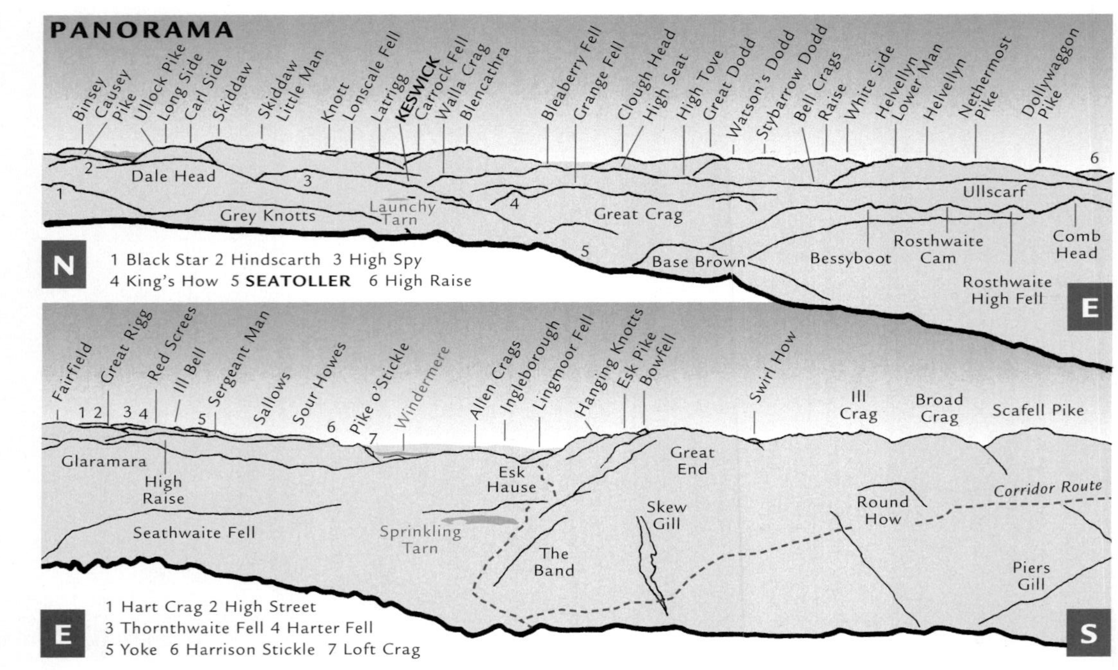
PANORAMA
Binsey
Causey Pike
Ullock Pike
Long Side
Carl Side
Skiddaw
Skiddaw Little Man
Knott
Lonscale Fell
Latrigg
KESWICK
Carrock Fell
Walla Crag
Blencathra
Bleaberry Fell
Grange Fell
Clough Head
High Seat
High Tove
Great Dodd
Watson's Dodd
Stybarrow Dodd
Bell Crags
Raise
White Side
Helvellyn Lower Man
Helvellyn
Nethermost Pike
Dollywaggon Pike
Dale Head
Grey Knotts
Launchy Tarn
Great Crag
Ullscarf
Base Brown
Bessyboot
Rosthwaite Cam
Comb Head
Rosthwaite High Fell
N
E
1 Black Star 2 Hindscarth 3 High Spy
4 King's How 5 SEATOLLER 6 High Raise
Fairfield
Great Rigg
Red Screes
Ill Bell
Sergeant Man
Sallows
Sour Howes
Pike o'Stickle
Windermere
Allen Crags
Ingleborough
Lingmoor Fell
Hanging Knotts
Esk Pike
Bowfell
Swirl How
Ill Crag
Broad Crag
Scafell Pike
Glaramara
High Raise
Esk Hause
Great End
Corridor Route
Round How
Skew Gill
Seathwaite Fell
Sprinkling Tarn
The Band
Piers Gill
E
S
1 Hart Crag 2 High Street
3 Thornthwaite Fell 4 Harter Fell
5 Yoke 6 Harrison Stickle 7 Loft Crag

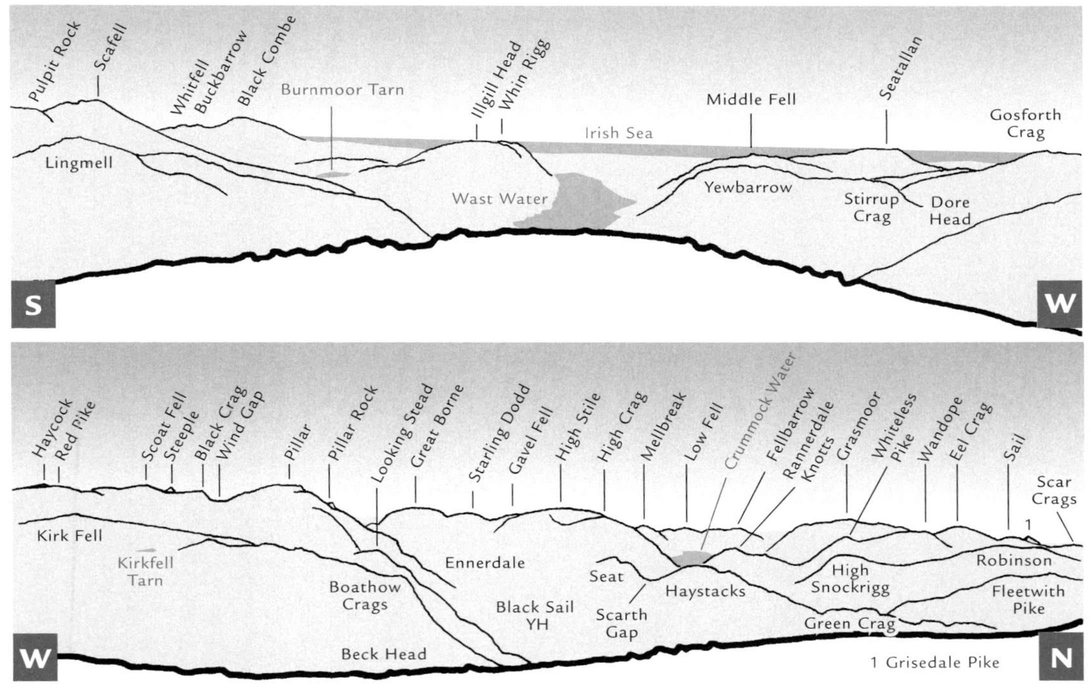
Pulpit Rock
Scafell
Whitfell
Buckbarrow
Black Combe
Burnmoor Tarn
Illgill Head
Whin Rigg
Middle Fell
Seatallan
Gosforth Crag
Irish Sea
Lingmell
Wast Water
Yewbarrow
Stirrup Crag
Dore Head
S
W
Haycock
Red Pike
Scoat Fell
Steeple
Black Crag
Wind Gap
Pillar
Pillar Rock
Looking Stead
Great Borne
Starling Dodd
Gavel Fell
High Stile
High Crag
Mellbreak
Low Fell
Crummock Water
Fellbarrow
Rannerdale Knotts
Grasmoor
Whiteless Pike
Wandope
Eel Crag
Sail
Scar Crags
1
Kirk Fell
Kirkfell Tarn
Boathow Crags
Ennerdale
Black Sail YH
Seat
Scarth Gap
Haystacks
High Snockrigg
Robinson
Fleetwith Pike
Green Crag
Beck Head
W
N
1 Grisedale Pike

7 GREAT HOW 523M/1716FT

Climb it from	Woolpack Inn **24**, Dalegarth Station **25** or Wasdale Head **2**
Character	Scarp at the culmination of the intriguing country east of Whillan Beck to the south of the main Scafell massif
Fell-friendly route	1
Summit grid ref	NY 197 040
Link it with	Slight Side

For some the broad slopes of Great How perform little more than the lead-in to Slight Side, either by the Woolpack Inn path or the Terrace Route, but there is a real sense of space about this rambling height. Set apart, its scarp overlooks Burnmoor Tarn and, but for the monster pile of Scafell, it would be a prime objective for expeditions from Boot.

When the higher tops are in doubt, perhaps lost in cloud, and a good walk is needed, Great How comes into its own. It is a special place from which to survey the rugged fells sweeping round the southern arc from Bowfell to the sea, with Burnmoor Tarn glistening in late afternoon sunlight. From the Eskdale slopes, fascinatingly rough with crags, tarns and pools to explore, Harter Fell and Green Crag also form shapely backdrops. Eel Tarn, overlooked by Great How, overtopped by Scafell, is particularly picturesque.

↑ *Great How from Lambford Bridge*

Three shorter approaches rise up from Eskdale (1–3) and you can make a day-long circuit from either Eskdale or Wasdale using Routes 4 and 5.

Ascent from the head of Eskdale 24

The two principal routes spring from the Woolpack Inn – a fresh place to start and a refreshing place to end. The more regular path leads by Eel Tarn (1).

Via Eel and Stony Tarns →*5km/3 miles* ↑*450m/1475ft* ⏲*2hr 20min*

1 Follow the lane signed from the road left of the pub 'Burnmoor and Wasdale Head'. This leads up behind the inn to a gate, rising to an obvious path divide with bracken looming. Go left with the enclosure wall, this path rises close by a roofless stone bothy over the brow to encounter **Eel Tarn**. The path skirts the blanket bog to the left, keeping to firmer ground. Watch for the branch right that effectively swings on round the tarn to head east into the irregular area of craggy knolls known by the surreal name **Peelplace Noddle**. The path trends up the ridge, negotiating marshy ground and keeps up to the left of **Stony Tarn** mounting onto a more definite ridge. Follow this only so far as it continues to rise up the undulating ridge. As it veers right to contour, head left. Drift slightly left of north to the summit outcrop and cairn.

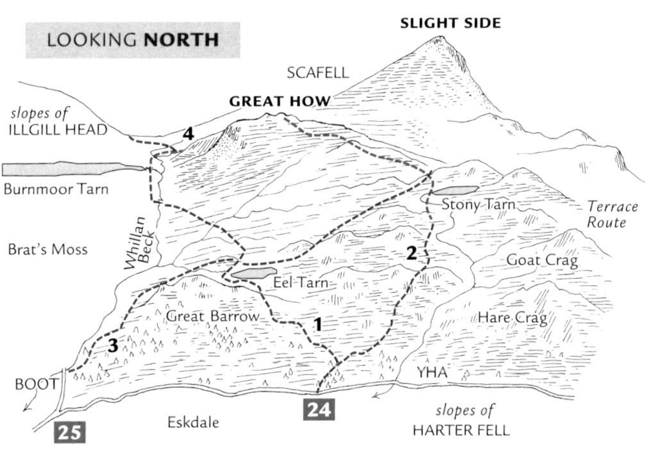

2 The second approach reaches this vicinity by branching right above the inn. This path rises naturally, in secretive spongy terrain, to come above the open marshy bowl of **Blea Beck**. Keep just to the left of the beck, into its upper amphitheatre. Ford the beck with small falls to the left. Climb a steeper bracken bank, with next to no evidence of a path, keep to the firmer ground in contouring to the natural dam rigg, then drop to the outflow of **Stony Tarn**. The tarn, backed by the craggy rim of **Dawsonground Crags**, has black plastic piping drawing water from its outflow. Cross the outflow heading north by the sheepfold and then climb onto the flat ridge to meet up with the path from Eel Tarn (**1**).

Ascent from Dalegarth Station 25

Via Eel and Stony Tarns →*5km/3 miles* ↑*450m/1475ft* ⏲*2hr 45min*

Eel Tarn

A short approach, on slightly confusing and eventually pathless terrain after Eel Tarn, heads up from Boot.

3 From the short village street, pass the Burnmoor Inn and bear right, signed 'Eel Tarn'. A roadway winds up behind the tree-shaded mill, the thunderous thrashings of **Whillan Beck** making an early impression. As the tarmac ends leave the farm-track leading to Gill Bank, with its two specimen monkey puzzle trees. Take the gate right and go left at the three-way footpath sign, again directing to 'Eel Tarn'. The green track threads through a walled passage. The path curves right and up. Do not be lured left onto the path to **Lambford Bridge**, but keep right to reach **Eel Tarn**. The boggy ground on this northern side has to be traversed before skirting to the east of the tarn to join Route **1**.

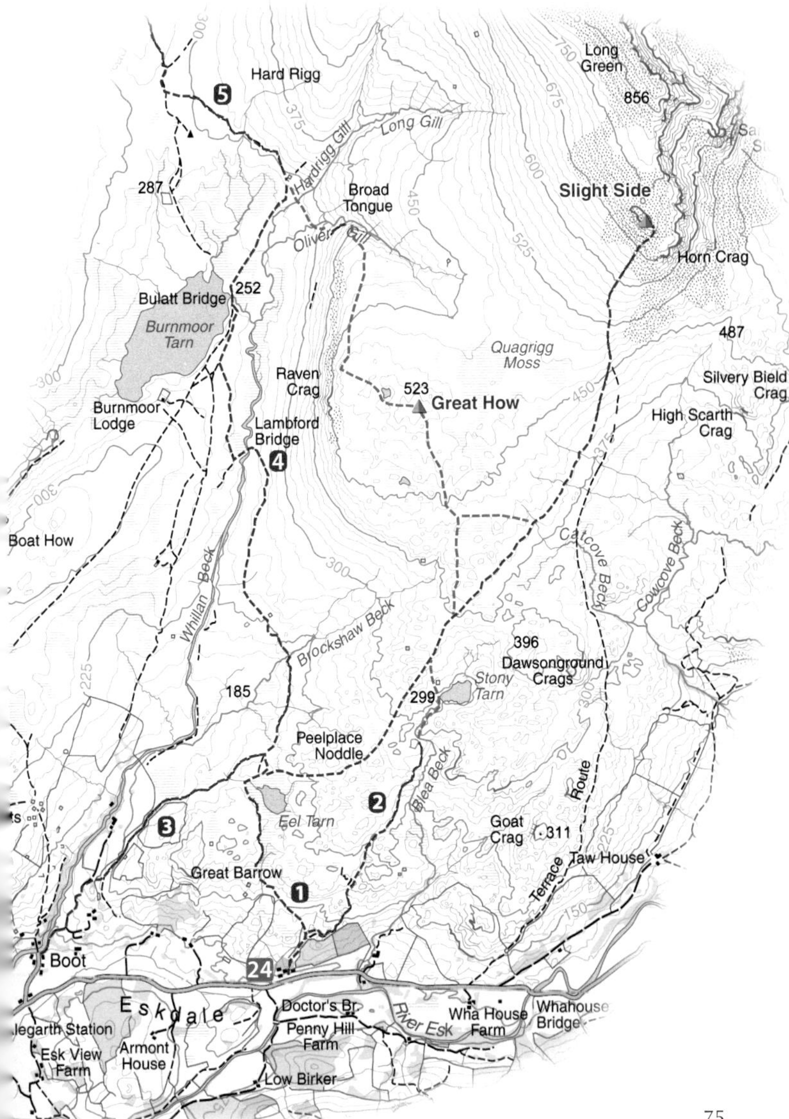
Hard Rigg
Long Green
856
Slight Side
Horn Crag
487
Silvery Bield Crag
High Scarth Crag
Long Gill
Hardrigg Gill
Broad Tongue
Oliver Gill
287
252
Bulatt Bridge
Burnmoor Tarn
Burnmoor Lodge
Raven Crag
523
Great How
Quagrigg Moss
Lambford Bridge
Boat How
Whillan Beck
Catcove Beck
Cowcove Beck
Brockshaw Beck
396
Dawsonground Crags
Stony Tarn
299
185
Peelplace Noddle
Blea Beck
Eel Tarn
Route
Terrace
Goat Crag
311
Great Barrow
Taw House
Boot
Eskdale
Doctor's Br.
River Esk
Wha House Farm
Whahouse Bridge
Penny Hill Farm
Dalegarth Station
Armont House
Esk View Farm
Low Birker

Scafell and Slight Side forming the backdrop from the summit cairn

Via Lambford Bridge and Oliver Gill →*6.7km/4¼ miles* ↑*510m/1675ft* ⏲*3hr 10min*

The other main line of ascent, from the north via Oliver Gill, could be used to make an excellent circuit from either of the Eskdale points of departure.

4 Begin as with Route **1**, continuing from **Eel Tarn** on this well-used path that was once consistently marked with white crosses daubed on stones. See one just before it curves down to Lambford Bridge. Cross **Lambford Bridge**, switching left and right to avoid the marshy patch beyond, the path angling up to join the main path from Boot to skip over the outflow of **Burnmoor Tarn** (the plank footbridge marked Bulatt Bridge on maps has washed away).

Forking half-right on the low path traversing the sheepfold at the foot of **Hard Rigg**, veer right to ford **Hardrigg** and **Oliver Gills**, climbing the south bank by the prominent waterfall: a huge rock block topped by a garden of heather. Keep up the rigg to the right of the gill, thus avoiding the loose scree within the actual gill. Grass predominates and soon easier ground is found. Ascend south on a gently rising scarp edge to the cairn above **Raven Crag**. From the cairn go east, passing two lovely sheets of water. Aim for the left of three outcrops and climb it to find the summit cairn.

Ascent from Wasdale Head 2 *off map N*

Via Oliver Gill →*4.5km/2¾ miles* ↑*485m/1590ft* ⏲*3hr*

A straightforward southerly, then southeasterly, line leads up from Brackenclose.

5 From the car park, go left crossing the broad bridge. Leave the farm-track following the gorse-lined path beside Lingmell Gill to enter the Brackenclose enclosure with a Fell & Rock Club Hut in its midst. Follow the Eskdale bridleway as it rises through gates to cross a twin-arched stone bridge over Hollow Gill. Continue on with the bridleway. As the ground levels out, and just after the **Hard Rigg** path has set off (NE) up the ridge, turn off half-left (SE) to follow a path contouring round to **Hardrigg Gill**. Where the path bends back SW, carry straight on, pathless, to ford the gill and join Route **4** by the waterfall and head steeply up to the summit plateau.

The summit

The highest ground is defined by a solid outcrop with a smaller pike of comparable height to the southwest. From here, Scafell looks a boring heap, the white-flecked peak of Slight Side having the greater visual impact. Between Illgill Head and the sleek slopes of Scafell there is a window into the Western Fells over Yewbarrow. The grander skyline sweep is the southeastern arc from Bowfell right round to Ravenglass.

Safe descents

The sense of isolation is emphasised by the total lack of paths in the upper reaches. The one cause for concern is the western scarp and the one course to avoid E across Quagrigg Moss. For ease of progress aim SE (**1**), watching for the several minor outcrops en route, to join the flimsy trail running S for Eel Tarn and the Woolpack Inn or, slightly better, cross and continue down the slope to join the more certain Terrace Route path beside Catcove Beck, again heading S.

Ridge route

Slight Side →*2.5km/1½ miles* ↓*45m/150ft* ↑*285m/935ft* ◷*3hr*
To minimise bog trotting across Quagrigg Moss, leave the summit aiming SE on line with Hard Knott, thereby joining the path from Boot. Switch acutely NE (left). As the grassy slope steepens the Terrace Route path joins from the right. The way is obvious but higher up the path is embroiled in loose stones. Keep right, onto the ridge – it's easier to climb onto the rocky summit ridge from the N side. It is simply superb.

8 GRIKE 488M/1601FT

Climb it from	Bleach Green **15**, Scarny Brow **14** or Scaly Moss **13**
Character	Western ridge of Crag Fell distinguished by a Bronze Age summit cairn
Fell-friendly route	4
Summit grid ref	NY 085 141
Link it with	Crag Fell

Grike forms a significant part of the headwater slopes of the River Calder, although few walkers will recognise this aspect of its situation, the cloak of conifers on its southern slopes annexing this part of the fell. In truth it is a rather plain fell, enlivened only by its steep northern slopes, incised by the various ravines of Goat and Ben Gills, falling to the meadows and woods of the River Ehen, below the outflow of Ennerdale Water.

The fell is most frequently climbed in conjunction with Crag Fell. To be honest, but for the considerable summit tumulus of Bronze Age origin – now rearranged into one huge and two smaller summit cairns – it would not register in a fellwalkers' log at all. However, for a half-day leg-stretch to a good height and view of the Irish Sea from the west coast, Grike could just fit the bill, or

↑ *Looking up towards Grike from Kinniside Stone Circle*

even as the first stop on a grassy circuit of the headwaters of the River Calder in company with Crag Fell, Iron Crag and Lank Rigg.

Ascent from Bleach Green 15

Choose from an easy, if partly pathless, approach from the northeast (Route 1) and a challenging clamber up Goat Gill – a rarely considered line of ascent for the intrepid, better tackled when the bracken is down.

Direct →*4.1km/2½ miles* ↑*380m/1245ft* ⌚*1hr 50min*

1 Step back over the access cattle grid and follow the roadway left, forking right by Bleach Green Cottage by a hand-gate beside a second cattle grid. Now head along the open track towards **Crag Farm**. As the track bears right, go straight on (with the garden fence left) to an integrated wall step-stile and hand-gate. On joining the track beneath the forestry, turn right and follow this track until the wall on the right ends. Here switch acutely left up into the forestry (no sign) on a green path that climbs steadily to a stile/gate onto the open fell. Rise above the impressive **Ben Gill** ravine overlooking the outflow of **Ennerdale Water**, come to a simple ford and bear off the obvious path to wander up the heather-clad tongue between the two feeder streams of Ben Gill. Cross the plain fence and continue up the ridge, coming above a large sheepfold in the left-hand gully. Cross the right-hand gill as it becomes subterranean, and ascend the featureless fellside SW to the summit.

2 Follow Route **1** to the point where the green path switches back up into the forestry. Now continue straight ahead on the level forest track (roughly west) finding a natural lessening in the dense growth as the first signs of the re-entrant are

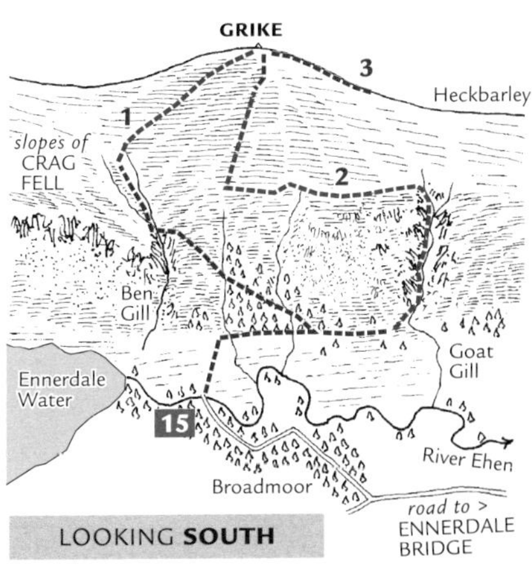

sensed left. So enter and begin to climb the secretive ravine of **Goat Gill**. There is no path, and the easiest ground – a relative statement – lies on the left-hand (E) side, clambering over pine roots. There are some lovely waterfalls, and particularly fine is the one tumbling into the main gill three-quarters of the way up. Near the top break left, grasping the heather to gain the fence along the top. Follow the fence left, with consistently handsome views. Arriving at the fence-junction simply slip through and bear up right to reach the summit. Job done, and quite some job!

Ascent from Scarny Brow 14

Direct →*3.2km/2 miles* ↑*260m/855ft* 🕒*1hr 30min*

The first of two direct ascents from the fell road.

Goat Gill ravine

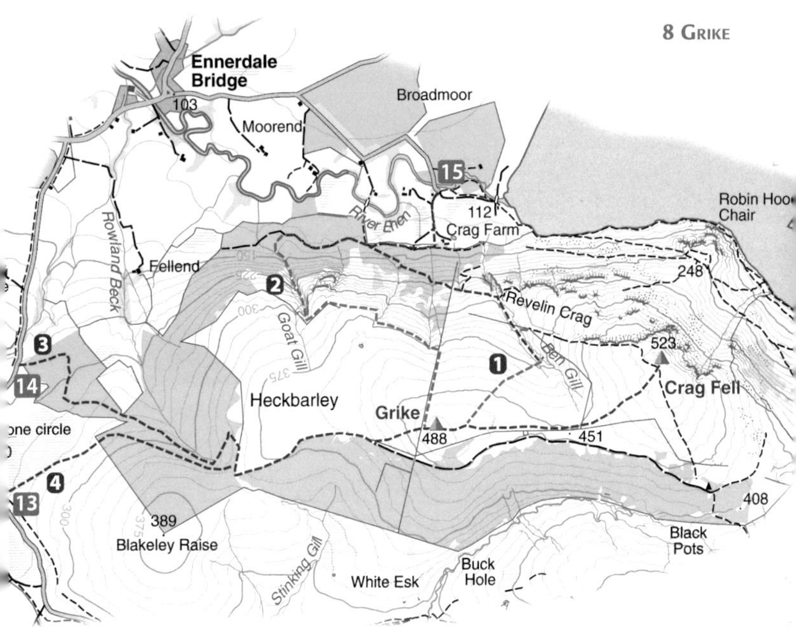

3 Find the (Forestry Commission) **Heckbarley** sign, cross the stile by the forest entry gate and follow the winding forest track. After about 1.5km it bends left (NNW) sharply and then back right (S) to follow a fence to a junction of five tracks.

Take the most left-swinging of the options, heading ENE along the northern boundary of the plantation to the right of a fence. After 750m seek a padlocked galvanised gate in the left-hand fence. Clamber over and follow the thin path directly up the fell, with a fence-stile visible on the horizon. This path leads quickly to the summit cairns.

Ascent from Scaly Moss 13

Direct →*4.2km/2½ miles* ↑*260m/855ft* ⏲ *1hr 30min*

4 Take the old mine road (bridleway), signed 'Crag Fell 3 miles'. This leads to a hand-gate into the forestry land. Some 60m below this point rests, at the angle of the forest fence, a large boulder with the grandiose name of the

Great Stone of Blakeley. This intricately patterned igneous rock appears to have been an ancient boundary stone. As such, it is more significant than the mock stone circle on the common beside the road, which long deceived casual observers, but was found to be a Victorian fraud. The old mine road is a good path and overlooks the forest track, eventually meeting it at a junction of five tracks. Follow Route **3** from this point.

Fence-stile above Heckbarley, looking to Blakeley Raise and Dent

The summit

Most visitors are drawn to this fell-top by its rather large shelter-cairn, built from the remnants of an ancient tumulus. The clear view is north and west to St Bees and the Irish Sea with Ennerdale Water sadly hidden behind its nearest neighbour, Crag Fell.

Safe descents

There is little in the way of difficulty in descent. You can retrace Routes **1**, **3** and **4** with the utmost ease. Just avoid the ravines of Goat and Ben Gills.

Ridge route

Crag Fell →*1.6km/1 mile* ↓*45m/150ft* ↑*80m/260ft* ◷*30min*

An evident path over damp pasture eases down the gentle slope due E, passing a mast and weather-station enclosure (gathering data for Sellafield). Cross a fence-stile near the fence-junction, from where the clear path drifts unimpeded NE to arrive at the summit.

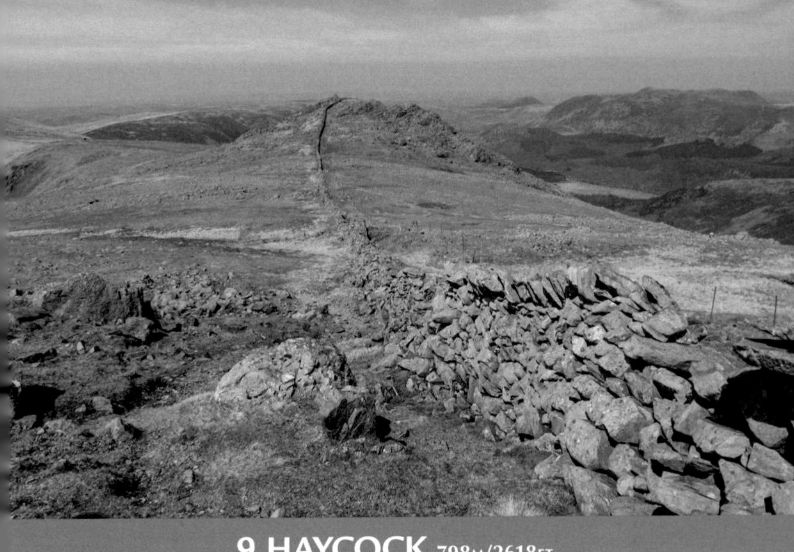

9 HAYCOCK 798M/2618FT

Climb it from	Bowness Knott **16**, Netherbeck Bridge **4** or Harrow Head **9**
Character	Mid-point of Ennerdale's long southern horizon
Fell-friendly route	4
Summit grid ref	NY 144 107
Link it with	Caw Fell, Scoat Fell or Seatallan
Part of	The Netherbeck Horseshoe

From most valley bases Haycock is a long march away, a great swelling mass on the Ennerdale and Wasdale watershed. Set back from Ennerdale proper by deeply entrenched gills, it features less obviously. Yet observed from Seatallan to the south it rises majestically above the wild hollow of Stockdale Head, at the source of the River Bleng. It has some craggy ground, with Little Gowder Crag a notable feature on the main ridge towards Caw Fell.

Offering clear views of the Scafell range from the summit but not well known, the fell makes a really good objective for the walker seeking something a bit different. Starting from Ennerdale (Routes 1 and 2), you could include it in a circuit with Caw Fell, Iron Crag and Crag Fell. Or strong walkers might take it in as part of a greater fell-round, with Pillar the crowning glory of a mountain

↑ *Looking towards Little Gowder Crag from the summit of Haycock (photo: Anne Bowskill)*

day, either from Ennerdale or from Wasdale. However, there is no denying the pleasure of the approach via the wild fastness of Stockdale Head or Nether Beck (Routes 3–5).

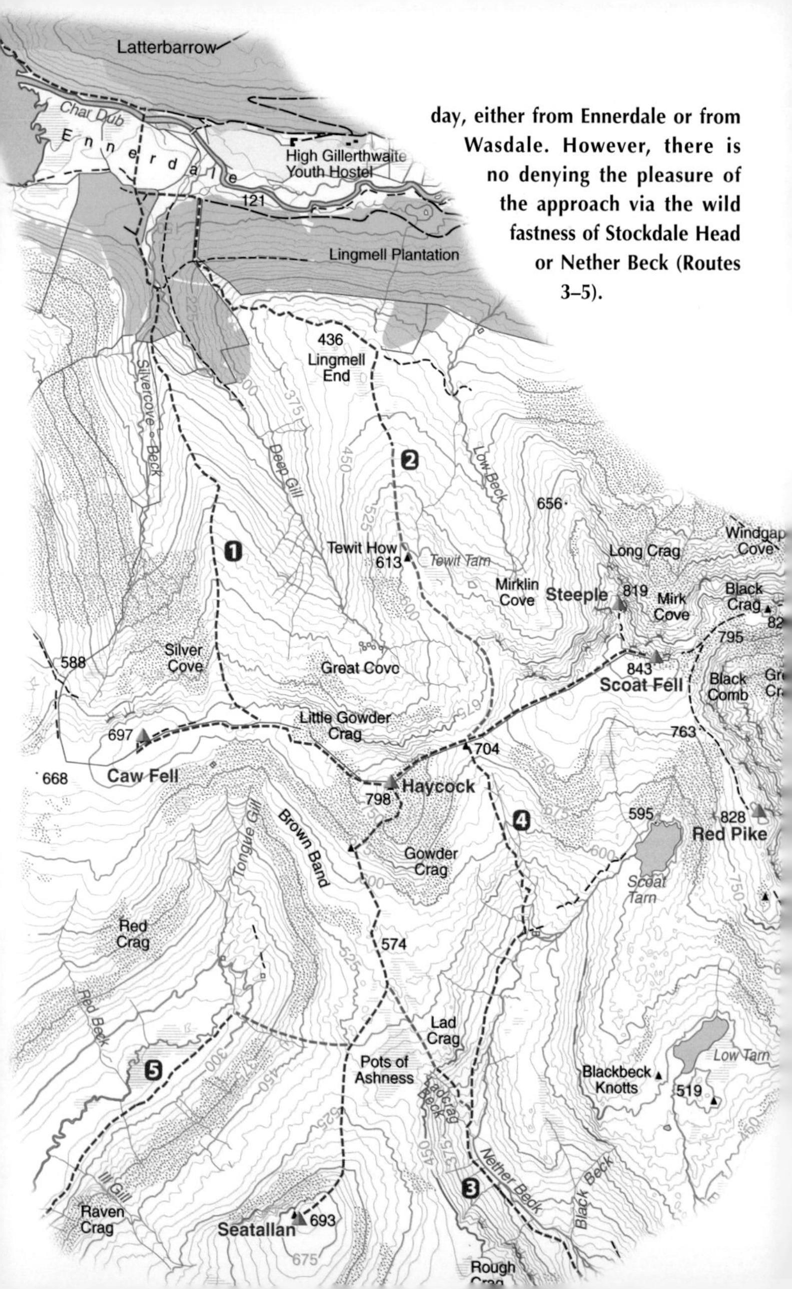

Ascent from Bowness Knott 16 *off map NW*

Two northerly spurs run down from the summit of Haycock to the head of Ennerdale. Route 1 fights up through the heather to the west of Deep Gill. Route 2 follows an ancient trans-dale connecting route over Tewit How, albeit largely without clear paths.

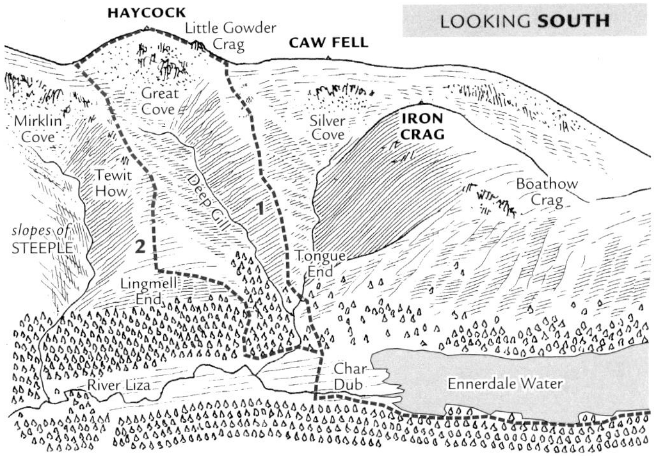

Via Tongue End →*8km/5 miles* ↑*700m/2300ft* ⌚*4hr 20min*

1 Follow the valley track beyond the lake-head and alongside the in-flowing River Liza, here called **Char Dub**. Take the first right-hand turn with the track to cross Irish Bridge, a concrete-culverted ford, and advance along the lane to a double-gated access into the forest. Keep forward, south, on the clear track leading through the mature trees. It comes by an awkward bank beside Woundell Beck, and passes the confluence to reach and cross a footbridge spanning **Silvercove Beck**. The path now ascends the rough-felled Tongue End ridge to reach a fence-stile. From here it embarks on the rank-heather fell proper. The going is quite tough as the eroded path works up through the heather. Eventually, after a cairn, the path shakes clear of it and runs on up the grassy ridge, evading outcropping to reach the Ennerdale Fence. Follow this left, keeping close to the wall to skirt to the right of **Little Gowder Crag**

– notice how the wall was cleverly stepped up to overcome this rocky obstacle – to reach the summit.

Via Tewit How →*8.8km/5½ miles* ↑*710m/2330ft* 🕒*4hr 30min*

2 Follow Route **1** over Irish Bridge to enter the forestry at the double-gate. Here bear left with the track, which crosses a second concrete-culverted bridge – this time crossing Woundell Beck. As the track rounds the next bend, after being joined by a track from the right, break off the firm track onto the soft, cattle-poached ground leading up the break to a hand-gate in a cross-fence. Continue past a seat on firmer ground. The forest gangway steps onto rockier ground, with heather leading ultimately to a fence-stile onto the ridge of **Lingmell End**. Continue beside the fence, heading east. After a large boulder, as the ground shapes to descend towards **Low Beck** and the **Steeple** ridge, veer right, with only a hint of a path initially through the heather. A path soon becomes apparent, leading up the broad ridge, but becomes less evident as the heather is left behind. The route rises onto the crest of **Tewit How**, with its cairn, above the marshy hollow of **Tewit Tarn**, now with barely enough open water to merit the description. Haycock is well in view from the cairn over the lonely hollow of **Great Cove**. As you reach the head of the cove, contour off the main ridge and rise S and then SW to the depression between Haycock and **Scoat Fell**. At the cairn bear right, following the Ennerdale Fence, on whichever side you prefer, to the summit.

Ennerdale Fence wall takes a serious step on Little Gowder Crag

Ascent from Netherbeck Bridge
4 *off map S*

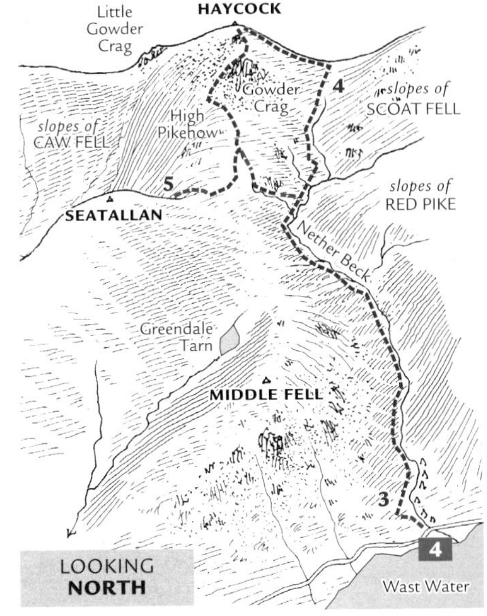

Two routes set off from the shore of Wast Water along the Netherbeck bridleway, Route 3 heading through bog and bracken to climb around the back of Gowder Crag to the summit while Route 4 offers a much more straightforward approach.

Via Ladcrag Beck
→6.4km/4 miles ↑785m/2575ft ⌚4hr 10min

3 Step up from the parking space and skirt the marsh, following the bracken-free passage on the left to join the lateral bridleway. The pathway up this long, deep, sinuous valley is stony, inhibiting a fast stride. Take a moment to admire the lovely waterfall early on, as falls further up are removed from the line of the path.

Upon fording **Ladcrag Beck**, about 2.5km from the parking space, travel some 30m further up the path before breaking off the bridle-path left into the bracken, short of the fence enclosure. A path exists, although the bracken can obscure it early on. This mounts under **Lad Crag** and follows close to the east bank of the beck to gain the marshy hollow close to the even more boggy **Pots of Ashness**. A tenuous path continues, which tends to drift towards the west side of the broad, undulating rising ridge. **This is critical to know, as there is no head-on way up Haycock from the south.** Seek a marker cairn, NY 142 104, set upon a boulder indicating the start of a grassy rake that slants steeply but easily through the scree to reach the saddle tucked behind the headland of **Gowder Crag**. Bear left, passing a second headland, with a prominent cairn, to reach the ridge wall and summit wind-shelter.

Haycock from Winscale Hows above Ladcrag Beck

Via the head of Nether Beck →*6.4km/4 miles* ↑*785m/2575ft* ⏲*4hr*

4 Start on Route **3** but stay with the old bridle-path after **Ladcrag Beck**. There is no mystery on its northward course – just avoid being lured right at the major waters-meet, the large sheepfold a clue. This path leads up to **Scoat Tarn**. Instead aim for the unnamed depression in the main ridge. En route you may be attracted to visit the huge boulder over to the right across the beck, projecting out from the slopes of **Scoat Fell** consistent with the fell's name. At the large cairn turn left (W), where the summit beckons.

Ascent from Harrow Head 9 *off map SW*

Via Stockdale Head →*8.4km/5¼ miles* ↑*710m/2330ft* ⏲*4hr 30min*

This is the connoisseur's approach. Meet another walker here and you'll meet a soulmate. If you don't mind the road-walking or can deploy a second car, it would make an excellent circuit with Route 3 or Route 4 back down to Wast Water.

5 Follow the concrete roadway rising towards Windsor Farm. Bear off right, as indicated by the bridleway sign, up the green track. Coming beside a wall, ford the gill, and move on between the fenced fold and the trench of the washed-out gill. A green way marches on free across the level moor. Gradually the path moves round the base of **Seatallan**, with Haycock coming into view on the skyline ahead, to the right of the bulky mass of Caw Fell. After fording Stare Beck, and just before Swinsty Beck, pass through a giant thick ring of stones, the remnants of a Viking stock enclosure. The path is largely consistent as it runs on into the dale head, aiming towards a fold. Steep slopes wall up the wild head of the Bleng valley. The easy route stops short of the fold and clambers up the north side of Rossy Gill to link up with the ridge path off Seatallan. This leads over the back of the skyline outcrops to join Route **3** from Ladcrag Beck.

The summit

There is a cairn on the south side of the broken ridge wall, although the ragged wind-shelter on the north side may be judged the summit. The all-round view is pretty good, with the Scafell range well displayed, while Scoat Fell intervenes to limit the choice of Ennerdale summits. Wander south to visit the cairn on the south top, and perhaps even go further down to stand on top of Gowder Crag for its view to Seatallan and the wilds of the upper Bleng valley.

Safe descents

The Ennerdale Fence is a godsend in mist – for Ennerdale follow it W. But be aware you must skirt Little Gowder Crag on the south side. As the ridge eases the swiftest route retraces Route **1** N down the Tongue End ridge. Alternatively, simply cling to the wall's course, keeping to the south side to cross Iron Crag, useful for Crag Fell and the forest track down by Heckbarley. For Wasdale, go

Scoat Fell from Haycock (photo: Anne Bowskill)

E down beside the wall (**4**), and in the first depression – with its cairn on the south side of the wall – bear right to follow Nether Beck on a consistent path.

Ridge routes

Caw Fell →*1.6km/1 mile* ↓*140m/460ft* ↑*40m/130ft* 🕒*25min*
The Ennerdale Fence does all the navigation for you, but watch out for Little Gowder Crag. Skirt it on the south side, but keep to the north side of the wall to reach the summit cairn.

Scoat Fell →*1.6km/1 mile* ↓*90m/295ft* ↑*140m/460ft* 🕒*35min*
Follow the Ennerdale Fence E, preferring the south side for underfoot comfort. After the depression, with grass from this point onwards, choose the north side for the fine scarp-edge views into Mirklin Cove and to Steeple. For all the ravages of time, the ridge wall is a substantial feature and the perfect companion all the way to the top.

Seatallan →*3.2km/2 miles* ↓*310m/1020ft* ↑*205m/670ft* 🕒*1hr*
Care is needed, especially in mist, to find the key point of departure off the high ground, as the south flank of the fell is well endowed with rock and scree. Head S from the summit, passing the first cairned top. Within a few paces of the second cairned crown find a modest cairn in the saddle. This indicates the top of a grassy rake that slants SW, with several minor cairns en route, down to a boulder capped with a cairn. The path turns left and weaves down the undulating, largely grassy/boggy ridge. Veer to the right of the worst wetness, the hollow bearing the charming name of the Pots of Ashness. The ridge path continues S, climbing up the steep plain ridge to arrive at the OS pillar and large tumulus cairn.

10 ILLGILL HEAD 609M/1998FT

Climb it from	Wasdale Head **2**, Dalegarth Station **25** or Miterdale Forest **27**
Character	Easternmost end of the famous Wasdale Screes ridge
Fell-friendly route	1
Summit grid ref	NY 169 049
Link it with	Whin Rigg

Illgill Head is the northern culmination of a great ridge born on Irton Pike above Santon Bridge, and shares custodianship with Whin Rigg of the majestic Wast Water screes, much admired by motorists pulling up all along the lakeside road to Wasdale Head. Above that arresting mural of rock and scree, on its high northern slopes, heather abounds – a joy to behold in August especially when flooded by the golden light of a late-afternoon sun.

This prime viewpoint for the Western Fells and the array of shapely fells encircling Wasdale Head has one natural line of ascent, with two strands of approach off the old corpse road which used to link Wasdale Head with consecrated ground in Eskdale. A circuit on the Wast Water side could be fashioned including both summits, making use of Greathall Gill, but only for

↑ *Illgill Head from Greendale*

those who are gluttons for punishment and ready to tackle the shoreline travail that is the Screes Footpath. There is nothing like it elsewhere in Lakeland, although the most punishing section resides in Whin Rigg's court, absolving Illgill Head from blame for twisted ankles.

The shortest approach is the southeasterly one from Wasdale Head (1) but fine expeditions can also be made from Eskdale (2) and Miterdale (3).

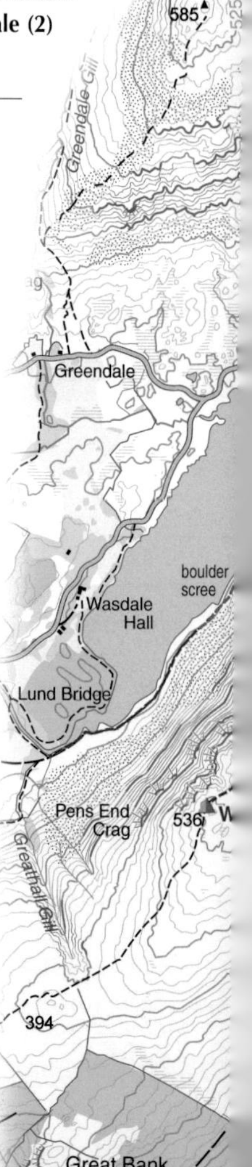

Ascent from Wasdale Head 2

Direct →*4km/2½ miles* ↑*535m/1750ft* ⏲*2hr 15min*

A clear path leads up to the summit through varied terrain and over a fairy-tale bridge.

1 Leave the car park, follow the trackway left to cross the broad farm-bridge spanning **Lingmell Gill**. Bear left, flanked by gorse, and wend upstream to a fork in the way at **Brackenclose**, a Fell & Rock Club property. Follow the path right, signposted 'Eskdale'. The track passes through three gates, then rises over the fairy-tale twin-arched bridge, where Hollow Gill and **Groove Gill** converge. Pass a group of ruined 18th-century peat huts. Shortly after the conifers end, the path forks, cairns indicating the old corpse road up to the saddle. Keep right to ford **Straighthead Gill** and begin the climb in earnest. Soon the wall on your left draws close to the path. Higher up the main path crosses this wall and pulls away from it. In misty conditions, you may choose to stay beside it (dashed green line on the map and topo) but beware that although it does draw back towards the summit path once again it leads to the top of a crag to the NW of the summit, not the summit itself. Nearing the prominent shoulder brow the path splits again, the regular path taking the ridge head-on by a cairn leading irrevocably to the shelter-cairned east summit.

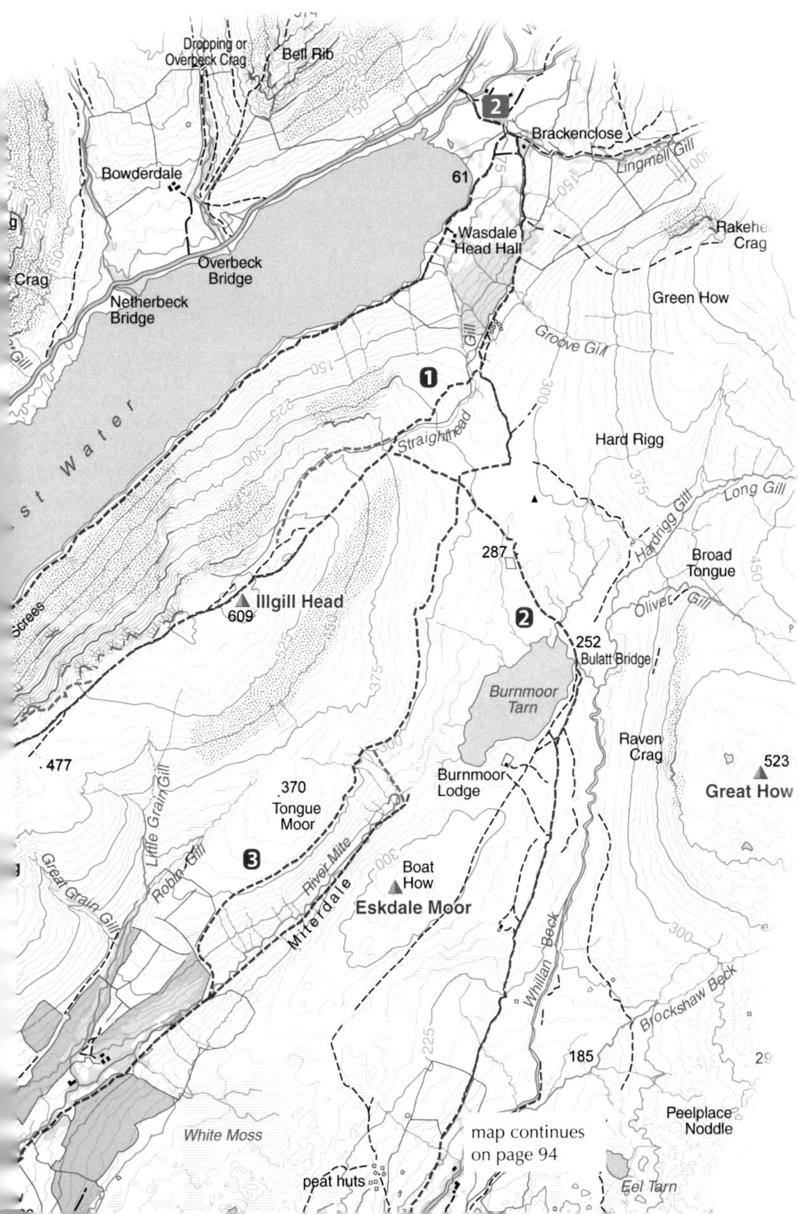

map continues on page 94

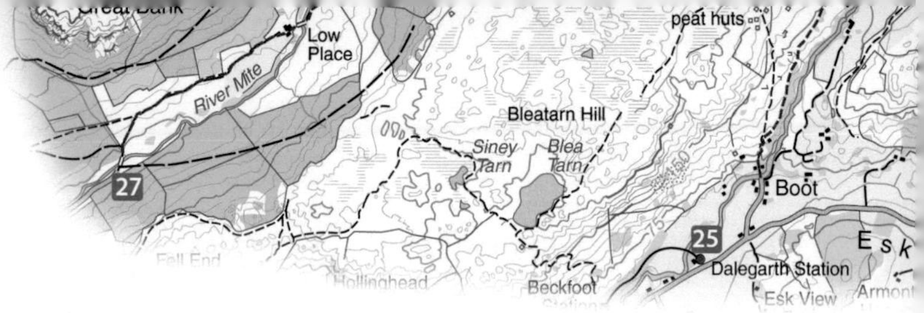

Ascent from Dalegarth Station 25

Via Burnmoor Tarn →*6.7km/4¼ miles* ↑*555m/1820ft* ⌚*3hr 10min*

Although somewhat remote from Eskdale, there is every good reason to make this excursion from Boot along the shores of Whillan Beck.

2 Leave the head of the village street at the gate beyond Eskdale Mill. Follow the green track branching right via gates – the old corpse road between Eskdale and Wasdale – up the steadily rising path onto **Eskdale Moor** parallel with **Whillan Beck**. Cross the plank footbridge at the outflow of **Burnmoor Tarn**, continuing level for a time, then, mounting a short rise, branch half-left at the top. An evident path leads through a shallow depression, rising diagonally northwest up the easy slope, crossing the Balcony Path from **Miterdale**, now tackling steeper ground to join the popular path at the top of **Straighthead Gill** (**1**).

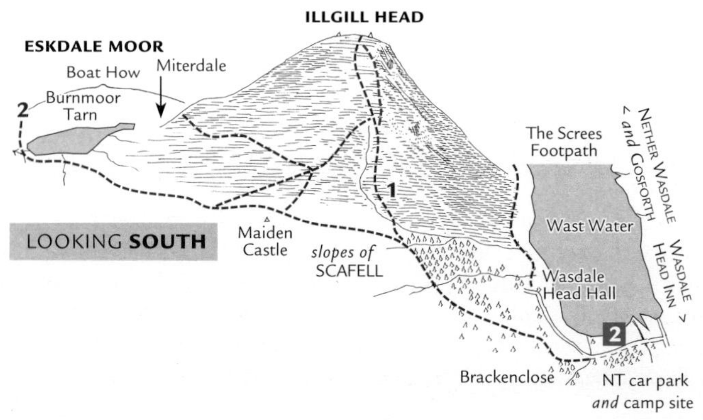

Fairy-tale twin-arched bridge above Brackenclose

Ascent from Miterdale 27

Via the Balcony Path →*8km/5 miles* ↑*835m/2740ft* ⏲*3hr 30min*

Rising from lower Miterdale a footpath draws up and along the edge of Tongue Moor as a balcony, continuing across the eastern slopes of Illgill Head, avoiding the soggy marshes en route to the summit.

3 Leave the open space crossing the broad bridge to follow the farm-track to Low Place. Pass between the farmhouse and the traditional barn and go right via the gate, curving round left with the wall. Notice the wooden board set into the wall. The farmer employed Cumbrian dialect, his wry humour prompted by frequent requests for directions from walkers. 'HOD REET FUR ESHDEL' speeds them on their way down the valley. Twenty metres after the ford cross the footbridge lurking in the bushes. Follow the rough open track leading through a gateway and then a gate into a lane. Ignore the green-way left to Bakerstead (an outdoor pursuits centre connected to the West Lakes Academy in Egremont). Instead advance on a path to a stile at the corner of the plantation.

The path next fords a gill, crossing a marshy patch and continues up the valley with conifers up to the left. At a ladder-stile and gate by a sheep handling pen the very narrow upper section of the dale is entered. However, you smartly turn left, ford the infant **Mite** to climb steeply beside the plantation. Rising onto a shoulder with a wall/fence left turn right to follow the balcony path on **Tongue Moor**: this overlooks the narrow defile of upper Miterdale.

Wasdale Head from the upper section of wall on Illgill Head

Sweeping easily through the bracken admire across the valley Boat How, overtopped by Harter Fell and Green Crag. Duly the path declines, crossing the feeder gills that spill into the quirky amphitheatre at the head of Miterdale. Burnmoor Tarn commands attention, as too the great mass of Scafell ahead. Contouring north to avoid marshy ground watch for a crossing path. Take this to go left, climbing to connect with (**1**) and rise steeply by Straighthead Gill.

The summit

Surveyors have fixed the highest point to be on the swelling plateau, south from the shelter-cairn. However, the cairn has been erected at a less momentous spot some 100m to the south, a point that at least gives a good view towards the Eskdale fells and the more distant Black Combe. Quite the majority of visitors are happy to stop at the shelter-cairn at NY 168 050, prizing its view of the head of Wast Water. Visit the large western cairn and stride 30 bold paces north to the brink of the scarp… now you know the real thrill of The Screes!

Safe descents

Leave the summit cairn NE, the wall quickly coming into view (**1**). Follow this down by Straighthead Gill to meet up with the N–S bridleway, then continue N, via gates, to the shelter of Wasdale Head.

Ridge route

Whin Rigg →*2.2km/1½ miles* ↓*135m/440ft* ↑*75m/245ft* ⌚*50min*
A clear path leads along the broad plateau to the west top, the ground falling steadily into the wide depression, or you could trend right to follow the narrow sheep trod along the very brink of The Screes escarpment. (Beware that there are sections where the continual process of slippage is revealed in fracture slumps. Note how even the sheep show due caution and keep to the firmer ground. There are also several places where arêtes allow you to venture onto spurs, offering precipitous views of the deep dark waters of Wast Water.) The main ridge path, which has two winding variants, passes a pair of tarns before ascending to the shelter-cairn on the slightly more certain summit knoll, on the north side of the path.

Illgill Head from Kirk Fell

11 IRON CRAG 640M/2100FT

Climb it from	Scaly Moss **13**, Scarny Brow **14**, Bleach Green **15**, Bowness Knott **16** or Coldfell Gate **11**
Summit	NY 123 119
Character	Great ridge between Crag Fell and Caw Fell, dividing the barren pasture of Kinniside Common from the rank heather of Ennerdale
Fell-friendly route	1
Link it with	Caw Fell, Lank Rigg or Crag Fell

Iron Crag's whale-back ridge forms a considerable skyline above the southern shores of Ennerdale Water, linking Crag Fell with Caw Fell. On its northern and eastern flanks, lovely birch wood fringes the lake and above a broad canvas of heather spreads over the pathless slopes of the Side, an ancient red-deer preserve. The upper slopes sustain a sub-alpine meadow. All this is in stark contrast to the barren western slopes at the headwaters of Worm Gill.

The main walkers' route follows the tidy wall of the Ennerdale Fence across the fell without a passing thought, intent on Caw Fell and Haycock. However, the curious wanderer will be rewarded by a minor deviation to visit the unusual scarp feature of Boathow Crag or the wild depths of secretive Silver Cove. An

↑ *The beautifully crafted Ennerdale Fence wall rising north to the summit*

impressive view northwards from the summit reaches over the upper slopes of Great Borne, Starling Dodd and the High Stile range towards the magnificence of the North-Western Fells.

A variety of routes lead up from all directions – from the fell road to the west (1), from the southern (2–4) and northern (5) shores of Ennerdale Water and from Wast Water (6). Do not however try to follow the bridleway clearly marked on OS maps from Worm Gill up Long Grain and directly over the edge of the crag! It does not exist.

Ascent from Scaly Moss 13 or Scarny Brow 14

Via Grike →*8km/5 miles* ↑*430m/1410ft* ⏲*3hr*

A straightforward path from alternative starting points on the fell road to the west.

1 The Scarny Brow route starts at the gate/stile entrance to the **Heckbarley** plantations (Forestry Commission), located beside the cattle-grid access to Kinniside Common, above Ennerdale Bridge. Follow the good gravel track winding up through the block-cleared forest to a track junction at the corner of Heckbarley pasture near Kinney How. From Scaly Moss reach this

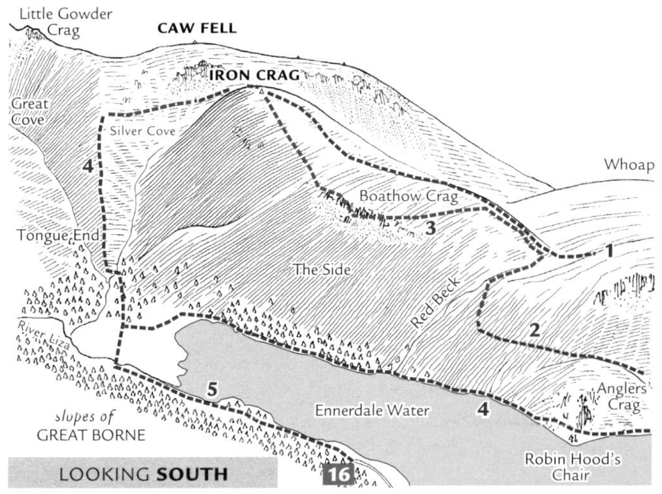

point more directly from the open road verge by following the signposted bridleway, which leads via a gate above the Great Stone of Blakeley.

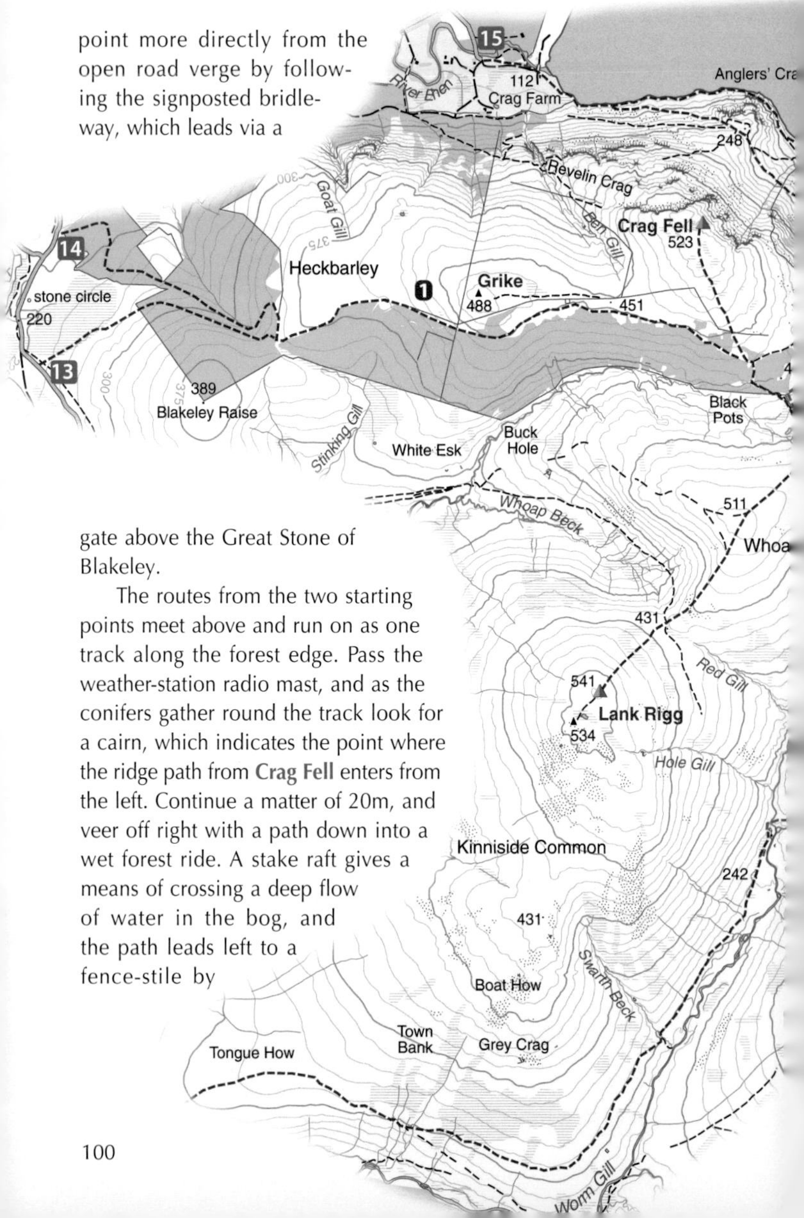

The routes from the two starting points meet above and run on as one track along the forest edge. Pass the weather-station radio mast, and as the conifers gather round the track look for a cairn, which indicates the point where the ridge path from **Crag Fell** enters from the left. Continue a matter of 20m, and veer off right with a path down into a wet forest ride. A stake raft gives a means of crossing a deep flow of water in the bog, and the path leads left to a fence-stile by

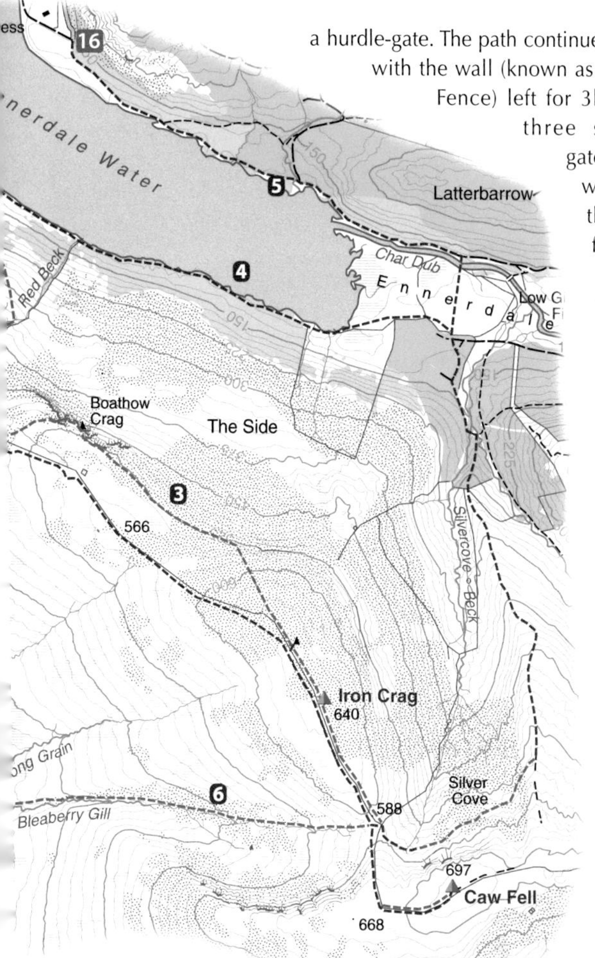

a hurdle-gate. The path continues, rising easily with the wall (known as the Ennerdale Fence) left for 3km. There are three small hand-gates set into this wall. At the third (after the fell levels) go through, continuing with the wall to the right to the summit.

Ascent from Bleach Green 15

Routes 2 and 3 make a fairly direct ascent from the north-west, with Route 3 just veering off path to make the most of the scarp edge above Ennerdale Water. Route 4 takes its time and combines the beauties of the lake and the wilds of the heather moor.

Via the Miners' Path

→7.6km/4¾ miles ↑555m/1820ft ⏲3hr 20min

Gate in the Ennerdale Fence (photo: Andrew Leaney)

2 Leave the enclosed car park by the hand-gate and follow the primary path to the outflow of **Ennerdale Water**, passing the outflow weir. Continue with the grand long view of Ennerdale ahead to go through a hand-gate in a wall bearing an Anglers' Crag National Trust signboard. This path runs along the stony shore of the lake. Watch for the rising path after some 300m, and climb with it to the grassy saddle at the top of the **Anglers' Crag** promontory. Directly after crossing the saddle avoid the trap of breaking left down the more popular path, after some 100m. Instead stick with the old miners' path as it contours (eventually fading) round to an adapted sheep-creep wall-stile, beyond a ford over **Red Beck** at NY 106 138. Turn right (uphill) here, keeping beside the left-hand wall (no path), and when a fence meets the wall continue within the wall/fence passage. Reaching the tip of the forestry, pass through by the unhinged gate to join the regular ridge path rising left, with the Ennerdale Fence on the left, and continue on with Route **1**.

Via Boathow Crag *→7.6km/4¾ miles ↑570m/1870ft ⏲3hr 30min*

3 Alternatively, go through the first hand-gate you come to (after the convergence of Routes **1** and **2**) in the Ennerdale Fence and climb a little further with the wall now to your right. As the slope and gullies ease a fraction, bear left through the heather to come along the brink of **Boathow Crag**. You may wish to venture down onto the slump ridge, with a cairn at the upper end, and then scramble up the stony connection with the rocky scarp. Follow the broken wall along this edge. As the wall begins to drift downhill, bear up onto the plateau top.

Via the lakeshore path *→10km/6¼ miles ↑560m/1840ft ⏲4hr 15min*

4 Follow the route of the Coast to Coast Walk along the lakeshore path, stepping over **Robin Hood's Chair** under **Anglers' Crag**, and continue via a hand-gate to the meadow at the head of the lake. Enter a lane at a kissing-gate and turn right to go through the double hand-gates at the end of the forest.

Keep forward, S, on the clear track leading through the mature trees. It comes by an awkward bank beside Woundell Beck, and passes the confluence to reach and cross a footbridge spanning **Silvercove Beck**. The path now ascends the rough-felled **Tongue End** ridge to reach a fence-stile. The going is quite tough as the path, worn by water in places, works up through the rank heather. Eventually when, after a cairn, the path shakes clear of the heather, branch off the ridge to the right before the outcropping. Dip down some 30m (90ft) to a small pointed rock, then slant across the broad damp shelf at the head of the valley. At this point you are without the aid of the reassuring path until, after fording a gill, one materialises and continues on the rise to the top of the wall climbing out of **Silver Cove**. Where the broken wall of the Ennerdale Fence is fenced, cross the wall-stile in the corner and ascend with the substantial wall on the left to the summit.

Bowness Knott from the top of Boathow Crag

Ascent from Bowness Knott 16

Via Tongue End →*9.6km/6 miles* ↑*560m/1840ft* ⌚*4hr 10min*

Another good day out, with a gentle walk-in along the north shore of the lake.

5 Follow the valley track beyond the lake-head and alongside the in-flowing River Liza, here called **Char Dub**. Take the first right-hand turn with the track to cross Irish Bridge, a concrete-culverted ford, and advance along the lane to a double-gated access into the forest to join Route **4**.

Ascent fron Coldfell Gate 11 *off map W*

Via Worm Gill →*9.6km/6 miles* ↑*525m/1720ft* 🕓*4hr*

A long approach, which would work well as part of a Worm Gill skyline walk if you add the summits of Whoap and Lank Rigg to your day.

6 From the parking space, adjacent to the road cattle grid, follow the track E into the valley, passing a barrier and continuing on down through the gated pens to cross the gated footbridge over the River Calder. Keep with the green bridle-track (damp in places) running along the lower southern slopes of Lank Rigg, especially wet as it descends in curving NE into the Worm Gill valley, fording Swarth Beck en route to the Intake Works waters-meet. Ford the southward-flowing beck beside the sheepfold and keep company with **Bleaberry Gill**, rising E. The lower third of this valley is a chaos of boulders and so progress cannot be speedy. Complete the pathless ascent to the broad saddle, which in effect links over into **Silver Cove**. Where the fence and wall join, cross the stile and turn left. Climb immediately over the wall-stile on the corner and follow the ridge wall up to the summit.

The summit

A modest cairn rests upon rock some 50m northeast of the wall-gate. Poignantly tucked into the walled hollow are pieces of fuselage from a Canadian F86 Sabre jet that clipped the fell-top and crashed into Bleaberry Hill on 29 June 1959. The summit is otherwise a confusing jumble of low outcropping rock intermingled with grass. There is a square fenced enclosure to the south, one of three near the ridge wall keeping sheep out in order to judge the effect of non-grazing on this sub-alpine meadow.

Deeply cut rock arrow pointing to Steeple beside the north cairn

Safe descents

The Ennerdale Fence (ridge wall) provides a sure guide in poor weather, leading back to the forest track in the long finger of conifer plantation (**1**), and continuing unerringly down by Heckbarley to Kinniside Common (about 6.4km). The western slopes are tame grass, leading by the often-damp Worm Gill bridleway to Coldfell Gate, almost 8km distant (**6**).

Ridge routes

Caw Fell →*1.6km/1 mile* ↓*55m/180ft* ↑*110m/360ft* 🕒*35min*
The Ennerdale Fence does all the navigation for you. Slip back through the gate and follow the wall left through the depression and up the scarp bank to the wall corner. Either cross the fence-stile or keep the wall on your left as you round the corner to find a further stile. Here the fence/broken wall becomes a secure wall, a matter of 50m from the summit cairn.

Lank Rigg →*4.8km/3 miles* ↓*110m/360ft* ↑*215m/705ft* 🕒*2hr*
Go through the gate and follow the Ennerdale Fence right. This descends in two easy stages. As the slope begins the second steep section towards the forestry, find a quad-bike track merging from the left. Bear off and follow this SW, crossing the featureless top of Whoap (pronounced 'warp'). The quad-track drifts W but maintain your SW course. A clear path comes underfoot, aiding progress down through a shallow depression at the head of the deep Whoap Beck comb, then climb on an evident path to the Ordnance Survey column.

Crag Fell →*4.5km/2¾ miles* ↓*235m/770ft* ↑*115m/375ft* 🕒*1hr 10min*
Again the Ennerdale Fence does much of the navigation work. Go through the gate and turn right. Keep strict company with the wall ridge path down to a fence-stile beside a hurdle-gate. The path leads through the peaty confines of the conifer plantation, negotiating a flow of water by a stake raft. Rising to the forest track, go left, and within 20m find a cairn guiding the ridge path off the track. Follow the path up the open glade in the conifers upon heathery ground to a fence-stile that exits the plantation. An evident path completes the task NW.

12 KIRK FELL 802M/2631FT

Climb it from	Wasdale Green **1** or Black Sail Hut **17**
Character	Steep slopes predominate, with twin summits on its gentle crown
Fell-friendly route	5
Summit grid ref	NY 195 105
Link it with	Great Gable or Pillar
Part of	The Upper Ennerdale Round

Stand by the porch of tiny St Olaf's Church, built in 1550 with, it is said, roof trusses from Viking longships, and your eyes are drawn to the simple conical lines of Kirk Fell. A delightful segment of leaded window inside is dedicated to Charles Pickles, one-time President of the Fell & Rock Climbing Club. It mis-quotes Psalm 121: 'I will lift up mine eyes unto the hills from whence cometh my strength', leaving out a vital comma! The mountaineer finds the mountains invigorating whereas the psalmist was asking God for strength to tackle the likes of Highnose Head (Route 2).

Kirk Fell from the head of Wasdale is a real scalp of fellwalking pride. The summit plateau is defended by crags and fiercely steep slopes. Ridge walkers all

↑ *Kirk Fell across Beck Head*

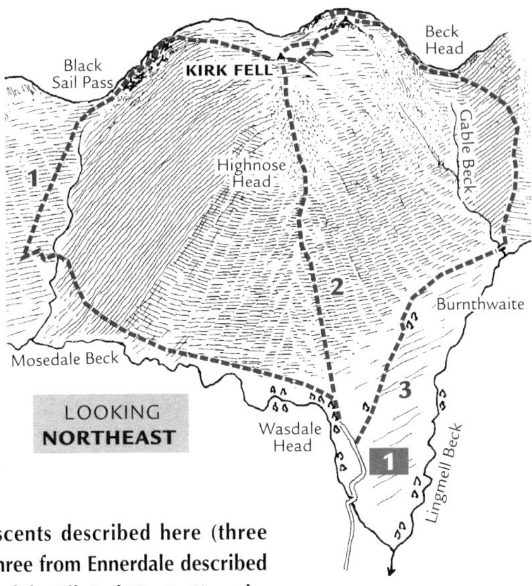

too frequently slip past underneath the summit on an terrace path along its northern flank that runs between Black Sail and Beck Head, leaving the very top only for the dedicated few. You may well have this unique view of the true giants of Wasdale to yourself.

None of the ascents described here (three from Wasdale and three from Ennerdale described here), unless you climb by Rib End (Route 3) or the head stream of Sail Beck via Baysoar Slack (Route 5).

Ascent from Wasdale Green 1

Most ascents stem from this impressive valley base, the fell being remote from roads on other fronts. Three routes offer themselves, each delectably different in character. One only, Route 3, via Gavel Neese, has the confident thumbs up for both ascent and descent.

Via Black Sail Pass →*5.2km/3¼ miles* ↑*715m/2346ft* ⏲*4hr*

1 Follow the bridleway leading N from the rear of the Wasdale Head Inn – the popular route to Black Sail Hut. This leads via hand-gates into **Mosedale**. Fording **Gatherstone Beck** it takes sweeping elbow turns then, as a pitched path, rises easily to the large cairn in **Black Sail Pass**. All seems serene. But Kirkfell Crags have now to be contended with. Head SSE, climbing first to the left, then up the spine of the overbearing ridge. Remnant metal estate-boundary stakes are a sure clue to the line of the steep rock-steps, and continue as you ease onto the plateau to the summit.

Via Highnose Head →*2.4km/1½ miles* ↑*710m/2330ft* ⏲*3hr 20min*

2 Many walkers like to get the hard work of ascent over and done with as early in the walk as possible and the route via **Highnose Head** lets you do this beautifully. However, it's an unremitting climb, with loose scree a torment on the final third. You will enjoy it more in hindsight. Pass through by the Wasdale Head Inn on the gated Mosedale bridleway. Where the path forks, head up through successive gates to begin the climb. Climb the first grassy stretch with plenty of opportunities to stop from time to time to witness the changing angle on the view back over the fields of Wasdale Head, Yewbarrow, Wast Water and The Screes. Higher still, the Mosedale circle of fells grows in importance, as too does Lingmell. Coarse scree and erosion by the downward passage of walkers make progress less comfortable higher up. But forge on irrepressibly, crossing the final rise and a slump dyke to reach the summit and cheer!

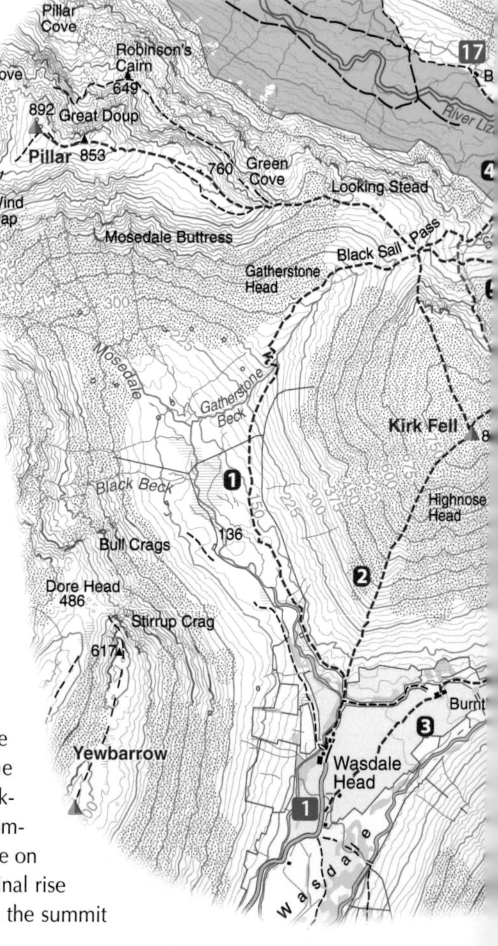

Via Gavel Neese →*4.8km/3 miles* ↑*745m/2445ft* ◷*3hr 50min*

3 Leave Wasdale Green by the lane leading from Lingmell House. As you pass by St Olaf's Church notice the circular stone-walled amalgams of beckstone that were picked up from the dale floor to maximise the haymeadow.

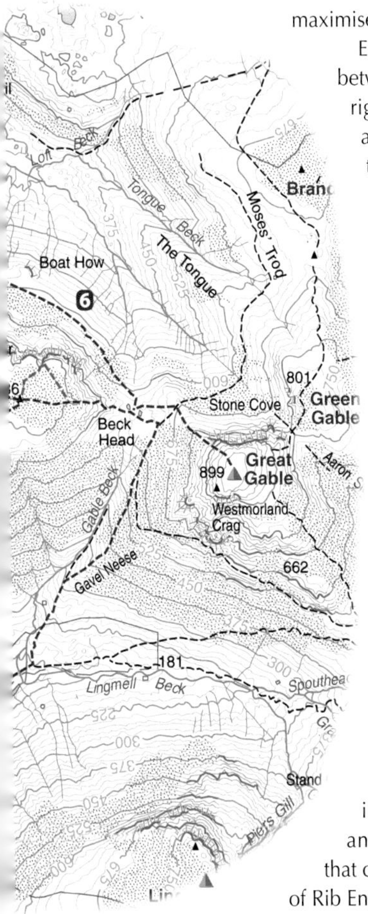

Entering the yard at **Burnthwaite**, go left between the barns to a gate. Beyond it, bear right, advancing along the rough track to a kissing-gate and continuing on to cross the footbridge spanning **Gable Beck**. At once step up left, beginning the steady climb of **Gavel Neese**. Well pitched, the path rises to a hand-gate at the intake wall, which gives the first excuse to gather breath. Look back to the massive slope of Lingmell and, up right, to the screes spilling from Great Napes on **Great Gable**, with Napes Needle discernible at the midst. Climbing on, you'll see, close at hand, Ill Gill falling impressively from the Kirk Fell. To the right are the massive craggy mass of Great End and the rough corried flank of Broad Crag, which draw the eye towards Scafell Pike – mountain Lakeland in its starkest expression.

At the onset of scree, with the stubby thumb of Moses' Finger in eyeshot above, take the first clear fork left. This leads steadily up to the broad saddle of **Beck Head**, with its surprise view into upper Fnnerdale. Pass the two tarns and embark on the uncomplicated path that clambers up through the low outcropping of Rib End to claim the east top of Kirk Fell. Metal stakes adorn this rocky top, a fine place to linger and admire an impressive scree-streaked view of Great Gable.

There is an interesting variant as you gain the high ground (see map) – bear right and visit the amazing gullies and arête at the top of Boathow Crags. From the east top a choice of grassy paths dips SW by Kirkfell Tarn, at the centre of the broad plateau, then rises to the summit wind-shelter.

Ascent from Black Sail Hut 17

This dale-head wild camp is the perfect base from which to take on Kirk Fell. There are at least three primary routes available to construct a compact circuit – direct to Black Sail Pass (Route 4), with Sail Beck (Route 5) or the fell-runners' short-cut traverse to Beck Head above Boat How (Route 6).

Via Black Sail Pass →*3.2km/2 miles* ↑*520m/1705ft* 🕒*2hr 40min*

4 The popular path leads SE from the hostel door to cross a substantial footbridge over the youthful **River Liza**, climbing in the company of **Sail Beck** but scrambling up the first rock obstacle rather than following the original path at the right-hand zig-zag. It later switches right to gain **Black Sail Pass** and join Route **1** in climbing Kirkfell Crags.

Steep rock path threading up Kirkfell Crags following the old ridge-fence stakes

Via Baysoar Slack

→*2.4km/1½ miles*
↑*520m/1705ft* 🕒*2hr 20min*

Take advantage of a valuable weakness in the fell's defences.

5 As the main path (**4**) angles away from the ravine, slant off the path, left, and resume contact with **Sail Beck**, keeping to the right-hand bank. There is evidence of the

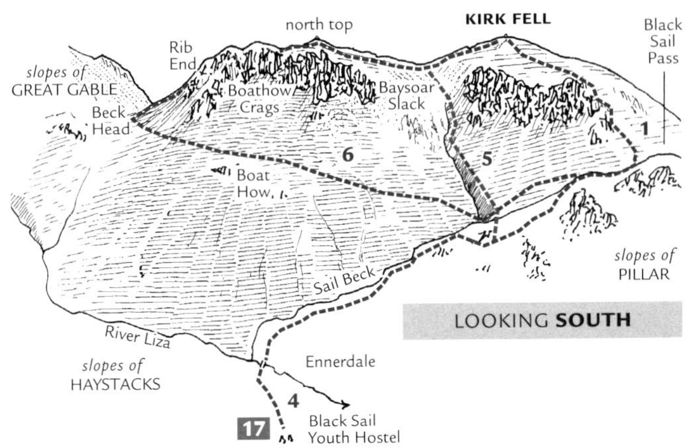

occasional progress of walkers where the way narrows and there are good views of the beck's tumbling course. Any hint of a path is lost as you enter the upper combe and follow a boulder-free route straight up to the high saddle. Turn right to complete the ascent swiftly.

The Boat How Traverse: Black Sail Pass to Beck Head →*1.6km/1 mile*
↑*145m/1706ft* ⌚*2hr 50min*

6 A regular fell-runners' short-cut has evolved to link **Black Sail Pass** with **Beck Head** across the northern slopes of Kirk Fell. The existence of this path – frequently in the shadows – can be turned to advantage when constructing a circuit of the fell from Wasdale Green (**1**).

The summit

A large wind-shelter gives some comfort on those blustery days when the summit is sorely exposed. On a calm day this is a wonderful place to idle away time, knowing that any walker who chances by will be of a similar bent. It is a conscious decision to climb Kirk Fell, so you should find common cause.

Sail Beck and Baysoar Slack

Safe descents

The surest path is by Bell Rib and Beck Head (**3**) to the E for Wasdale. However, if you descend NW from the Kirkfell Tarns down by Baysoar Slack (**5**) and keep to the left bank of Sail Beck, the going is comfortable and gives you a sheltered way down to Black Sail Pass (for Wasdale) and the hostel (for Ennerdale). The main ridge path by the stakes over Kirkfell Crags direct to Black Sail Pass is steep and quite a scramble in places. Dismiss all thought of going down Highnose Head – it's Purgatory.

Ridge routes

Great Gable →*2.4km/1½ miles* ↓*180m/590ft* ↑*280m/920ft* 🕒*1hr*
Head NE, descending into the depression where Kirkfell Tarns lie. Slip between them or skirt to the N – either way rising onto the east top outcrop. Continue E with the odd metal stake as guide to descend Bell Rib to reach Beck Head. Keep course beyond the tarns, holding the high-bias path which duly mounts Gable's rough northwest ridge, with the odd boulder to hop as you head direct to the summit.

Pillar →*4.1km/2½ miles* ↓*250m/820ft* ↑*340m/1115ft* 🕒*2hr*
The normal practice is to follow the stand-alone fence posts NNW to N on a tangible ridge path to tackle the steep descent of Kirkfell Crags. Progress during this descent should – and will – be slow. As a variant you could descend Baysoar Slack and the left bank of Sail Beck from the Kirkfell Tarn saddle to join the path coming over Boat How and rising left to Black Sail Pass. Cross the pass NW and adhere to the very evident ridge path that climbs in two definite stages WNW via Looking Stead to arrive at the Ordnance Survey column.

13 LANK RIGG 541M/1775FT

Climb it from	Blakeley **12** or Coldfell Gate **11**
Character	Spacious western outlier embraced by the upper Calder and Worm Gill
Fell-friendly route	1
Summit grid ref	NY 092 120
Link it with	Iron Crag or Crag Fell

Lying off the natural ridge-line of the range, Lank Rigg (locally pronounced 'Lancrig') seldom registers high on walkers' radar. But this wide-open viewpoint seems, from the presence of a tumulus just southwest of the summit, to have played a significant part in the lives of the indigenous people living to the west long before the Roman occupation. From this point they must have surveyed their homeland, bounded to the north by the Solway and to the west by the Irish Sea.

Every drop of rain that falls here drains into the Calder, either directly or via Worm Gill (perhaps the biggest 'gill' in Lakeland). The Calder, forming the western boundary, is curiously spanned by a beautifully crafted, if rather precarious, single-arched packhorse bridge, known as Matty Benn's, or Monk's, Bridge, whose sole purpose seems to be to connect the remote in-bye pasture of Farthwaite with the open common.

↑ *Lank Rigg from the Coldfell road*

Five one-fell ascents from the fell road to the west are described here – two from the north (1–2) and three from the south (3–5). Strong walkers will spot that a circuit from Coldfell Gate, including Caw Fell, Iron Crag, Whoap, Lank Rigg and Latterbarrow, would make a mighty fine 20km endeavour.

Ascent from Blakeley 12

From here you have the choice of the low road (up the valley with Route 1) or the high road (skirting the top of neighbouring Whoap on Route 2).

Via Whoap Beck →*4.1km/2½ miles* ↑*430m/1410ft* 🕒*2hr*

1 A green track leads off from the road bend, easing down into the valley of the **River Calder** and gaining a first view of the rather featureless western aspect of fell. After fording **Stinking Gill** a path continues E, well above the north bank along the slopes of **White Esk**. At the next significant ford keep to task now above **Whoap Beck**. More of a sheep trod, the path duly curves up to the head of the amphitheatre to reach a small saddle in the ridge. Turn right, SW, climbing with the slope on a strong path to the summit.

Via Whoap →*4.5km/2¾ miles* ↑*500m/1640ft* 🕒*2hr 20min*

2 This skyline alternative breaks from Route **1** at the second ford, after White Esk, and steadily gains height on a quad-track to skirt right along the upper plateau of **Whoap** (pronounced 'warp'). The ridge draws S, curving SW to pass some rocky ground where a small wind-shelter has been constructed off the strict line of the path. The path comes

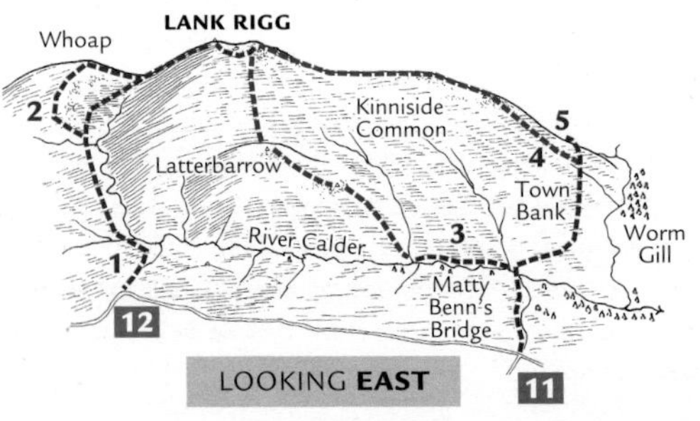

down to the small saddle at the head of **Red Gill** and marches straight on up the slope to the summit pillar.

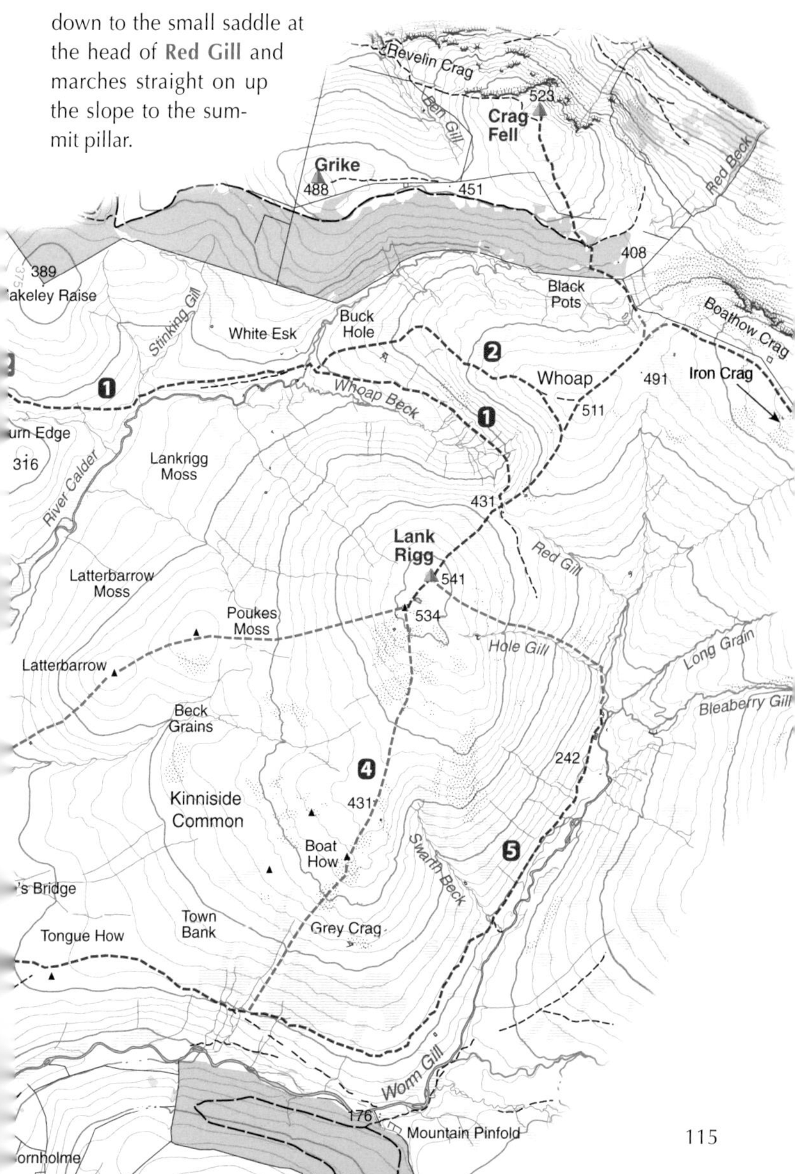

Ascent from Coldfell Gate 11

Two routes explore Kinniside Common and so could form the basis of a short circular tour. Walk out via Latterbarrow (Route 3) and return by Town Bank (Route 4).

Via Latterbarrow →*5.4km/3½ miles* ↑*400m/1312ft* ⌚*2hr 10min*

3 From the parking space adjacent to the road cattle grid follow the track E into the valley, passing a barrier and continuing on down through the gated pens to cross the gated footbridge over the **River Calder**. Bear left, following the obvious track upstream to inspect the curiously sited **Matty Benn's Bridge**. Keep to the right-hand bank on a sheep trod, avoiding the rushy low ground close to the river. Ford Latterbarrow Beck by the large double-compound sheepfold and head NE, climbing **Latterbarrow** and passing a sheepfold with a long, low west–east connecting wall. Thread through the light gorse and, higher, a boulder slope to reach the multi-cairned top of Latterbarrow.

A grassy ridge skips on to a second top before declining to the rushy hollow of **Poukes Moss**. Beyond the rushes the grassy slope of Lank Rigg proper looms welcomingly. Ascend it direct E to the southwest top. Cross the shallow saddle on a clear path NE to reach the Ordnance Survey pillar.

Via Town Bank →*6km/3¾ miles* ↑*385m/1265ft* ⌚*2hr 30min*

4 At the footbridge over the **River Calder**, keep forward on the green-way, forking left at the obvious split in the way that leads over **Tongue How**, passing to the left of a massive ring enclosure of unknown antiquity. Escaping the rushes for a while, a grass bridle-track runs on with minimal gradient. Resist the temptation to aim pathless for the far horizon of Boat How – you only get an added dose of torrid marsh for your pains. It is better to keep with the track, tilting gently down through the rushes, and ignore the inferior bridle-fork right. As watercourses drain across the line of the green-way, take leave left and head

Matty Benn's Bridge and the River Calder

Summit tarn, looking east to the Pillar range

up the slope NNE, finding drier ground as you go. A large broken bield leads to a cairned top, from where you angle half-right to the cairn on **Boat How**. Take a moment to look ESE to see, left of Seatallan, in tight composition, Great End, Lingmell, Ill Crag, Scafell Pike and Scafell. Curiously the term Boat How crops up on the northeast side of the continuing ridge, too, on the slopes of Iron Crag – an odd local duplication that must cause confusion. From here the ridge is pathless, and for some distance nearly level, until it passes a sheepfold at the edge of a boulder slope and the ground rises to the southwest top of Lank Rigg.

Via Worm Gill →*8km/5 miles* ↑*390m/1280ft* 🕒*3hr 20min*

A back-door approach to the summit

5 Keep with the green bridle-track (**4**) (damp in places), and continue with it as it runs along the lower southern slopes of the fell. It is especially wet as it descends and curves NE into the **Worm Gill** valley, fording **Swarth Beck**. Pass to the left of the waterworks compound and the following sheepfold at the confluence. All hint of a path is lost as you continue N with the tributary beck, fording **Hole Gill** to ascend the grassy slope WNW direct to the summit.

The summit

A small cairn provides the only company for a stone-built Ordnance Survey column. The situation offers a 'big scene', although it is largely unremarkable – unusual subjects to spot are Great Carrs and Swirl How (SE) and Blencathra (NE). Inevitably it has a wide coastal horizon. A path runs SW by a shallow wind-whipped pool to a further cairn amid outcropping, with a tumulus a further 100m distant, suggesting that this high point played a significant part in the lives of the indigenous people living to the west long before the Roman occupation.

Safe descents

All ascents are safe to retrace in poor conditions.

Ridge routes

Iron Crag →*4.8km/3 miles* ↓*215m/705ft* ↑*110m/360ft* 🕒*1hr 40min*
This route is simply a matter of setting the compass NE and following the needle. Descend to the saddle and rise over the plateau of Whoap with evidence of a quad-bike track, coming by marshy ground to meet the handsome wall of the Ennerdale Fence. Turn right with the wall, passing through a hand-gate to arrive upon the summit.

Crag Fell →*3.2km/2 miles* ↓*230m/755ft* ↑*210m/690ft* 🕒*1hr 15min*
Traverse Whoap in similar fashion, NE, only turn N with the track and descend by the Ennerdale Fence down to a fence-stile into the plantation. Keep left and step gingerly over the stake raft in the marsh then continue up the damp ride to reach the forest track. Turn left, and after 20m branch right at the cairn, traversing the heather-clad open space to cross a fence-stile leading out of the conifer enclosure. Follow the evident rising path on the open fell NNW.

14 LINGMELL 807M/2649FT

Climb it from	Wasdale Head **1–2**
Character	Strictly one of the pikes of Scafell, projecting northwest of the main massif with amazing northern cliffs and ravines
Fell-friendly route	3
Summit grid ref	NY 209 082
Link it with	Scafell Pike
Part of	The Roof of England

Nestled under the Scafells, handsome Lingmell has two personalities – smooth and debonair to the south and west but rough and tough to the north and east. The mighty gash of Piers Gill, torn into the northeastern flank of the fell in alpine proportions, is a great monument to the ravages of ice and rain. The ferocity of storms has, down the millennia, brought boulders in profusion into Lingmell Beck, which constantly shuffle towards the lake.

Side show? Not a bit of it. Lingmell is a star performer. The circuit from Wasdale Head, climbing via Piers Gill to Lingmell Col (Route 1) and descending the west ridge (Route 3), is pure magic from start to finish. The rise over the fell-top from the high col is stunning, revealing the most exciting aspect of Great

↑ *Lingmell from the Corridor Route*

Gable, the sheer gullies leading down into the dizzy depths of Piers Gill, and the course of the Corridor Route from Sty Head, overtopped by Great End and Broad Crag. During the traverse of its southern slopes (Route 2) Scafell Pike and Scafell Crags are also seen to their very best effect.

Note that the path between the National Trust camp site and the Wasdale Head Inn is often put beyond practical use by flooding from the Beck.

Ascent from Wasdale Green 1

Via Piers Gill →*5km/3 miles*
↑*730m/2390ft* ◷*3hr 10min*

A clear route with lots of striking views and following the edge of the spectacular Piers Gill ravine, with a rock-step that may make this a better choice for ascent than descent.

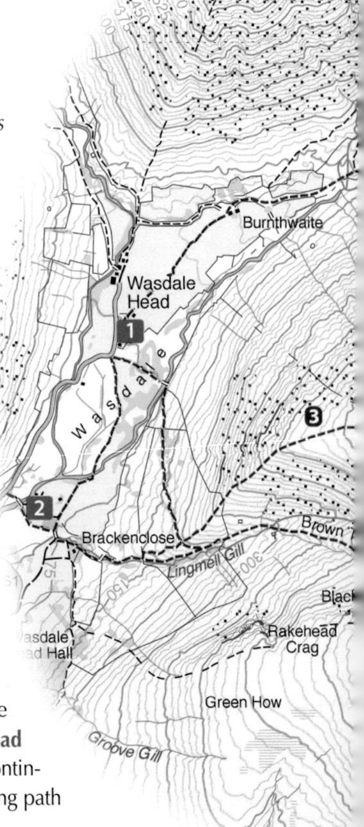

1 Follow the farm lane from the village green car park, leading by the yew tree-shaded St Olaf's Church directly to **Burnthwaite Farm**. The path is ushered left of the farm buildings to a gate. Go through and bear right, passing through a gate en route to a footbridge spanning **Gable Beck**. Take the right-hand of two paths at dale-floor level, leading to a hand-gate in a descending wall. The crags of Great Napes pierce the sky above the massive scree bank up to the left, with the dark shaded bulk of Lingmell overbearing to the right. At the gill confluence the path fords **Spouthead Gill** to reach a clear zig-zagging path continuing up the rigg. Watch for the branching path right, keeping company with the lower ravine of **Piers Gill**. Ford the stony foot of **Greta Gill**, continuing with ever-heightening excitement beside Piers Gill. The path climbs to a nine-metre rock-step, which might be considered a problem for descending walkers. But the hand- and foot-holds are very sharply angled, making it a straightforward exercise in ascent. Above this, the path comes close to the deepest section of Piers Gill. You may be tempted to peer over the edge at the right-angle bend and, if you do, **immense care is needed**. There is a curious white solution spilling from the facing gully, beneath a crag capped by an apron of scree. A little further on, look up the ravine and admire the view towards Dropping Crag on Scafell Pike. Finally, the path meets up with the **Corridor Route** passing another great viewpoint in the same direction. Go right, fording the gill near the lip of the ravine and traverse up to the broken wall on the saddle of **Lingmell Col**. The fell-top is easily gained. Make a point of keeping right to note, halfway up, the view down Piers Gill and across to Great Gable.

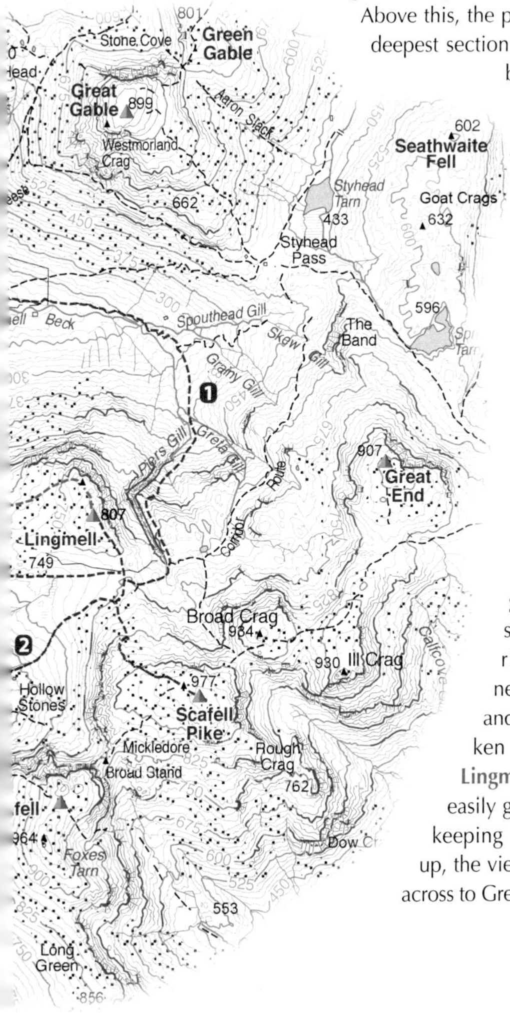

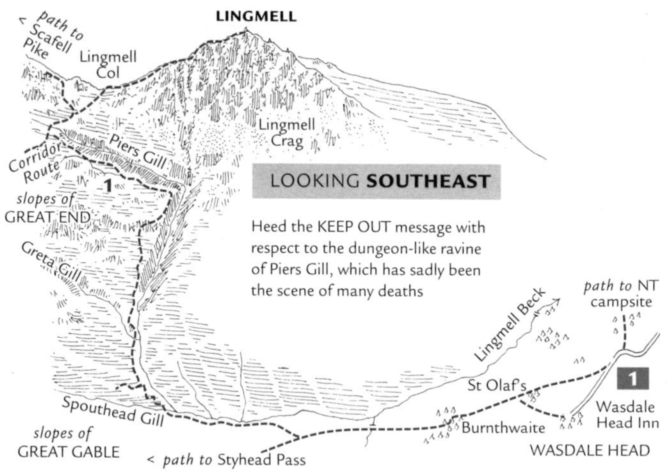

Ascent from Wasdale Head 2

Route 2 is another natural ascent, following a popular Scafell Pike approach as it does for much of the way. On Route 3 a steep climb gives way to a grassy slope, which might be gentler on the knees in descent.

Via Lingmell Gill →*4.7km/3 miles* ↑*730m/2390ft* 🕒*3hr 20min*

2 Start out along the farm-track from the National Trust car park and cross the broad bridge spanning **Lingmell Gill**. Follow upstream to the gated

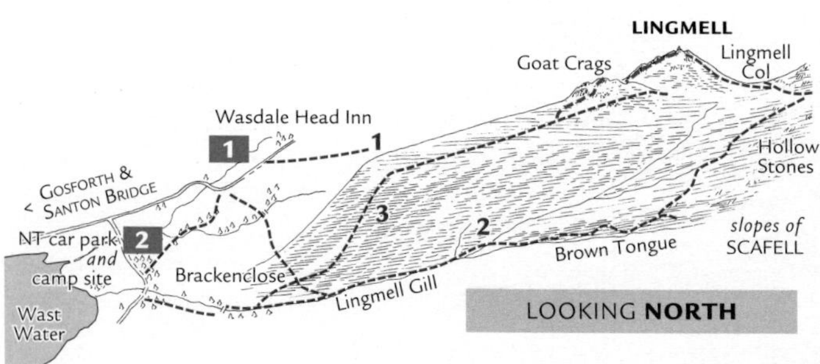

footbridge, cross the bridge, then keep up the valley via two hand-gates, the path pitched throughout much of its course because of its inevitable popularity as a primary route to Scafell Pike. The path climbs onto the green rigg of **Brown Tongue**. Watch keenly for the left branch of the path which draws up **Hollow Stones**. As the path bends right to address the broad northwest ridge of **Scafell Pike**, bear off towards the easy saddle of **Lingmell Col**, identified by its wall. Continue with Route **1**.

Via Goat Crags →*4.3km/2¾ miles* ↑*745m/2450ft* ⏲*3hr*

3 Early in the ascent of **Lingmell Gill** (**2**) with the footbridge just crossed, rise to the next hand-gate in a fence (NT collection box close by). Leave the gill path slanting up left onto the rising rigg, crossing over the path swinging over the ridge from Wasdale Head bound for Lingmell Gill (which it joins at the top hand-gate). Ahead sweat and toil on the steep climb mounting the prow

Above the spectacular ravine of Piers Gill

of the west ridge. Near the top the inevitable loose gravel adds to the effort but once topped an ocean of grass on a gentle gradient lies before you. The route either crosses over the broken outcropped subsidiary top of **Goat Crags**, or takes the earlier half-right branch bypassing on the south side to join and follow the wall to **Lingmell Col**. The former is the direct option and it comes up to the broken wall. At the point where an erratic has been integrated into the wall, quaintly topped with a crown of walling stones, leave the wall heading due north. Traverse the western slopes, reaching the north ridge at the lower scarp brink and follow the edge up, via several steps and cairned tops, above the spectacular **Lingmell Crag**.

The summit

The cairn is an edifice of pride, befitting a noble vantage point. The summit is a personal favourite, running a close second to Great End in the mid-western Lake District fells, with Scafell chasing up in third place. The view is dominated by the almost perpendicular aspect of Great Gable, while from the cairnless south top you get a peerless view of Scafell.

Summit cairn looking towards Great Gable, enveloped in mist

Safe descents

The first concern is to avoid Lingmell Crag which plummets from the northern edge. By walking generally S from the summit you will encounter a wall. If you go precisely SE from the summit it is easy enough to reach Lingmell Col and link up with the path (**2**) descending from Scafell Pike into Hollow Stones and, by this means, reach the shelter and security of Lingmell Gill. Alternatively, follow the wall W until you find the large erratic boulder crowned by a ring of stones, where you join the W ridge path (**3**).

The sleek west ridge from Rakehead Crag on Scafell

Ridge route

Scafell Pike →*1.6km/1 mile* ↓*85m/280ft* ↑*255m/840ft* 🕒*45min*
Descend SE to Lingmell Col, cross the broken wall, and lead on through the irregular outcrops to link up with the Corridor Route (from the left) and then the path ascending from Hollow Stones (from the right). At a ledge slant half-right and then half-left, following an excess of cairns along the broad NW ridge (N of Pikes Crag) to a large cairn at the plateau edge. A stony but not too troublesome path leads to the summit, distinguished by an old trig pillar and crumbling walled tower.

15 MIDDLE FELL 585M/1919FT

Climb it from	Greendale **6** or Goat Gill **5**
Character	A craggy-faced ridge above the middle reaches of Wast Water linking to Seatallan
Fell-friendly route	1
Summit grid ref	NY 151 072
Link it with	Seatallan
Part of	The Nether Beck Horseshoe

Occupying a suitably central situation in Wasdale, Middle Fell's craggy southern and eastern slopes match Buckbarrow's fierce scarp and seem to defeat all thoughts of assault and ascent. But a soft turf 'overbelly' ridge runs from the jaws of Greendale Beck to the fell's union with Seatallan and circumvents those bewildering battlements. The wild upper valley of Greendale Beck by Greendale Tarn is a further weakness in the ridge's defences.

However you get there this is a real fellwalkers' summit. Enjoy a grand outlook all around – right across to the Scafells and, a little closer, the Screes and, further off to the west, the great sweep of the Irish Sea – and relax in the low chances of a convoy of casual visitors heading by to break your communion with a wonderful high-fell world.

 ↑ *Summit of Middle Fell looking towards Yewbarrow*

Four routes are described here, Routes 1–2 taking the gentler approach from Greendale. The determined fellwanderer, on the other hand, undeterred by the crags, will spot a natural line to the high skyline defined by Goat Gill (Routes 3–4). This is the better ascent, walking steeply up thrillingly pathless terrain straight to the ridge.

Ascent from Greendale 6

When it comes to climbing Middle Fell on a first visit, Route 1 is the way to go. For a longer walk and more of an expedition, try Route 2.

Via the southwest ridge →*2.4km/1½ miles* ↑*505m/1655ft* ⏱*1hr 40min*

1 A clear path leads N from the verge, rising towards the portals of the Greendale Gill ravine. As you brush past the gorse, watch for the fork where the southwest ridge path begins. You will soon discard the bracken on a regular trail to the summit.

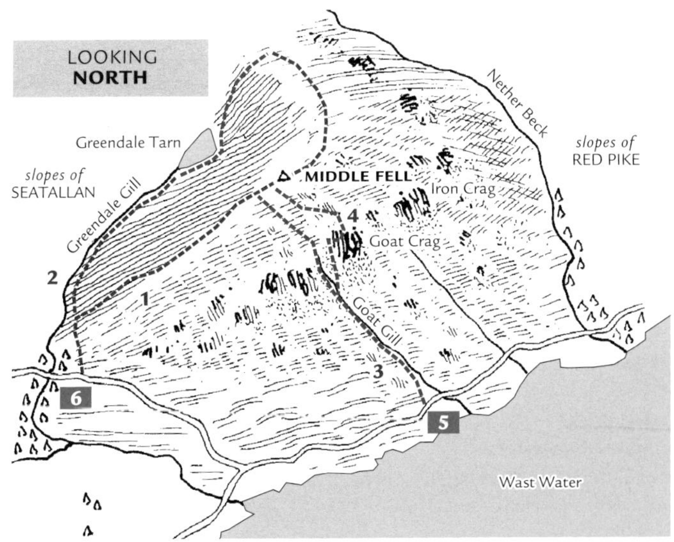

Via Greendale Tarn →*3.7km/2¼ miles* ↑*510m/1675ft* ⏲*2hr*

2 Where Route **1** branches off right, stay on the path within the gorge, but keep to the east bank. The path diminishes and is lost at **Greendale Tarn**. Keep along the damp east shore, taking pleasure in this off-the-beaten-track sheet of wild water. Sombre tones prevail. Continue to the saddle, where you join the ridge path, switching back acutely S and passing a striking outcrop.

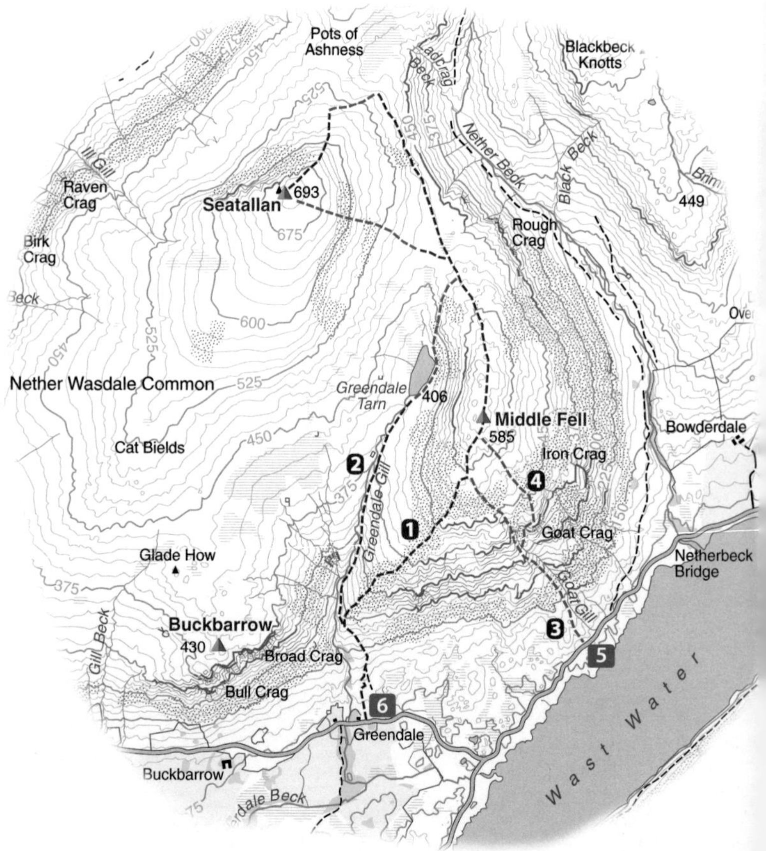

Yewbarrow overtopped by Great Gable, from the summit

Ascent from Goat Gill 5

The rough southern slopes of Middle Fell seem, to the casual eye, uninviting. But all is not what it seems.

Via Goat Crag → *1.6km/1 mile* ↑*510m/1675ft* ⏲ *1hr 20min*

3 Look up the hillside and see the great mass of **Goat Crag**. To the crag's left a grassy breach at the headwaters of **Goat Gill** is the clue to a direct and uncommon route of ascent. Bracken is easily beaten as you head up by glacial bedrock ridges and gorse patches, keeping to the left-hand side of the rising gill. There are no hazards on this route nor a hint of a path. Enjoy your pioneering progress! The grassy upper portion of the fell, still intermingled with minor outcropping, leads easily to the ridge path to join Route **1**.

4 As a special treat you can traverse the gill above the screes spilling from the main face of **Goat Crag** and mount a rake above, with brief evidence of climbers' and sheep's feet underfoot. The ridge of easy boiler-plate slabs leads to the top of the rock headland, turning right onto the ridge path to reach the summit.

Goat Crag and the Scafells

The summit

The summit is a solitary cairn atop a (solitary) grassy tump but what a view! Inevitably the Scafells and The Screes take centre stage in a fine panorama. If atmospherics oblige, you may also see the Isle of Man floating like a battleship on the horizon above Glade How.

Safe descents

The descending ridge path leading SW (**1**) holds all the certainty you need for a safe return to Greendale.

Ridge route

Seatallan →*2.4km/1½ miles* ↓*110m/360ft* ↑*220m/720ft* ⏲*1hr 30min*
Follow the ridge path N. This descends to the marshy saddle at the head of the Greendale Beck valley. There are two options. You can veer half-left to avoid the rushes and climb the steep pathless east slope of Seatallan unimpeded. The more comfortable route, however, accepts the rushes and follows on with a strong sheep path along the northeast slope above the Nether Beck valley, coming round to join the path climbing the north ridge above the Pots of Ashness and heading to the summit.

16 PILLAR 892M/2926FT

Climb it from	Wasdale Green **1**, Bowness Knott **16**, Gatesgarth **18** and Black Sail Hut **17**
Character	Great whaleback ridge whose projecting 'rock' commands upper Ennerdale
Fell-friendly route	1
Summit grid ref	NY 171 121
Link it with	Kirk Fell or Scoat Fell
Part of	The Mosedale Round

Pillar is a commanding presence in Ennerdale – one mighty, imperious column of naked rock, amid a tangled wall of rock and high coves casting shadows into the upper dale – with the projecting buttress of Pillar Rock a longstanding landmark for shepherds.

It has been the scene of heroic climbing deeds over the years. One such was the first ascent, recorded by a shepherd in the 19th century. He scrambled over Pisgah and made his way up by the 'Slab and Notch' to the top – and, perhaps even more impressively, returned to tell the tale! Many years later nearby Black Sail Hut evolved from a shepherd's shieling into a hostel especially to provide a base for climbers intent on the famous rock.

↑ *Pillar from Black Sail Pass*

But it is a fine fell for walkers, too, many attracted by its remoteness. For competent fellwalkers who love to get to the heart of their mountains, the High Level Route, combined with the Shamrock Traverse (both Route 9), ranks as one of the best fell paths in Lakeland. This is balanced by the scree-torn descent from Wind Gap into Mosedale (Route 2), which rates among the worst! Other approaches lead up from Bowness Knott (4–6), Wasdale (1–3) and even over from Gatesgarth in Buttermere for a really good fell day (7–8).

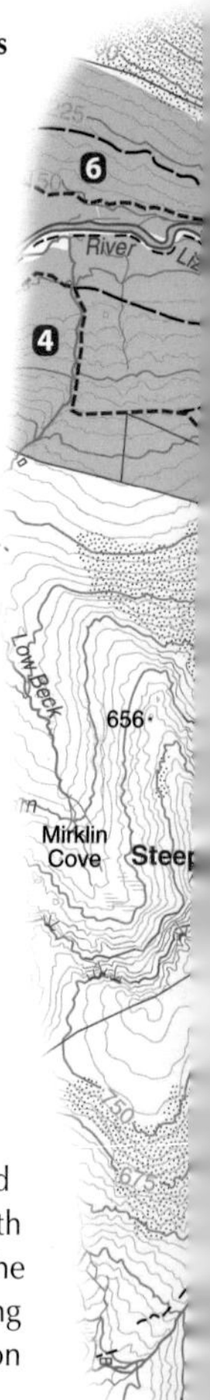

Ascent from Wasdale Green 1

There are two routes to the top – one a standard classic, the other more punk rock! The former, via Black Sail Pass (Route 1), by convention forms part of a natural skyline round, the Mosedale Horseshoe. Like all rough mountain routes, where steep ground is involved, this route can be tricky in bad weather, but under normal conditions it has few awkward moments and promises good sport. The Wind Gap routes (Routes 2 and 3), by contrast, are wet underfoot.

Via Black Sail Pass →*7.2km/4½ miles* ↑*825m/2705ft* ⏲*3hr 40min*

From behind the Wasdale Head Inn set off past the beautiful single-arched stone bridge through hand-gates and swing left into Mosedale.

1 Rising through the bracken, the path comes onto pitching and addresses the handsome cascades of **Gatherstone Beck**. The path fords the beck, hairpins left and right, and heads reliably towards the pass, with good pitching (thanks to the efforts of Fix the Fells) ending just short of the saddle. Advance beyond the large cairn to the iron stakes, where the ridge path crosses from **Kirk Fell**.

Turn up left. Either hold to the worn path or break up onto the natural ridge-top to accompany the old fence. There are small tarns to find in lovely settings en route to the crest of **Looking Stead**, offset from the main ridge. The ridge path itself keeps left, but the view from the grassy crest, marked by iron stakes, is too good to ignore. The generous outlook is a

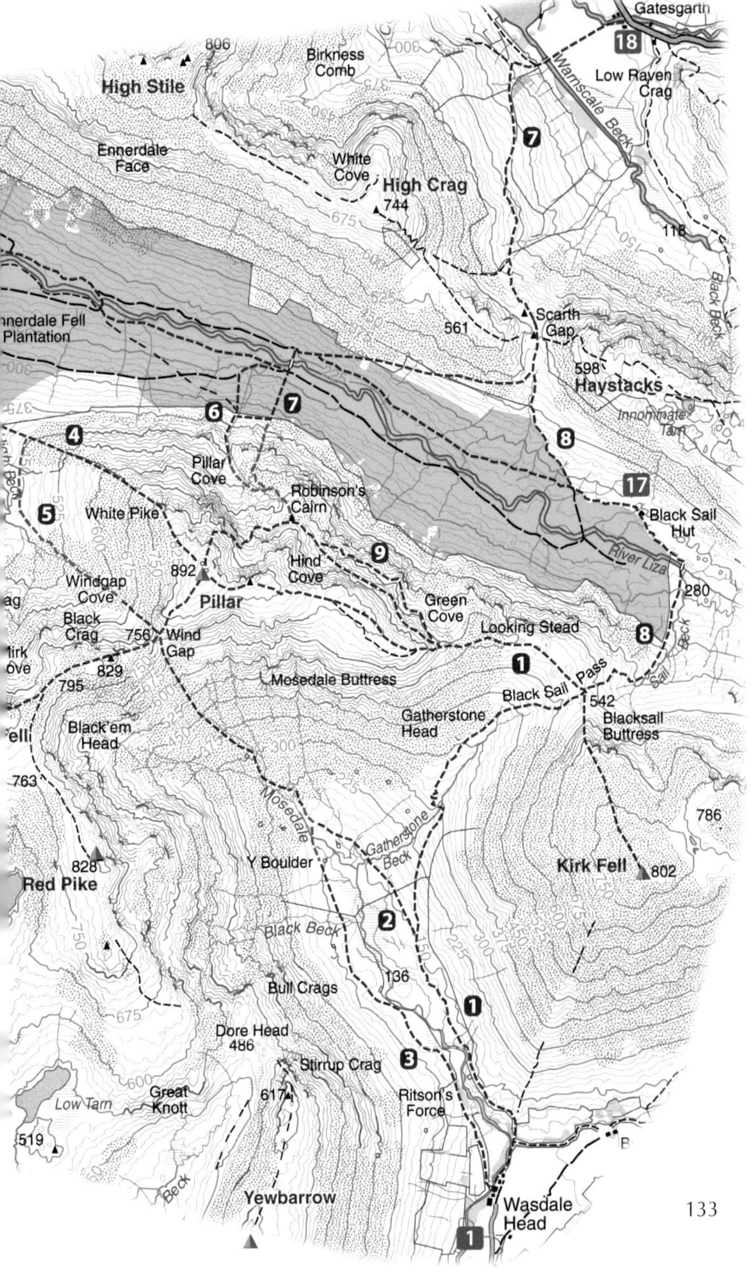

Gatesgarth
18
806
Birkness Comb
High Stile
Low Raven Crag
Warnscale Beck
7
Ennerdale Face
White Cove
High Crag
744
118
Black Beck
Scarth Gap
561
598
Haystacks
Innominate Tarn
Ennerdale Fell Plantation
6
7
4
8
17
Pillar Cove
Robinson's Cairn
Black Sail Hut
5
White Pike
9
Hind Cove
River Liza
892
Windgap Cove
Pillar
280
Black Crag
756
Wind Gap
Green Cove
Looking Stead
8
829
1
Mosedale Buttress
Black Sail Pass
795
542
Black'em Head
Gatherstone Head
Blacksail Buttress
763
Mosedale
786
Gatherstone Beck
Y Boulder
Kirk Fell
802
828
Red Pike
2
Black Beck
136
Bull Crags
1
Dore Head
486
Stirrup Crag
3
Great Knott
617
Ritson's Force
Low Tarn
519
Beck
Yewbarrow
Wasdale Head
1

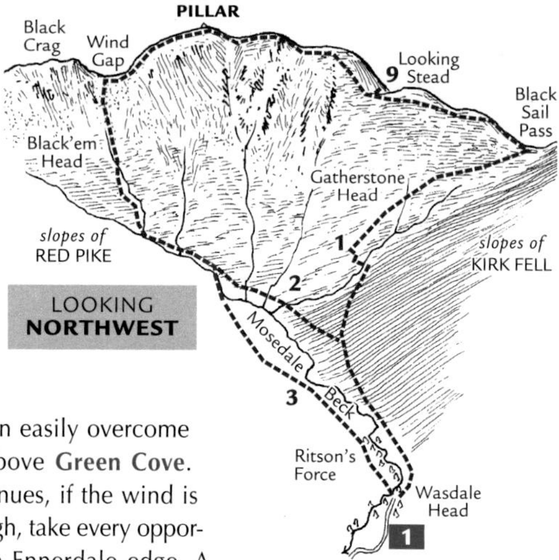

real 'looking' place, peering down upon Black Sail Hut and the wild head of Ennerdale, and along the craggy northern flank of Pillar to the high-perched Robinson's Cairn. The ridge path turns upward, tackling an easily overcome rocky sequence above **Green Cove**. As the climb continues, if the wind is not whistling through, take every opportunity to study the Ennerdale edge. A second pull brings you above **Pillar Cove**, the pinnacled scenery quite thrilling, and the path eventually arrives upon the summit plateau.

Via Wind Gap →*5.2km/3¼ miles* ↑*825m/2705ft* ◷*3hr 40min*

The final stretch to Wind Gap, common to both these routes, probably evolved as a rapid descent, so do not undertake it unless you really are prepared for the discomfort.

2 Follow Route **1**, watching for the large cairn at NY 183 103, where a path bears left off the main trail. Keep below the bracken crossing the valley floor by an area of possible ancient cairns and go through a fenced pen and gate in the wall. Footprints on the ground confirm the impression that most walkers on this path are heading back to Wasdale Head, no doubt nursing their jaded joints! The wet, mossy valley of Mosedale lives up to its name. Ford **Mosedale Beck** and angle half-left by an old sheepfold. The path is intermittent and less evident than may be expected, keeping close to the beck.

The west face of Pillar Rock from high on White Pike

Advance up the grass ridge, aiming for the extended ribbon of scree. With the screes gained, the going gets even less appealing with every stride – find the firmer footing, predominantly on the left-hand side. Reach the **Wind Gap** saddle up the boulders, half-left, avoiding the final fellside insult of scree. Turn right, completing the ignominious ascent with a less than comfortable rough scramble up the ridge – oh, what bliss, the summit plateau!

3 A variant approach begins by crossing the lovely single-arched stone bridge directly after the stile behind the Wasdale Head Inn. Follow the walled drove-way leading N, and soon come above the pines shrouding **Ritson's Force**. From the succeeding gate the path contours through the bracken – avoid being lured up towards the path to **Dore Head**. You need to hold a lower line, advancing to a ladder-stile after fording **Black Beck**, and heading on to the prominent, tall fractured rock known as **Y Boulder**, for obvious reasons. Skirt left to evade the marsh and ford **Mosedale Beck** to join up with Route **2**.

Ascent from Bowness Knott 16 *off map NW*

Via White Pike →*8.8km/5½ miles* ↑*775m/2545ft* ⏲*4hr 30min*

A high-level ridge route (Route 4) or a beckside adventure (Route 5) are available from a common walk-in starting on the shore of Ennerdale Water.

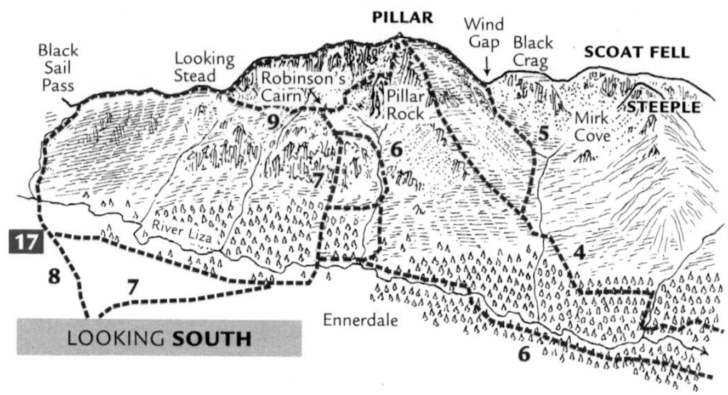

4 Head up Ennerdale upon the main track, turn right after Char Dub (**River Liza** on map) and cross Irish Bridge, designed to resist the Liza's flood waters. Enter the trees at the double-gate, bear left and cross the next concrete ford-bridge over Woundell Beck. Pass through a gate and keep to the dale-floor forest track. After 2km come to a second conventional bridge crossing. Immediately after, turn up right (this is easy to miss), keeping close to **Low Beck**. The path, sorely worn in places, leads up through a hand-gate beside the ravine to step up onto a forest track. Follow this track left for 400m, keeping a sharp eye out for a path stepping off the track into the trees on the right. This then escapes the trees into rough cleared ground and follows an old wall up to a fence-stile. Turn left and gingerly ford **High Beck**, scrambling up the facing bank by the fence.

Follow the old wall-line up the grass slope to mount the northwest ridge – rockier ground comes with the stiffer gradient as you work up over **White Pike**. The rewards are higher up as the mighty west face of **Pillar Rock** is progressively revealed, and the route continues on steeply to the summit unhindered.

5 Alternatively, after fording High Beck (**4**) venture right into **Windgap Cove**. Having begun the ascent by the old wall, find a sheep trod contouring right to slip through the broken wall. The path becomes less certain thereafter as marshy ground predominates. As height is gained, ford the beck. Evidence of a path is resurrected only as stonier ground is encountered in the midst of the upper cove leading to the saddle. Continue on to the summit.

Via Pillar Cove →*9.2km/5¾ miles* ↑*780m/2560ft* ⌚*4hr 45min*

The more adventurous may be tempted to climb by Pillar Cove to get intimate with Pillar Rock.

6 Follow the main forest road up Ennerdale. Some 2.5km beyond High Gillerthwaite Youth Hostel take the track forking right, signed 'Pillar Rock'. This crosses the **Liza**, amid dashing waters. Keep to the up-dale track to reach an acute bend. Swing up with the hairpin track to find what was once termed the Pillar Ride. Felling has somewhat obscured the path, which heads up the slope to cross the forest-bounding fence. Clamber up the west bank of Pillarcove Beck on a very evident path, although even this disappears as height is gained in the cove. Aim for the headland surmounted by **Robinson's Cairn**, to join Route **9**.

Pillar Rock from Scarth Gap

Ascent from Gatesgarth 18

Via Pillar Cove →*6.8km/4¼ miles* ↑*1050m/3445ft (*↓*240m/788ft)* ⌚*4hr 45min*

This entails crossing Scarth Gap. Not necessarily time or energy-saving in comparison to the long march up Ennerdale, one of the special thrills of this approach is the late-spring vision of a rapture of bluebells, with Haystacks a wonderful mountain backdrop.

7 Traverse the meadows at the head of Buttermere lake by the gate-marshalled lane. Cross **Warnscale Beck** via Peggy's Bridge, and through the gate rise directly beside the small copse on a pitched path. At the acute corner, where paths radiate, bear up left, maintaining company with the fence and pitched path. The path mounts onto Wax Knott, a pronounced shelf where many walkers pause to admire the great basin of Warnscale, encircled by the craggy heights of Fleetwith Pike and Haystacks. The path leads through a wall and continues up to **Scarth Gap**. As the ground begins to fall away, veer along the rocky margin and over the saddle. A clear path ensues, which takes a long diagonal line, via three stiles, down to the forest track. Turn right, and after 120m go left, descending the bank to cross the memorial footbridge and arrive at a second forest track.

There are three options from here. Two start by continuing straight ahead, higher up the slope confined by conifers, to cross a fence-stile. At this point either bear right, following the fence on a path to ford Pillarcove Beck and join the more regular path (**6**). Alternatively, keep straight on up the grass gully – there is little evidence of footprints, so there is a sense of pioneering. There is one very minor rock-step high up, but otherwise it is simple. It has the advantage of putting you on the ridge above the cove, and by bearing up left, via a patch of boulders, you naturally arrive at **Robinson's Cairn** to join Route **9**.

The third option, and the more common route from the forest track, is to go right, forking left at the track junction to join Route **6**.

Via Black Sail Pass →*8.4km/5¼ miles* ↑*990m/3250ft* ⌚*4hr 30min*

A clear-pathed, conventional connection to Route 1

8 Cross **Scarth Gap** (**7**), keeping to the conventional path, which descends with pitching and beside the forest fence. Reaching the track, follow this in natural order, left, to reach **Black Sail Hut**. Follow on with the more obvious path SE, cutting down the edge of the moraine to cross the Liza footbridge. A strong path climbs on S, scrambling up, rather than deftly rounding, the first minor rock-step, as the old zig-zag survives. The path is never in doubt thereafter to **Black Sail Pass**, where you join Route **1** to the summit.

Ascent from Black Sail Hut 17

Via the High Level Route →*4.8km/3 miles* ↑*640m/2100ft* ⌚*3hr 20min*

An exciting route above precipitous cliffs to the rocky Shamrock Traverse.

The iconic Black Sail Hut

9 Go SE from the hut, following the path to **Black Sail Pass** (**8**), where you go right to **Looking Stead** (**1**). A third of the way up the initial rise from the dip after Looking Stead, a cairn indicates a short lateral path to the right. This route to the summit involves 340m (1115ft) of ascent. The loose path zips down a short gully to embark upon a sure-footed contouring course high within **Green Cove**. Watch out early on for a split in the path, with higher and lower braided ways. You can take either, but be warned that they become far removed. The lower route has an awkward downward rock-step early in its course – if you reach it and don't fancy chancing your arm (or neck!) then it is easy to backtrack and take the higher path. Both paths have their moments requiring a cautionary step, but both can be relied upon. **Choose one and stay with it** as there are precipitous cliffs below. Eventually the two paths come back into union in **Hind Cove**, short of **Robinson's Cairn**. The headland brings Pillar Rock's eastern face into view in all its majesty. As the memorial implies, surely John Wilson Robinson and all his mountaineering chums loved this place, as will you.

From here the very clear path continues declining before rising beside a low bare-rock ridge almost in the shadow of **Pillar Rock**. Stepping onto scree, zig-zag up to join the Shamrock Traverse – an easy ramp terrace conveniently located above the sheer Shamrock Buttress leading to the nick behind Pillar Rock. Apart from an early wet slab at a narrow cleft, which could be dicey when icy, the going is not problematic. Slabs lead excitingly to a good stance, from where you may admire the upper portion of the great protruding cliff, with Pisgah separated from the main mass of Pillar Rock by a startling gap, the point of access to the top for mountaineers and climbers only – walkers take the more reassuring fellside path.

Soon you can stand in the nick and, dismissing all thought of scrambling over Pisgah, begin the steady clamber up the fellside, frequently looking back to give Pillar Rock a reverential glance and espy its 'remote' cairn. The open fell-top arrives, as ever, with an element of surprise. March past the marker cairn at the plateau edge to reach the Ordnance Survey column and wind-shelter.

The summit

A large wind-shelter constructed upon a low outcrop stands beside a stone-built Ordnance Survey pillar and cairn. A feeble horseshoe wind-break a few strides to the northwest needs dismantling. At the northern brink a cairn indicates where the path down to Pillar Rock commences. Difficult ground makes this a place for the sure-footed only.

Safe descents

The summit is no place to meander in mist. For all you may dislike retracing your steps if you came by Black Sail Pass, this is the **only** safe way back to both upper Ennerdale and Wasdale Head, so leave the summit seeking cairns due E (**1**). For lower Ennerdale you can descend directly NW (**4**), or SW (**5**) via Wind Gap and then NW down into the uncomplicated hollow of Windgap Cove, the two routes converging on High Beck. As already mentioned the Wind Gap path into Mosedale is a horror story, evolved from walkers leaving the ridge in haste and

Looking east from the summit

realising their error too late. The only sane and comfortable early descent in that direction is by Black'em Head (not described here), oddly adopted by very few.

Ridge routes

Kirk Fell →*4.1km/2½ miles* ↓*340m/1115ft* ↑*250m/820ft* ⏲*2hr 10min*
Head E on a clear ridge trail that permits a brisk pace, although stirring views over the edge warrant frequent pauses. The path takes in two big steps and makes confident progress down to Black Sail Pass. Across the saddle the metal fence posts persist, guiding the ridge path S up the rock headland of Kirkfell Crags – far easier in ascent than descent. Once free of the rocks upon the plateau, the stakes continue their guiding role SSE to the summit.

Scoat Fell →*2km/1¼ miles* ↓*140m/460ft* ↑*90m/295ft* ⏲*1hr*
Leave the wind-shelter/Ordnance Survey column in a SW direction. The descent to Wind Gap is, lower down, uncomfortably loose in places. Cross the gap and ascend through the boulders to the cairn on Black Crag. This impressive mass of fell comes very close to meriting separate status. Certainly this is a fine place to linger – take your time and peer over the northern edge, lined by amazing cliffs imposing on Windgap Cove. Heading further W take a moment to visit the top of the northwest spur facing into Mirk Cove – a wonderful place to stand and study Steeple. The ridge path drifts naturally SW and forks. Keep right, on the lower part boulder-hopping, and eventually encounter the Ennerdale Fence wall-end on Scoat Fell.

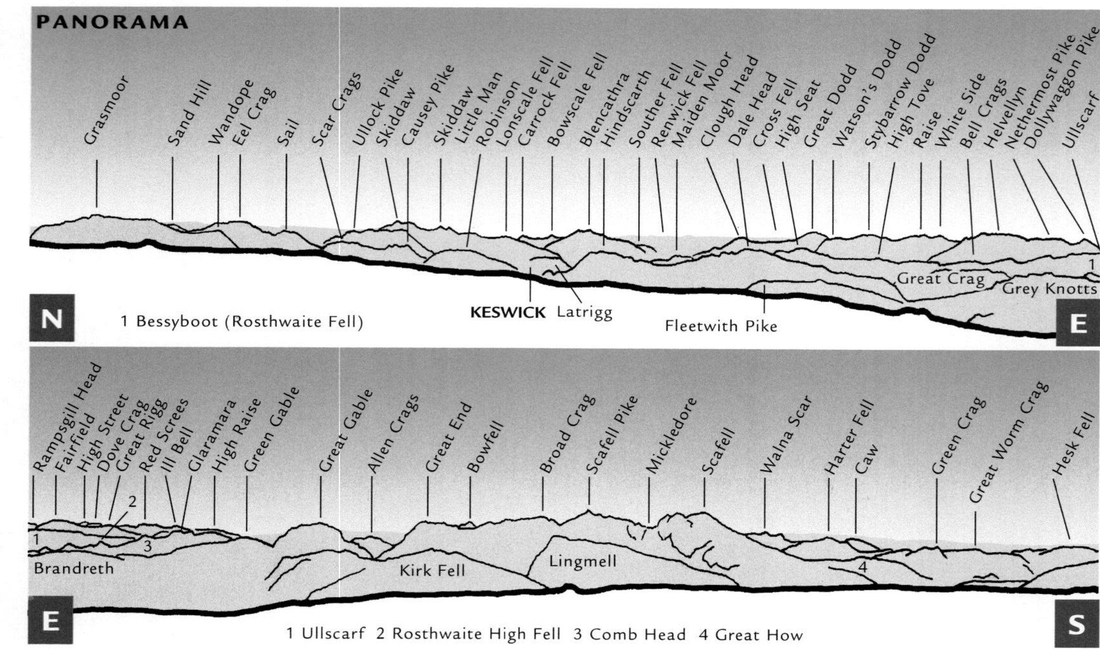
PANORAMA
Grasmoor
Sand Hill
Wandope
Eel Crag
Sail
Scar Crags
Ullock Pike
Skiddaw
Causey Pike
Skiddaw Little Man
Robinson
Lonscale Fell
Carrock Fell
Bowscale Fell
Blencathra
Hindscarth
Souther Fell
Renwick Fell
Maiden Moor
Clough Head
Dale Head
Cross Fell
High Seat
Great Dodd
Watson's Dodd
Stybarrow Dodd
High Tove
Raise
White Side
Bell Crags
Helvellyn
Nethermost Pike
Dollywaggon Pike
Ullscarf
Great Crag
Grey Knotts
KESWICK
Latrigg
Fleetwith Pike
N
1 Bessyboot (Rosthwaite Fell)
E
Rampsgill Head
Fairfield
High Street
Dove Crag
Great Rigg
Red Screes
Ill Bell
Glaramara
High Raise
Green Gable
Great Gable
Allen Crags
Great End
Bowfell
Broad Crag
Scafell Pike
Mickledore
Scafell
Walna Scar
Harter Fell
Caw
Green Crag
Great Worm Crag
Hesk Fell
Brandreth
Kirk Fell
Lingmell
E
S
1 Ullscarf 2 Rosthwaite High Fell 3 Comb Head 4 Great How

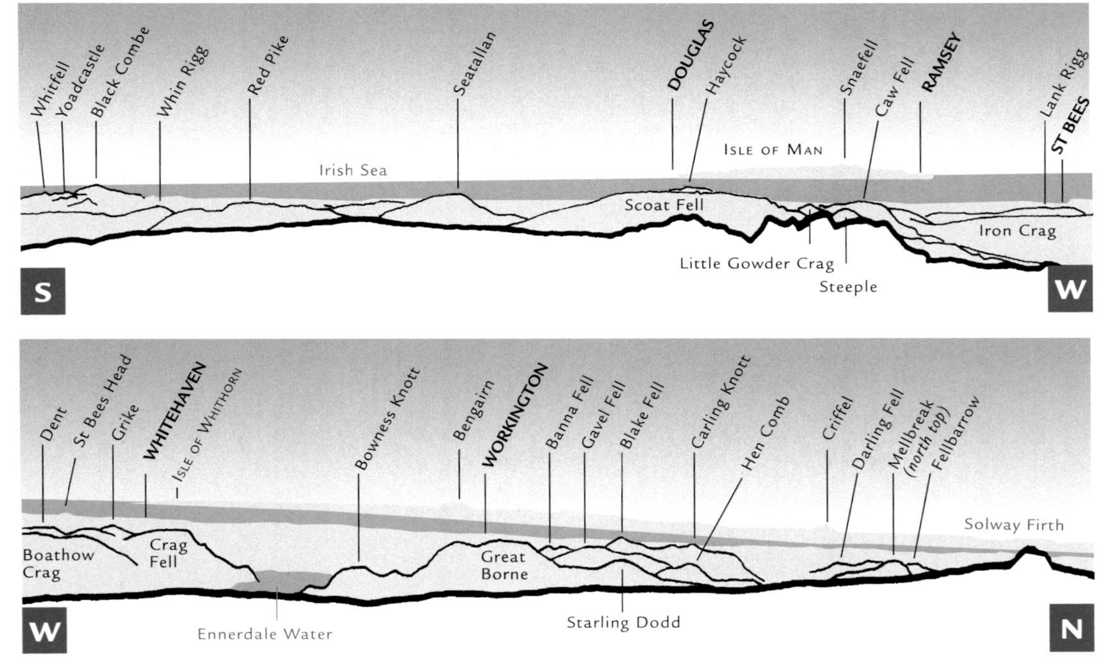
Whitfell
Yoadcastle
Black Combe
Whin Rigg
Red Pike
Seatallan
DOUGLAS
Haycock
Snaefell
Caw Fell
RAMSEY
Lank Rigg
ST BEES
Irish Sea
Isle of Man
Scoat Fell
Iron Crag
Little Gowder Crag
Steeple
S
W
Dent
St Bees Head
Grike
WHITEHAVEN
Isle of Whithorn
Bowness Knott
Bengairn
WORKINGTON
Banna Fell
Gavel Fell
Blake Fell
Carling Knott
Hen Comb
Criffel
Darling Fell
Mellbreak
(north top)
Fellbarrow
Solway Firth
Boathow
Crag
Crag
Fell
Great
Borne
Starling Dodd
Ennerdale Water
W
N

17 RED PIKE 828M/2717FT

Climb it from	Netherbeck Bridge **4**, Overbeck Bridge **3** and Wasdale Green **1**
Character	A north-south ridge with a broken cliff forming an impressive western wall to Mosedale
Fell-friendly route	5
Summit grid ref	NY 165 106
Link it with	Scoat Fell or Yewbarrow
Part of	The Mosedale Round and The Nether Beck Horseshoe

Red Pike is a fell of striking contrasts. To the east it's short and ferociously steep, casting deep shadows from its impenetrable craggy scarp face down into Mosedale, the only let-up the high combe of Black'em Head. An implausible dry-stone wall climbs the wild slope between Black Beck and Black'em Head. To the west, wide slopes spread down to the Nether Beck valley touching Wast Water at Bowderdale. In this rough fell pasture the wanderer can locate a sure line of ascent or descent with comparative ease, in spite of the absence of paths.

Two lovely pools are cradled in high basins – the little-visited Low Tarn is embraced by a series of rocky knots, while Scoat Tarn, visited by a long trail up Nether Beck, is the perfect place to find solitude. But it is the high ridge that

↑ *The dramatic summit escarpment (photo: Anne Bowskill)*

most captivates. Stand on this airy summit, or beside the Chair on the south top, and you really feel aloof.

Unlike its near neighbour in Buttermere, Wasdale's Red Pike has only fleeting blushes of red in its scree and rocks. Perhaps Mosedale Pike would have been a better name for such a commanding presence in this vast mountain-rimmed basin.

Ascent from Netherbeck Bridge 4

Via Nether Beck →*6.4km/4 miles* ↑*750m/2460ft* ⌚*3hr 45min*

A long march in lonely fell country, this route is perfect for a getaway day, visiting a lonely yew and a high-set sheet of wind-whipped water.

1 The path steps up from the layby and skirts the marsh to find a brief weakness in the bracken where it bears up left to join the bridleway. Turn right and accompany this age-old trail, sustaining a historical wild connection with Ennerdale. The path is prone to stoniness, which may cause a brisk stride to falter. The best 'water show' occurs early on, as **Nether Beck** crashes down – a notable fall among the last of the trees. The valley is hemmed in and offers few views of note, and the beck is hidden where it runs in a ravine beyond **Lad Crag**.

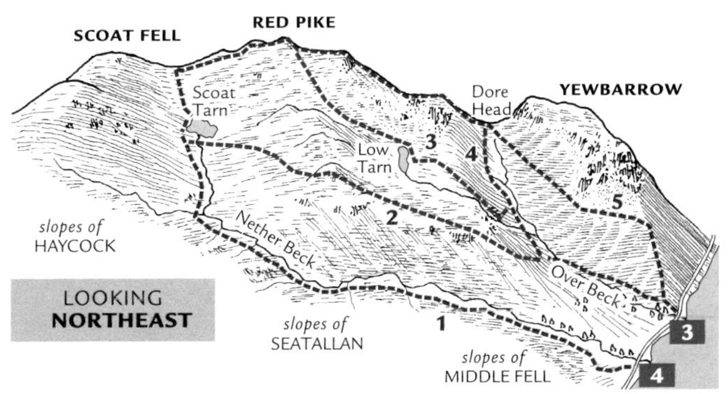

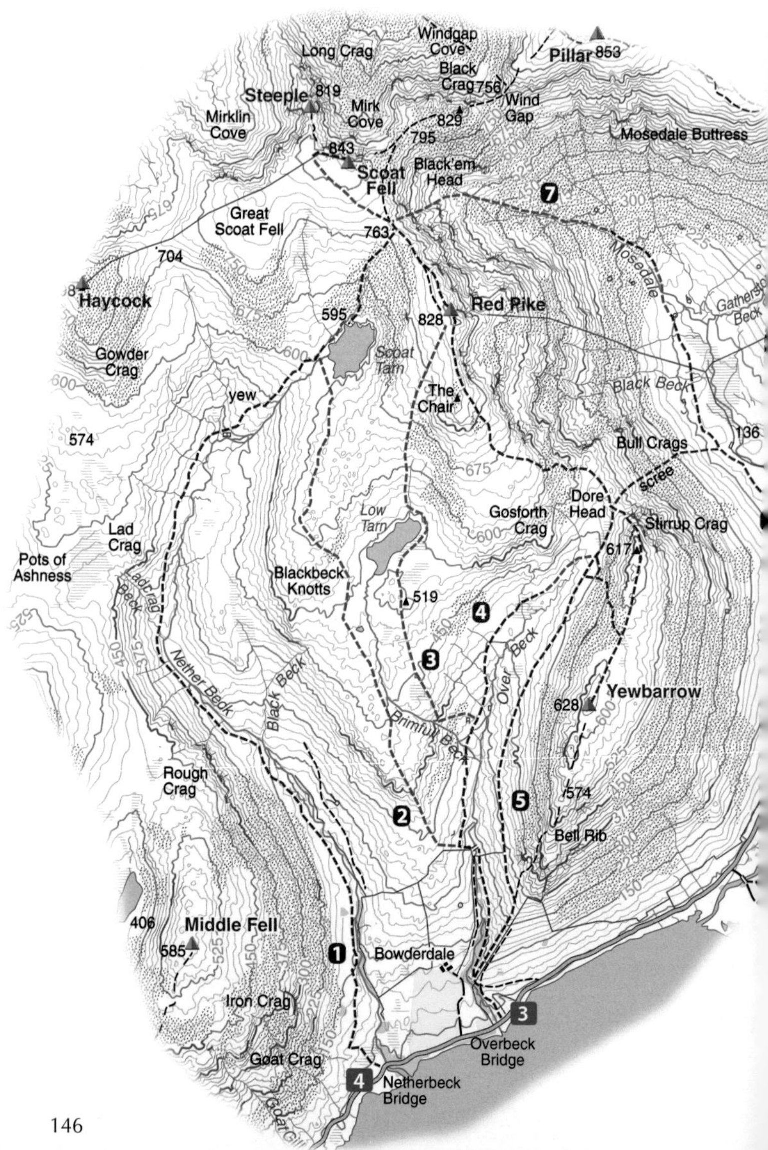
Windgap Cove
Long Crag
Pillar 853
Black Crag 756
Steeple 819
Mirk Cove
Wind Gap
Mirklin Cove
829
795
Mosedale Buttress
843
Scoat Fell
Black'em Head
7
Great Scoat Fell
763
Mosedale
704
Haycock
Red Pike
828
595
Gowder Crag
Scoat Tarn
Gatherstone Beck
The Chair
yew
Black Beck
574
Bull Crags
136
675
scree
Dore Head
Gosforth Crag
Stirrup Crag
Low Tarn
617
Lad Crag
Pots of Ashness
Blackbeck Knotts
519
4
Ladcrag Beck
3
Nether Beck
Black Beck
Over Beck
Yewbarrow
628
Brimfull Beck
Rough Crag
5
574
2
Bell Rib
406
Middle Fell
585
1
Bowderdale
Iron Crag
3
Overbeck Bridge
Goat Crag
4
Netherbeck Bridge
Goat Gill

The main path-fork occurs at a waters-meet below an obvious crag and beside a ruined fold. Ford the beck and follow the rising path aiming NE. Curiosity draws you left when eyes light upon a solitary yew tree. It's a must-visit spot, and makes you wonder how this little tree made it down the centuries. The path runs up close to the outflow of **Scoat Tarn**, where you can see a weather station on the far bank. The path falters as it leads along the western shore to resume on the northerly rise beyond the tarn. Switch sides along the tiny tributary hollow and continue up to the high saddle. Bear right with the ridge path, and be aware that most passing walkers inexplicably 'miss' the summit.

Ascent from Overbeck Bridge 3

There are two ways up the Over Beck valley, the more sure-footed route on the east side (Route 5). That to the west (Route 4) is a springboard from which you can explore Red Pike's wider fell dominion (including Routes 2 and 3).

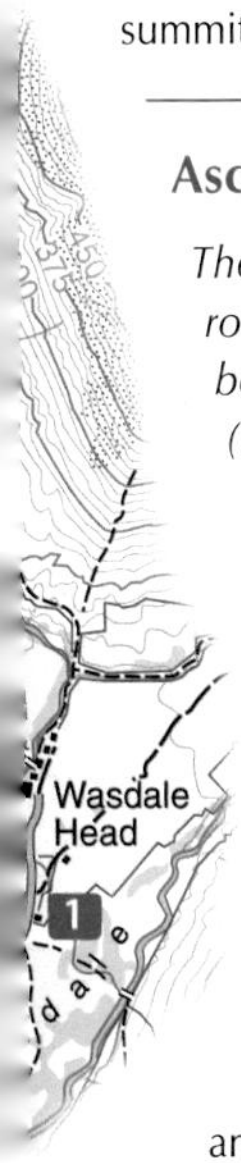

Via Scoat Tarn →*6.4km/4 miles* ↑*760m/2495ft* ⏲*3hr 50min*

Visit two secluded tarns on this route, making use of a pathless northerly ridge for excellent views.

2 Head up from the car park, shunning the inviting stile and brushing past the gorse to go through a gate on a path close above the deepening ravine. Pass an embowered oak, and take a dramatic glimpse into the boiling tumult. The downward gradient from this point on is such that the slope is prone to slippage amid the bracken. The path reaches a gate, smartly followed by a footbridge that crosses the lively waters of **Over Beck** in an attractive rocky gorge. Slipping over the wall, the path is ushered right to a stile, then climbs the bank beside the rising wall to a lateral path, which emanates from the inbye pastures of **Bowderdale Farm**, from where there is no recreational access.

With Low and Scoat Tarns as the primary objectives en route, ignore the lateral path and continue up with the wall. At the top, simply head up the ridge, with faint evidence of a shepherding path, onto the first brow – beyond here only sheep paths exist on the open fell. The views are really handsome

Low Tarn, with The Screes the striking backdrop

across the Nether Beck valley to Seatallan. Draw towards **Brimfull Beck** and pass the outflow of **Low Tarn**, keeping to the western flank of the fell and mounting onto **Blackbeck Knotts** – an indefinite knolled ridge, where you may lose yourself in thought, but not direction. Keep N to ford the outflow of **Scoat Tarn** and join Route **1**, running along the northern shore, to the summit.

Via Low Tarn →*4.8km/3 miles* ↑*750m/2460ft* ⏲*3hr 20min*

Another pathless route, with a little easy scrambling, yields great views of the delightfully named Brimfull Beck ravine.

3 An entertaining variant to the former route follows the lateral path up the valley, crossing the plank-bridge over **Brimfull Beck** to reach the remnants of an old sheepfold. Here, cut back left, pathless, over the boulders and continue up to the cascades and water-shoots of the higher Brimfull Beck ravine. Again there is no evidence of a path, but the scrambling is easy and the animated waters tremendous fun to observe. Follow the beck to the tarn, or, better still, angle part-right to gain the old shepherds' cairn on the High Fell knoll, with its fine view to the Gosforth Crag face of Red Pike and Yewbarrow.

Cross the peaty moor to skirt round the east side of **Low Tarn** and evade the obvious problems of **Gosforth Crag**, which looks like a stand-alone peak from the shores of the tarn. Work N up the slopes on grass all the way to the top.

Via Dore Head →*4.8km/3 miles* ↑*760m/2495ft* 🕒*3hr 30min*

Choose between a waterfall walk crossing marshy ground (Route 4) or a steady ascent on strong paths (Route 5).

4 With the head of the valley the first target, you may simply stick with the lateral path after Route **3** turns off left, with two good waterfalls to admire. The path eventually is released from bracken's grip, but only to run into marshy ground. From **Dore Head** the real climbing starts, and a series of certain steps brings you purposefully onto the crown of the fell above **Gosforth Crag**. (Make sure you visit **The Chair** viewpoint to the left.) Now on easy ground, edge close to the audacious scarp to reach the summit – again, this is off the regular line of the path.

5 The best path, and for many walkers the first choice for the ascent of Red Pike, leaves the car park and takes advantage of the first inviting fence-stile. From here it ascends the lower ridge of **Yewbarrow** beside the fence, with the impressive **Bell Rib** prow of the fell strikingly in view up ahead. A ladder-stile puts you on the left side of the fence and onto a lateral path that contours below Dropping Crag to a hand-gate. The path runs on at an easy gradient to the head of the side-valley to join Route **4**.

Ascent from Wasdale Green 1

Via Dore Head →*4.1km/2½ miles* ↑*750m/2460ft* 🕒*3hr 20min*

A tough start to the ascent of Red Pike on a far more agreeable trod than in days gone by, when it followed the infamous scree-run to the left.

6 Begin from behind the Wasdale Head Inn and cross the elegant stone footbridge to advance along the walled drove by a gate and on beside the pine-shaded **Ritson's Force**, a lovely place to idle and admire the crashing waters of Mosedale Beck. From the ensuing hand-gate, the path leads through bracken above the beck-lining wall.

At a fold, the path switches up left, aiming for the grassy strip below the scree. Follow this up and angle half-right across the lower portion of scree to find the beginnings of a more earnest grass path that climbs to the saddle of **Dore Head** to turn right with Route **4**.

Via Black'em Head →*4.8km/3 miles* ↑*775m/2545ft* ⏲*3hr 50min*

This is quite the most engrossing ascent, if contrary to the normal practice of seeking the liberation of a rising ridge.

7 Begin with Route **6** but at the fold cut over the moraine through the bracken following a path that keeps to the lower ground and aims for a ladder-stile at the foot of an amazing wall. You cannot but be startled by this wall, which beetles straight up the east slope of Red Pike for little obvious advantage. It must have resolved a keenly felt grazing dispute. Advance to the Y Boulder, a startling block split as by an earthquake. Here you could skirt left round the marshy patch to ford **Mosedale Beck**, joining the path to the **Wind Gap** screes. But it's much more pleasurable to wander up the pathless slope in harmony with Mosedale Beck, close beside a sequence of entertaining waterfalls. Where three gills converge to form the single beck, turn your attention

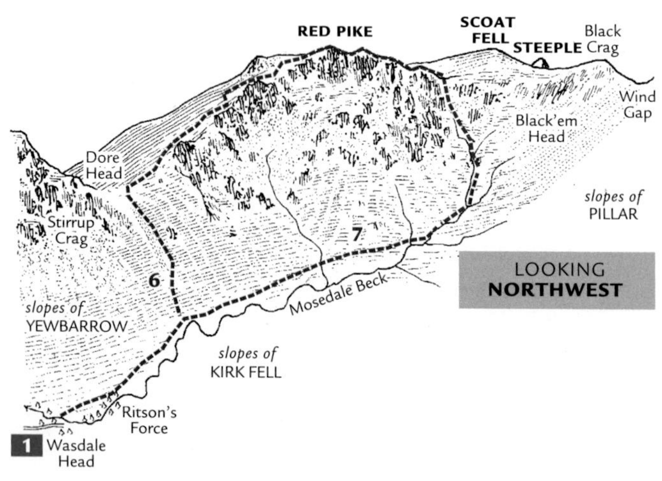

Red Pike from the ridge above Black'em Head

to the one and only escape to the skyline ridge out of **Black'em Head**. To the right, screes spill from Black Crag, and to the left all seems conclusively rock girth. However, it is a simple matter, your good fell-sense prevailing, to spot a narrow gully left of the headwall. Weave up to surprise yourself with the ease of its discovery and your prompt delivery upon the saddle above. Turn up left for the summit (**1**).

The summit

Two tops seem to vie for the summit accolade, but a perilously perched cairn on the southernmost peak attests which has assured seniority. Contrast the breathtaking drop to the east with the gentle sheep pasture to the west. Stand warily if the wind is gusting – you do not want to fall from here. A peak it may be, but there is a further high rocky eminence to enjoy, situated some 500m due south. This is also crowned with a cairn, and at the brink to the southwest of it find a stone-built seat, long known as The Chair, 25m/80ft lower than the summit but commanding a great westward prospect.

Top of the exit gully out of Black'em Head onto the ridge

Safe descents

The best advice is to follow the ridge path S down to Dore Head (**4**), descending the east side of Over Beck valley along the flanks of Yewbarrow to reach Wast Water (**5**). Avoid getting embroiled in the bouldery slope off the south top or The Chair, as this is unnecessarily troublesome. You can also descend due SW from the summit cairn over pathless but navigable territory into the Over Beck valley (**3**). From the saddle depression to the north you can retrace Route **1** via Scoat Tarn and the Nether Beck valley. Canny walkers may be tempted to pit their wits against Black'em Head in the other direction (**7**), sheltered from the full force of strong westerlies.

Ridge routes

Scoat Fell →*1.2km/¾ mile* ↓*70m/230ft* ↑*80m/260ft* 🕒*30min*
Follow the scarp N down to the saddle, and here veer half-left, traversing the mild boulder slope to slip through the broken Ennerdale Fence. Turn right to the summit.

Yewbarrow →*2.8km/1¾ miles* ↓*360m/1180ft* ↑*160m/525ft* 🕒*1hr 15min*
Keep rigidly to the descending ridge path heading S to Dore Head. There are now two options depending on your capacity or inclination. Head straight across the gap to tackle Stirrup Crag. There are weaknesses in its armour, a cleft squeeze for one and several scrambly gully sections, but all are do-able with normal fell endeavour. This route leads over the north top and on along the ridge, which dips before reaching the summit. However, you are not obliged to lock horns with Stirrup Crag. By turning right and following the dale path down past a cluster of boulders you will find a path that heads up the stony slope and veers right under the outcropping to work up onto the ridge at the saddle, from where turn right to the summit.

18 SCAFELL 964M/3163FT

Climb it from	Brotherilkeld **22**, Wha House **23**, Wasdale Head **2** and Dalegarth Station **25**
Character	Forbidding, compelling, mightier than its more illustrious and higher namesake neighbour
Fell-friendly route	8
Summit grid ref	NY 207 065
Link it with	Scafell Pike or Slight Side
Part of	The Roof of England

Scafell was once thought to be higher than Scafell Pike, hence the name 'Pike', as if it were merely an adjunct. Of the two mountains Scafell is also more of a peak. Its convex slopes, craggy to the east and north and smooth to the west, keep the summit constantly in view and prospects from the summit are unhindered. Whether from Crinkle Crags or Wast Water, Scafell does look the higher but triangulation eventually proved the naked eye wrong.

Today peak-baggers home in on Scafell Pike but there is still much to enjoy on demoted Scafell. North-facing Scafell Crag, plummeting from Symond's Knott, once drew the bolder fellwalker's attention, with Lord's Rake and West Wall Traverse accessing Deep Gill offering thrilling scrambles. But the remarkable Lord's

↑ *Scafell from Long Green*

Rake was rendered far too dangerous by a rockfall in 2002 and can no longer be recommended. The main gully rearing from the foot of Scafell Crag, notoriously full of loose rock, is also now dire, and access to the West Wall Traverse has been compromised too.

Instead, the first five routes here pick their way up to the summit through the easterly crags, starting from the foot of Hardknott Pass. From Wasdale, three routes (6–8) head up the smooth western slopes with Route 9 curling round the summit to scramble up via Mickledore. Routes 10 and 11 describe an elegant circuit from Boot, in Eskdale.

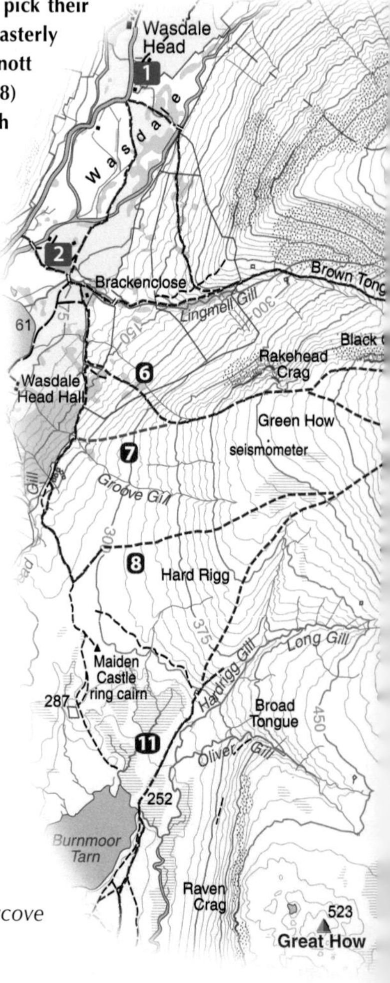

Ascent from Brotherilkeld 22 *off map S* and Wha House 23 *off map S*

The journey into upper Eskdale from the foot of the Hardknott Pass is one of Lakeland's dale-approach treats. In terms of reaching Scafell the key point is Cam Spout. Two paths draw in to this point, from either side of the Esk. Route 3 then continues up towards Route 5 to Foxes Tarn and the summit ridge, while Route 4 heads off in search of a stunning arête and direct route to the summit. The scenery both within and without the dale is pure fell delight.

Via Cam Spout →*7.5km/4¾ miles* ↑*640m/2100ft* ⌚*4hr 30min*

The speediest route is via the Cowcove zig-zags.

1 Embark along the farm track to Brotherilkeld from the old red telephone box, guided left of Brotherilkeld farmyard to a hand-gate, and a matter of a few metres on, go left, crossing the wooden footbridge spanning the wonderfully tree-shaded **River Esk**. Traverse the pasture, with a wall right, to a ladder-stile entering the farmyard at Taw House. Leave the Taw House farmyard by the gate at its northern end and follow the lane to a gate, thereafter on an open track, via two gateways, to a gate/ladder-stile at a sheepfold. A clear track continues to Scale Bridge, crossing the embowered cascades of Scale Gill. Ignore a path taking a cavalier direct diagonal line up to the zig-zags from the bridge and take the footpath signed further up the track. This becomes the lesser-used route up the west side of the valley, rougher than its parallel path to Lingcove Bridge, particularly above Esk Falls, but nonetheless fascinating to tramp. Watch for the acute turn left up through the bracken – the path is clear enough. Higher, the zig-zags afford a view into the Cowcove Beck ravine laced with

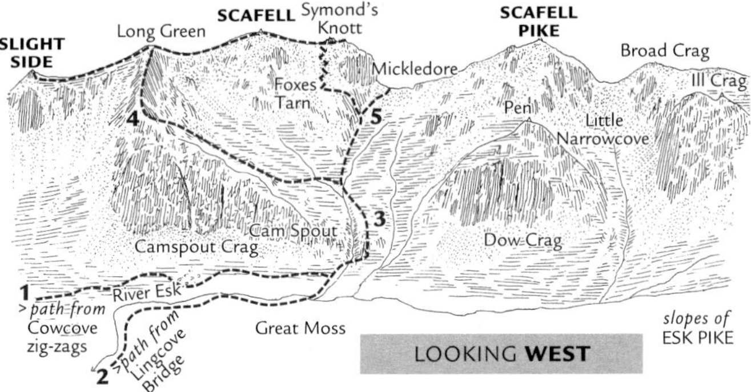

birch and rowan, before entering the first of two marshy hollows. Keep to the dry western edge, crossing a plank over Damas Dubs, the natural drainage for the two, apparently separate, hollows. The path, well evidenced underfoot, leads into the Esk catchment and meets up indistinctly with the west-side path to carry on through a multi-penned sheepfold, curving round a low spur, littered with huge erratics, known as Sampson's Stones, set beneath the massive cliff of **Camspout Crag**. Keeping to the fringe of **Great Moss** marsh, bear up half-left to reach the foot of **Cam Spout**, the most handsome of pencil-thin waterfalls. Follow Route **3** from this point.

2 The main valley approach holds tight to the east bank of the **Esk** beside a fence. Notice the curious erosion that has left an oak tree's roots bare some 20m short of the hand-gate into the pastures. A clear path leads on, via a gate in a wall, continuing to a ladder-stile beside a gate and small fold, where a path that began above the cattle grid at the foot of the Hardknott road converges. The valley soon narrows with three great cliffs catching the eye – Yew Crag up to the right on Hard Knott, and Brock Crag and Heron Crag with its large, free, climber-friendly face to the left. Soon after, The Steeple is visible up to the right. The undulating path becomes smoother as it reaches the sheep-wash fold at the elegant single-span **Lingcove Bridge**. From here The Steeple takes on the appearance of a Roman thumbs-up. Close to the bridge is quite the most excited passage in the Esk's beautiful career. Deep pools and falls abound, and in high summer its crystal cool waters are the happy haunt of swimmers and dippers. Cross the bridge and follow the path up **Throstle Garth**, passing too high to catch a glimpse of Esk Falls – known only to the infinitely rougher west-side path. As the mass of Throstlehow Crag is left behind we see the river taking wide meandering sweeps through a landscape reminiscent of a remote Highland glen, the path keeping close under Scar Lathing. As the vast amphitheatre surrounding **Great Moss** takes centre stage, see a turf-topped wall close right. This is the remnant of a medieval deer compound built by the monks of Furness Abbey. Wet marsh is unavoidable, but once the Esk shallows are forded the sponge is less of a problem as you trend northwest to the foot of **Cam Spout**, where the real rigours (and Route **3**) begin!

3 The path climbs steeply up on naked rock close to the falls – two thin tails of water spilling down the gully, intermingled with a few smaller spills. **4** As the slope eases a variant approach appears, the objective the little-visited delights of the **Camspout Crag** ridge. Angle across the grassy slope avoiding a band of rock to the right. Work up through the skyline outcrops, no trace of a path until at last the ridge is joined. This is a stunning, safe, grassy arête leading handsomely to the cairned ridge-top of **Long Green**. Make sure you stop to take in the fine views across Green Cove to Scafell's East Buttress and south to the craggy eastern declivity of Slight Side. An easily found stony trail leads north to the summit.

5 The normal recourse is to follow the path up the combe beneath **Mickledore**, branching into a gully below East Buttress. Steep, stony but not rotten, this clambering stair leads to **Foxes Tarn** – a constant horseshoe of naturally dammed water around a large boulder. A pitched path zig-zags up the loose fellside south of East Buttress reaching the skyline at a cairn. The summit is located left upon a final rough stony rise. Make sure not to miss the head of Scafell Crag to the right from this saddle. Climb the prominent headland of **Symond's Knott** to gaze tentatively over the brink into the abyss of this famous climbing arena. Pass on by the head of Deep Gill to be impressed by what you've just achieved! Stride cautiously a little further, gaze over the **Broad Stand** brink to Scafell Pike and down upon Pikes Crag towards Lingmell and Great Gable, a supremely beautiful prospect.

The combe path from Cam Spout climbs, close under East Buttress for the most part, to **Mickledore** (the big gap), the narrow saddle connection linking the two Scafells, but this currently gives **no safe access to the summit**. Although Broad Stand may **seem** a modest step from the saddle there are several wildly exposed moves involved. **Do not entertain taking this route** unless you are fully equipped with rope and belays and have rock-climbing expertise – every year there are deaths here!

Ascent from Wasdale Head 2

There are two main lines of ascent, either via Rakehead (Routes 6 and 7) or the much more exciting route up Lingmell Gill (Route 9). On the latter you need to cross over Mickledore, descending some 90m to climb a gully on the east side of the mountain. Route 8 offers a less demanding but less exciting option over Hard Rigg.

Via Rakehead →*3.5km/2¼ miles* ↑*900m/2950ft* 🕒*3hr 20min*

6 To take the route over **Green How**, from the car park go left crossing the broad bridge. Then leave the farm-track to follow the gorse-lined path beside **Lingmell Gill**. Enter the **Brackenclose** enclosure with a Fell & Rock Club Hut in its midst.

A left turn leads up to a footbridge, from where a very poor path embarks, climbing the steep pasture via stiles to tackle the excessively steep scarp slope on the west side of Rakehead Crag. The path is horrid in ascent and wretched beyond words in descent, so be kind to the fell and leave it alone. Better bear

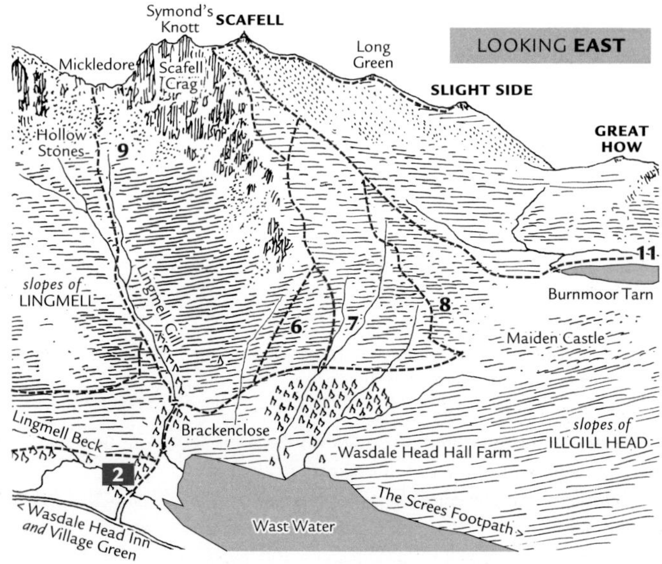

The Pinnacle at the top of Deep Gill, looking to the Mosedale Horseshoe

right with the Eskdale bridleway via a gate onto a green track into a field. Approaching the next gate, bear up the shallow hollow-way to a gate in the fence. Slant half-left up the pasture interspersed with thorn scrub to a stile in the intake wall/fence. A steep grassy trod leads directly up the scarp. At the brow keep along the edge above **Rakehead Crag** (spurning a path which would link through to Route **8**).

Beyond this point, gain height gradually with a certain rhythm made lyrical if you keep to the northern edge with breathtaking views into the **Hollow Stones** amphitheatre. The latter part of the climb is inevitably stony and leads up by the top of **Lord's Rake** (a famous old way now blighted by rockfalls), with stunning views. Reaching the saddle, identified by the quartz cross, bear up right to the summit.

7 The kindest option, for fell and feet, is to continue up the bridleway to where it crosses **Groove Gill** by a twin-arched stone bridge. Climb left, initially beside a smaller gill and then slanting pathless across to the left to join the scarp edge path.

8 You could even continue higher up the bridleway from Brackenclose before branching onto the broad open ridge climbing to join the **Hard Rigg** path, but the walking is easy and without excitement. When a path comes in from the right, take it to climb in straightforward fashion onto the stony western slope, aiming for the high saddle some 40m north of the summit.

Via Lingmell Gill →*5.5km/3½ miles* ↑*975m/3200ft* ⌚*4hr 20min*

9 Start with Route **6** but keep left before Brackenclose to join the pitched path up **Lingmell Gill**. When you reach the right-hand fork on **Brown Tongue** bear right up to **Hollow Stones**, a truly stony hollow beneath the huge north-facing Scafell Crag. A loose gravel gully leads up to the **Mickledore** saddle. **Broad Stand should not be considered unless you have a high level of climbing competence.** A torrid 90m descent, beneath the East Buttress, leads to an obvious gully to your right. Follow Route **5** to climb this to the summit.

Ascent from Dalegarth Station 25 *off map SW*

These two good routes from Boot make the perfect circuit.

Via Eel Tarn →*8km/5 miles* ↑*915m/3000ft* ⌚*4hr 45min*

10 From the short village street, passing the Burnmoor Inn, bear right, signed 'Eel Tarn'. A roadway winds up behind the tree-shaded mill, the thunderous thrashings of **Whillan Beck** making an early impression. As the tarmac ends leave the farm-track leading to Gill Bank, with its two monkey puzzle trees. Take the gate right, go left at the three-way footpath sign, again directing to 'Eel Tarn'. The green track threads through a walled passage, the immediate surroundings reminiscent of Yorkshire limestone country. The path curves up right. Do not be lured left onto the path to Lambford Bridge, but keep right to reach **Eel Tarn**.

Broad Stand – not an option any more

The boggy ground on this northern side has to be traversed before skirting to the east of the tarn, from where a path weaves on up through a confusing terrain leading by Peelplace Noddle. In mist

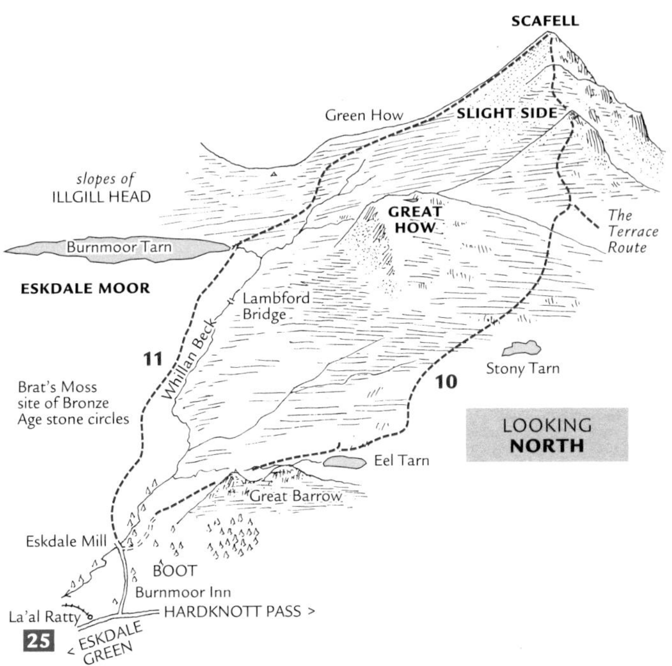

you certainly do have to use your noddle and a compass would not come amiss. The path mounts onto a more definite ridge above **Stony Tarn**, and generally contours across marshy ground due northeast, fording several minor gills, latterly a grassy trod that meets up with the **Terrace Route**, as the slope steepens... now gird your loins for a final push for the top of **Slight Side**. The ridge path thereafter could not be simpler. There is nothing but the occasional gravel patch to slow your progress to the top of the **Long Green** ridge, a handsome intermediate high point. The ridge dips then climbs again, with moderate toil, to the skyward crest of Scafell.

Via Burnmoor Tarn →*7.5km/4½ miles* ↑*905m/2970ft* ⏲*4hr 15min*

11 Cross the stone bridge passing **Eskdale Mill** to a gate. The path zig-zags. Go through the gate on the right beneath a pine tree. A gated path leads through the enclosures onto the open moor. Keep to the principal path and, about half a kilometre after crossing Ramshaw Beck, keep straight on, leaving the hardcore path which bends left to the Eller How barn. The green-way reaches the outflow of **Burnmoor Tarn** which you need to step across with care. Take the path forking half-right north-northeast across the low ground to reach a sheepfold. The path forks. Take the ascending left-hand path out of the bracken onto the grass prairie of **Hard Rigg**. (The right-hand path leads up Hardrigg Gill but any shelter this more minor route provides is lost when it meets Route 8.) Follow Route **8** to the summit from here.

The summit

The summit cairn

The summit is marked by a modest cairn on a tilted pedestal, close by a low circular wind-shelter all set up upon a rough rocky crest. On the north side two short walls serve as shelters from contradictory winds. The view matches up to expectations. Anyone who makes the serious effort to combine the two Scafells in one expedition, and it is no light undertaking, will recognise this as a distinctly different point of view. More than just different, it might be thought the pick of the two, being the culmination of a narrow ridge, and sufficiently set apart to give perspective on Scafell Pike and upper Eskdale. The Western Fells above Wast Water and Mosedale are well displayed, as too Burnmoor Tarn and Miterdale, with the Isle of Man, as if afloat in the Irish Sea, beyond.

Safe descents

There are two simple ways off. The easiest of all heads for Wasdale Head (3km) and leaves the summit immediately N of the summit outcrop.

A cairned path takes to the stony fellside heading due W (**8**), the loose trail easing as grass takes over on the route down Green How (**6**). Ankles are less stressed by linking to the Burnmoor bridleway at the foot of Groove Gill, rather than by being drawn off the scarp beyond Rakehead Crag.

For Eskdale (7km) follow the stepped ridge SSE (**10**), then due S to Slight Side, a well-marked path leading off that top into Cow Cove following the Terrace Route bound for the Wha House car park.

Ridge routes

Scafell Pike →*2km/1¼ miles* ↓*275m/900ft* ↑*290m/950ft* ⌚*1hr 20min*
Ignore old guides and maps: there is now only one way to Mickledore. Lord's Rake and Broad Stand are out-of-bounds for walkers. From the shallow saddle 60m north of the summit, turn abruptly SE (right) by the cairn descending the zig-zags to Foxes Tarn. Follow the tarn outflow down the bouldery gully. At its foot, bear up left, clambering up the gravelly slope below East Buttress to reach Mickledore. Go right passing the Mountain Rescue stretcher box, the stony ground seldom relenting, though the slope eases heading NE to the summit, identified by an old Ordnance Survey column and a raised memorial cairn, suitably flat-topped with access steps – a place of congregation and elation. The whole process will take at least an hour and considerably more if you are tired!

Slight Side →*2km/1¼ miles* ↓*210m/690ft* ↑*30m/100ft* ⌚*30min*
The south ridge falls in easy stages with some rough bouldery ground, but nothing to trouble an accustomed fell foot. Should you be tempted to curve with the initial ridge to take advantage of the splendid view from the ridge-end above Green Cove, viewing Foxes Tarn and Scafell Pike beyond, you may notice evidence of old aeroplane wreckage on the scree. Mid-point on the ridge is the shapely summit of Long Green (marking the top of the Camspout Crag ridge, and a novel route down into Eskdale). A simple, if occasionally loose path, leads on S. The ground levels before the final easy scramble on this perfect termination of the massif.

19 SCAFELL PIKE 977M/3206FT

Climb it from	Old Dungeon Ghyll **21**, Seathwaite **20**, Wasdale Green **1**, Wasdale Head **2**, Brotherilkeld **22** or Wha House **23**
Character	Remote and rugged, daunting and deserving of great respect
Fell-friendly route	4
Summit grid ref	NY 215 072
Link it with	Great End, Scafell or Lingmell
Part of	The Roof of England

Scafell Pike must be the monarch of all Lakeland mountains, following hard on the heels of Helvellyn as the most popular climb of the major fells. It is, in every dimension, a real mountain. Crag and scree abound on all fronts meaning that care is needed both in ascent and descent and the summit contrives to keep itself remote from the gaze of valley observers.

It is not the most beautiful, does not have the very best ascent, does not offer the finest panorama and is not home to the most challenging crags, but Scafell Pike is the highest, roughest, toughest and assuredly the most revered ground. In a district simply bristling with shapely peaks there is inevitably a strong impulse to stand atop the highest of the lot.

↑ *Scafell Pike from Bowfell*

Your judgement on when to go, and by which route, needs to be tempered with much forethought. The fell can be climbed from four directions: Wasdale Head (5–7), Seathwaite in Borrowdale (2–4), Great Langdale via Esk Hause (1) and lonely Eskdale (8–10). There are two hot-favourite ascents. Two paths come together in the vicinity of Lingmell Col, from Lingmell Gill (6) and the Corridor Route (2). The other popular approach is from Great Langdale via Rossett Gill and Esk Hause (1). Being closer to the M6 this route comes under disproportionate pressure, but it is nonetheless a grand route.

Ascent from the Old Dungeon Ghyll 21 *off map E*

Via Rossett Gill and Esk Hause →*11km/6¾ miles* ↑*955m/3130ft* ⏲*5hr*

Scafell Pike is a distant, almost surreal, notion from the Old Dungeon Ghyll, with the added fear that it may be lost in the clouds. The adage 'better to travel hopefully' applies, as too 'retreat is the better part of valour', an option if, having reached Esk Hause, it is, indeed, befogged.

1 Starting from the Old Dungeon Ghyll, you can soon pick up your stride in Mickleden but don't overdo it – energy levels will be tested today. Crossing the footbridge at the foot of Stake Gill, engage on the pony path which fords Rossett Gill, then via an exaggerated double zig-zag steps ascend to the saddle at the head of the gill. The path goes down to the outflow of **Angle Tarn**, a place to pause and study the reflections of Hanging Knotts in the hanging waters. The continuing path rises northwestward up **Tongue Head**.

Closing in on the saddle, drift half-left to the cross-wall shelter. This is an important landmark and its existence is no coincidence. The terrain here has a nasty habit of confusing even confident ramblers and it is a meeting of the winds too! Be aware there are two saddles – the east–west link to **Sprinkling Tarn** and **Sty Head** and the higher col of **Esk Hause**, situated 250m to the southwest of the wind-shelter. Esk Hause, the broad depression between **Esk Pike** and Great End, is littered with cairns. Clearly many people come this way bound for Calf Cove. Go west on the all-too-palpable trail. The path winds up the damp hollow wherein lies a small shelter and the last running water.

Climb onto the plateau saddle. So far so good, but the terrain is about to deteriorate. The ridge draws up southwestward to an innominate rocky

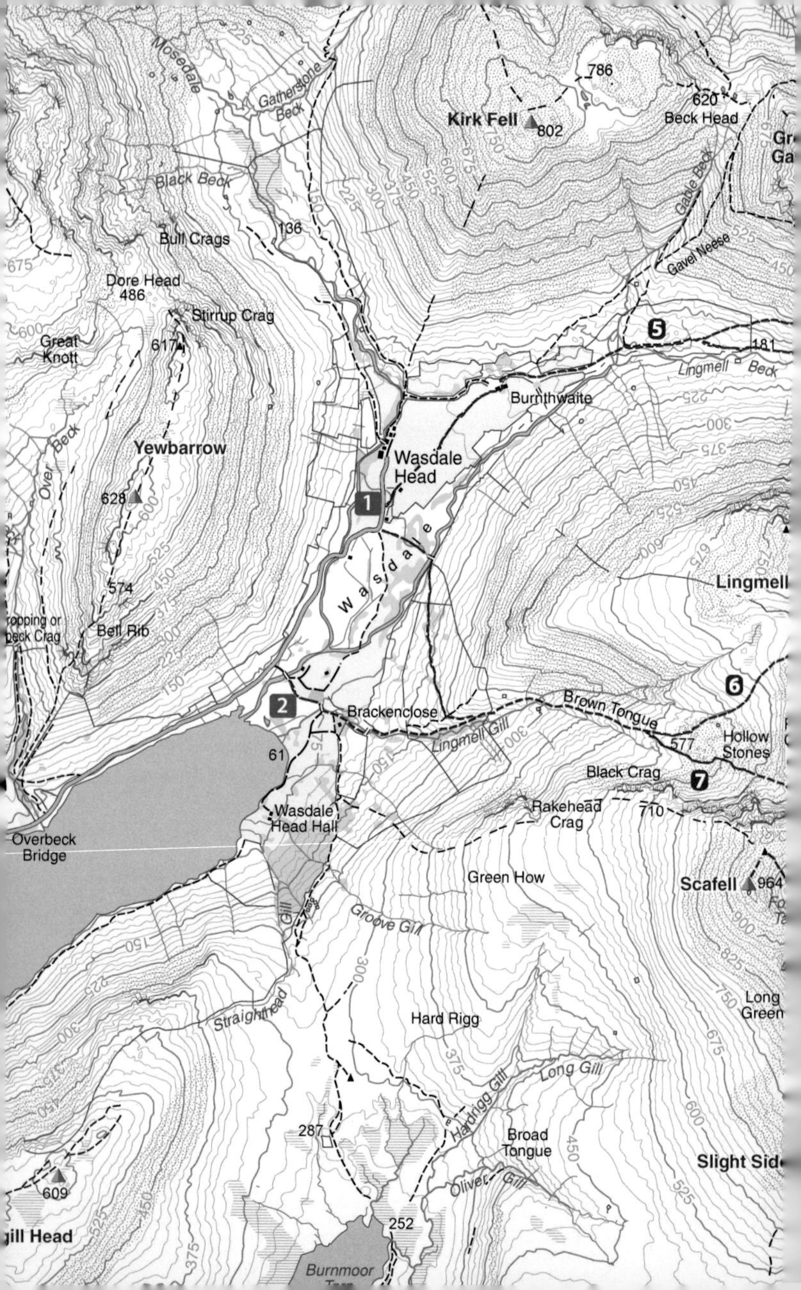

Mosedale
Gatherstone Beck
Kirk Fell
802
786
620
Beck Head
Gable Beck
Gavel Neese
Black Beck
136
Bull Crags
Dore Head
486
Stirrup Crag
Great Knott
617
5
181
Lingmell Beck
Burnthwaite
Wasdale Head
1
Yewbarrow
628
Over Beck
574
Bell Rib
Wasdale
Lingmell
6
2
Brackenclose
Brown Tongue
Lingmell Gill
577
Hollow Stones
61
Black Crag
7
Wasdale Head Hall
Rakehead Crag
710
Overbeck Bridge
Green How
Scafell
964
Groove Gill
Long Green
Straighthead
Hard Rigg
Long Gill
Hardrigg Gill
287
Broad Tongue
Slight Side
609
Oliver Gill
252
Burnmoor

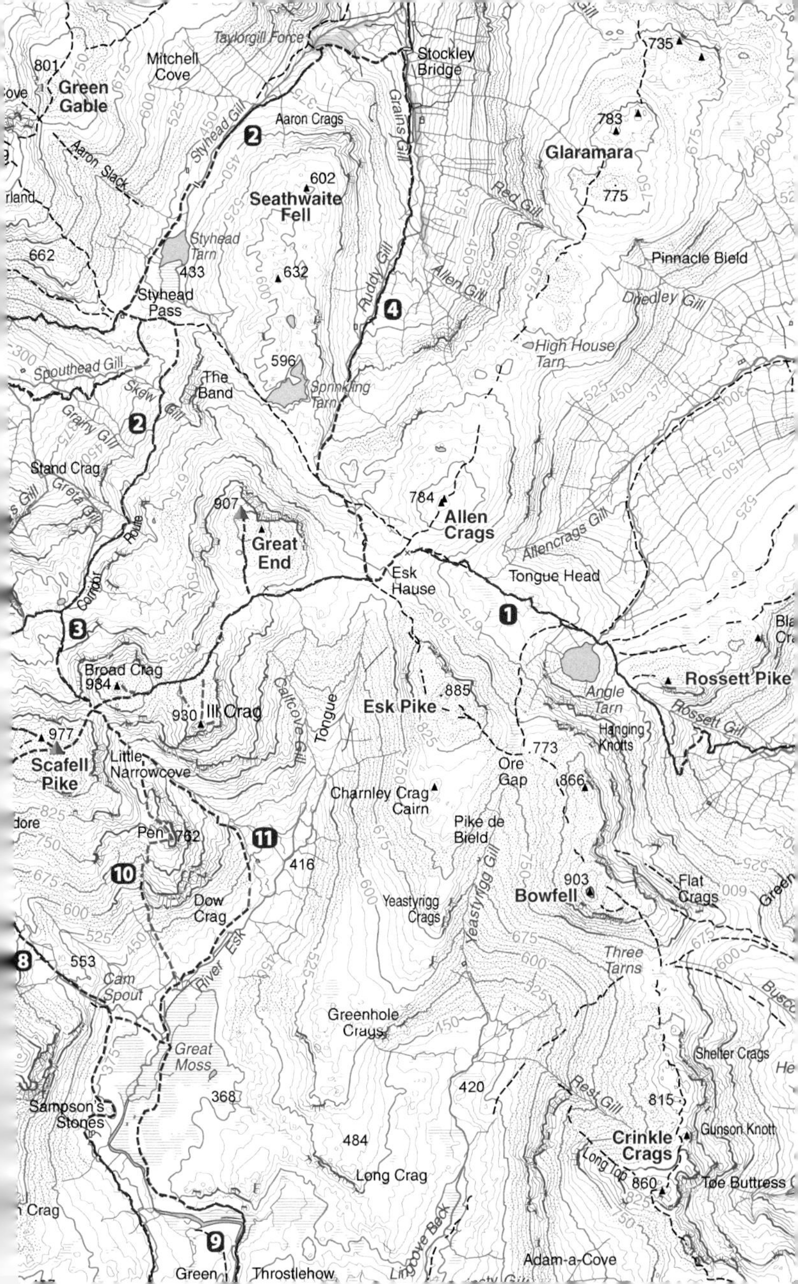

Taylorgill Force
Mitchell Cove
Stockley Bridge
Green Gable
Grains Gill
Aaron Crags
Styhead Gill
Aaron Slack
Seathwaite Fell
Glaramara
Red Gill
Styhead Tarn
Styhead Pass
Ruddy Gill
Allen Gill
Pinnacle Bield
Dudley Gill
High House Tarn
Spouthead Gill
The Band
Skew Gill
Sprinkling Tarn
Grainy Gill
Stand Crag
Greta Gill
Great End
Allen Crags
Allencrags Gill
Corridor Route
Esk Hause
Tongue Head
Broad Crag
Rossett Pike
Angle Tarn
Rossett Gill
Ill Crag
Calfcove Gill
Tongue
Esk Pike
Hanging Knotts
Scafell Pike
Little Narrowcove
Ore Gap
Charnley Crag Cairn
Pike de Bield
Pen
Bowfell
Flat Crags
Dow Crag
Yeastyrigg Crags
Yeastyrigg Gill
River Esk
Cam Spout
Three Tarns
Greenhole Crags
Great Moss
Shelter Crags
Rest Gill
Sampson's Stones
Crinkle Crags
Gunson Knott
Long Top
Long Crag
Toe Buttress
Lingcove Beck
Green
Throstlehow
Adam-a-Cove

crest. Weave through the boulders, the path inevitably vague. The boulders relent as the summit of Scafell Pike comes tantalisingly into eye shot – more distant than you may have hoped! Here the path sweeps majestically over the gravelly shoulder of the **Ill Crag** plateau, dipping into Illcrag Col, before yet more boulders on the traverse of the east shoulder of **Broad Crag** into Broadcrag Col. Views from the col, left down Little Narrowcove to Pen and right to Lingmell, are quite stirring. Wearying legs need to make one final effort on the sorely eroded scramble up the narrow arête leading to the summit boulder-field. All but the keenest walkers will dally on the summit, perhaps wandering to the various plateau brinks for differing perspectives, knowing that long, rough crossing has to be repeated.

Sadly the tiresome trek across the plateau causes most walkers to ignore Ill Crag and Broad Crag, both considered part and parcel of the Scafell Pike ensemble. In fact, they fully deserve the attention of well-informed fellwanderers and the high-country connoisseur. Broad Crag is a serious adjunct, serious in its utter rockiness. You can count the grass by the blade! The cairnless top lies only a matter of metres to the west of the ridge path, with easiest access from the north. Ill Crag is actually quite a separate entity as you clearly appreciate if you view it from Pen across Little Narrowcove, removed but at one with the mountainous setting.

Ascent from Seathwaite 20 *off map N*

For all its tantalising distance from the target summit a circular expedition can easily be created courtesy of the paths that fork at Stockley Bridge. The valley to the left (4) leads to Esk Hause, while that to the right (2) makes unerringly for Styhead Pass, thereby joining the Corridor Route.

Via Styhead Pass and the Corridor Route →*6.7km/4¼ miles* ↑*855m/2800ft* ◷*4hr 15min*

2 From Seathwaite Farm follow the regular bridleway via **Stockley Bridge**. This bears up right via gates climbing above the trees of **Taylorgill Force**, with excellent pitching underpinning a heavily used trail. Though the way is stony on the approach to the **Styhead Gill** footbridge, a more comfortable trail ensues passing **Styhead Tarn** to reach the pass, identified by the stretcher box.

There is nothing passage-like about the **Corridor Route**: it is a deceptively long and quite tough traverse, frequently congested with human traffic.

Broad Crag summit (photo: Anne Bowskill)

Ongoing pitching works on the steep open sections have made it more comfortable. You can start directly from the Sty Head stretcher box, angling half-left, short-cutting across the headstream of **Spouthead Gill**, but it's better to take the original route which branches right after the initial rise on the east-bound path, as to **Sprinkling Tarn**. Cross the vestige of a short wall, dipping and contouring to the mouth of the **Skew Gill** ravine. Climb the facing slope, pass through a short cutting on a hard staircase rising to a ridge crossing. Beware: the far-side step down is awkward. The path weaves on by two headstream fords of **Greta Gill** before a parting in the way.

Bear right to continue on the Corridor Route and ford **Piers Gill** just where it spills almost innocently into its notoriously deep and treacherous ravine. Eschew the dubious trace of a path that branches up the rough northern slopes west of Dropping Crag. The main path avoids the Lingmell Col. Work up among the outcrops to link with the path from **Hollow Stones** on the broad, stony, but otherwise unthreatening, northwest ridge to the summit.

3 Or, at the junction just after **Greta Gill**, take a clear set of steps to the left which marks the start of a less than savoury direct route to Broadcrag col. The latter stages of the climb up the wild combe to the narrow, rough saddle will test your tempo and temper. The route to the summit (**1**) lies up the blunt eroded arête to the right.

Pool beside the Corridor Route looking to Great Gable

Via Esk Hause →*6.5km/4 miles* ↑*905m/2970ft* ⌚*4hr 40min*

4 The Esk Hause route follows the left-hand path from Stockley Bridge up **Grains Gill**, which becomes **Ruddy Gill** after a footbridge. Pitching is evident right up to the point where the upper ravine is forded. Link to the path rising from **Sprinkling Tarn** and **Sty Head**. Take the first path branching right, leading up to Esk Hause to join Route **1**.

Ascent from Wasdale Head 1–2

Via Styhead Pass and the Corridor Route →*5.7km/3½ miles* ↑*915m/3000ft* ⌚*4hr 30min*

The direct route up from the head of Wasdale, with a choice of a steady ascent or a pleasant valley approach to Styhead Pass.

5 Leave the village green car park, following the lane by St Olaf's to **Burnthwaite**. Pass to the left among the farm buildings to a gate. Keep right – the obvious way heads on between varying walls, via a gate, to cross a footbridge spanning **Gable Beck**. Soon you face a choice of routes. Both are equally sound routes to Sty Head. The standard route sticks religiously to the rising path which passes through a hand-gate before taking on the scree section. The passage of several hundred years has ensured a well-defined shelf has been padded down and, but for one brief stumbly section, and a good deal of ball-bearing gravel, the path delivers the walker with minimal fuss.

The more pleasant option lies up the valley. Either bear off as bracken begins to encroach or wait a further hundred metres to find a clear path slanting down to the hand-gate near the foot of the descending wall. Keep alongside **Lingmell Beck**, fording the stream just after the confluence with **Piers Gill**. A clear green trail winds up the rigg, then fords to the left a gill. Cut across the next rigg to ford **Spouthead Gill** and then zig-zag up to **Styhead Pass** to join Route **2**.

Via Lingmell Gill →*4.5km/2¾ miles* ↑*915m/3000ft* ⏱*3hr*

Route 6 offers the shortest and most trouble-free ascent, while Route 7 up to Mickledore will involve discomfort, if short-lived, but no navigational difficulty. The latter path may never have been all that sweet, but certainly the

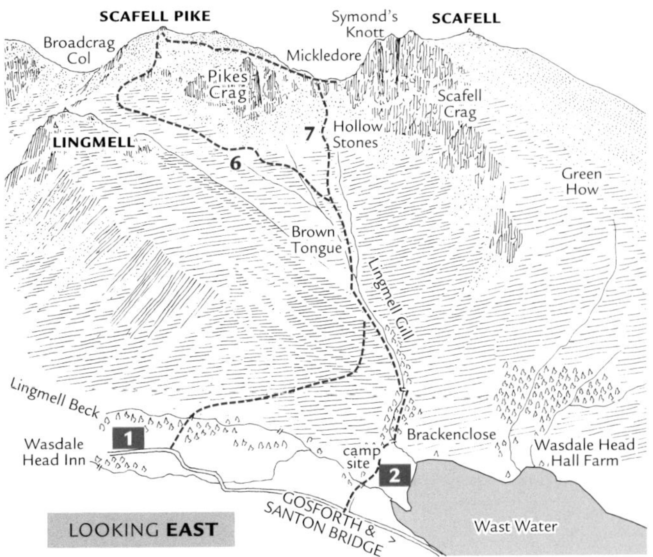

relentless scouring of fell boots has taken its toll.

6 There are two prime approaches to the Lingmell Gill valley. Direct from the NT camp site, follow the path left off the **Wasdale Head Hall** track by **Brackenclose**, rising beside the beck to a footbridge and subsequent hand-gates. From the village green follow the road back to the first bend where a stile and footpath sign direct across the dale floor to a footbridge spanning the stony-bedded **Lingmell Beck**. The path bears right, gradually ascending across the fellside to draw over the ridge-end contouring into **Lingmell Gill**.

Pikes Crag from below

Where the path splits as the **Brown Tongue** ridge begins to flatten out, take the left fork. This leads to the well-worn trail below **Pikes Crag**, and onto the northwest ridge, winding up to a large cairn on the lip of the summit plateau.

7 The right branch at the top of **Brown Tongue** leads up to a quite breathtaking intimacy with Scafell Crag on the way to **Mickledore**. Once on the narrow neck of ridge connecting the two great Scafells, turn left, passing the Mountain Rescue stretcher box. The path to the summit remains clear. For a brief diversion, once onto the plateau, bear half-left and, with modest effort and a hint of bravery, clamber onto the top of Pulpit Rock. A cairn marks the spot. From here you can enjoy a jealously guarded and airy new angle on Scafell Crag.

Ascent from Brotherilkeld 22 *off map S* or Wha House 23 *off map S*

There are two approaches to Cam Spout and then three choices thereafter – direct and scrambly up via Mickledore (8 and 9) or looping round via Broadcrag Col (10 and 11).

Via Mickledore →*8.5km/5½ miles* ↑*1050m/3450ft* ⏲*5hr*

8 The speedier route to Cam Spout is via the Cowcove zig-zags. Embark either along the farm track from Wha House direct to Taw House, or take the farm-track from Brotherilkeld from the old red telephone box, guided left of Brotherilkeld farmyard to a hand-gate, and, a matter of a few metres on, go left, crossing the wooden footbridge spanning the wonderfully tree-shaded **River Esk**. Traverse the pasture, with a wall right, to a ladder-stile entering the farmyard at Taw House.

Leave the farmyard by the gate at its northern end and follow the lane to a gate, thereafter on an open track, via two gateways, to a gate/ladder-stile below a ladder-stile at a sheepfold. A clear track continues to Scale Bridge, crossing the embowered cascades of Scale Gill. Ignore the direct path up from the bridge, and take the footpath signed further up the track. Watch for the acute turn left up through the bracken. (The path is clear enough.) Higher, the zig-zags afford a view into the Cowcove Beck ravine laced with birch and rowan, before entering the first of two marshy hollows. Keep to the dry western edge, crossing a plank over Damas Dubs. The path, well-evidenced

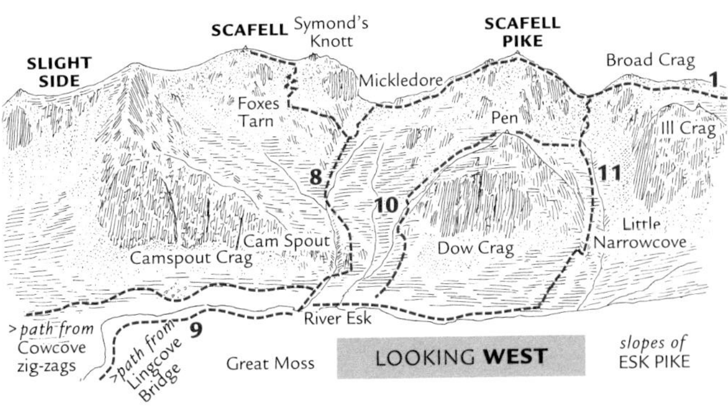

underfoot, leads into the Esk catchment and meets up indistinctly with the west-side path. It then leads through a multi-penned sheepfold, curving round a low spur, littered with huge erratics, known as **Sampson's Stones**, set beneath the massive cliff of Camspout Crag. Keeping to the fringe of **Great Moss** marsh, the path now bears up half-left to reach the foot of **Cam Spout**.

The lower mare's tail of Cam Spout – the path scrambles up the slabs to the right

9 Alternatively, the main valley approach holds tight to the Esk beside a fence. A clear path leads, via a gate in a wall, continuing to a ladder-stile beside a gate and small fold, where a path that began above the cattle grid at the foot of the Hardknott road converges. The valley soon narrows with three great cliffs catching the eye – Yew Crag up to the right on Hard Knott, and Brock Crag and Heron Crag to the left. The undulating path becomes smoother as it reaches the sheep-wash fold at the elegant single-span Lingcove Bridge. From here Eskdale Needle (aka The Steeple) to the south takes on the appearance of a Roman thumbs-up. Cross the bridge and follow the path up Throstle Garth. As the mass of **Throstlehow Crag** is left behind we see the river taking wide meandering sweeps through a landscape reminiscent of a remote Highland glen, the path keeping close under Scar Lathing. As the vast amphitheatre surrounding **Great Moss** takes centre stage, see a turf-topped wall close right. This is the remnant of a medieval deer compound built by the monks of Furness Abbey. Wet marsh is unavoidable, but once the Esk shallows are forded the sponge is less of a problem trending northwest to the foot of **Cam Spout**, the most handsome of pencil-thin waterfalls.

Clamber up the bare rocks to the right of Cam Spout, ascending the increasingly rough combe above you, beneath Scafell's East Buttress. There is a path all the way, though it is inevitably loose nearing the saddle. From **Mickledore** head up the southwest ridge with Route **7** to reach the summit.

Via Little Narrowcove →*8.7km/5½ miles* ↑*920m/3020ft* 🕒*5hr 30min*

Arguably the most impressive of Scafell Pike's chest of crags is Esk Buttress (Dow Crag), the Central Pillar face commanding upper Eskdale. It is quirkily surmounted by a pimple of banded rock bearing a distinctly Celtic name, Pen. The route to this fabulous little top is arduous and largely pathless, but the summit well rewards the effort.

10 Bearing off right from Route **9**, a path contours along the edge of **Great Moss** and, after fording two gills, it is time to bend to the ascent. The rigg tapers to a gill to the left of **Dow Crag**. A worn path materialises, the climbers' descent route off the back of the crag. Don't be drawn into the gully, but keep on the steep rigg. As the slope gradually eases drift right to scramble to the top of **Pen**. There is a cairn and cause for much inner revelry at reaching this less than orthodox viewpoint. Ill Crag's stunning southern buttress simply steeples even from this elevated spot. Briefly follow the spine of the ridge, then work round to the left to find the breach in the ridge. A sheep path leads easily through into **Little Narrowcove**.

11 The direct route into Little Narrowcove does not hug the outflowing beck. To find the point of entry continue beside the infant **Esk**. After a large cairn, angle up the rigg left. A path emerges on approaching a gully. Clamber up, exiting right then left on a path drawing up beside Little Narrowcove Beck. The rarely seen beauties of this secret corrie deserve to be savoured. The final stages of the ascent zig-zag up the scree at the head to reach **Broadcrag Col**. It's a feather in your cap to have made this point by this means. Walkers converge here from Esk Hause and up the combe from the Corridor Route, but precious few from Little Narrowcove! Turn left, SW, for the summit.

The summit

A domed plateau well blessed with boulders and a few precious grassy patches culminates in a sturdy circular drystone-walled platform, which displaced the Ordnance Survey from the actual crown of the fell. All summits with loose rock seem to attract windbreak-makers and Scafell Pike is no exception. There are several of the normal, tumbledown type and one, situated towards the eastern brink, which lacks only a roof. I recommend visitors make the effort to wander around the plateau edge and enjoy some stunning new perspectives, the pick of the bunch that from above Dropping Crag.

Safe descents

For all its many year-round visitors, in nasty weather there can be no lonelier place than the summit of Scafell Pike. And once you've made it there, getting back is an altogether different proposition. Psychologically, the energy that drove you ever upward disappears in the instant you turn back, you may be tired and objectives are downbeat. Great Langdale, for instance, lies to the east, smack into the teeth of winter winds. Wasdale Head, by contrast, catches the prevailing ocean-borne breeze, by definition warmer, if potentially no less fierce.

For Wasdale Head (4km): start from the extra large cairn on the plateau edge 250m W of the summit. Descend the cairned path down the NW ridge (**6**). Short of Lingmell Col the path veers left down into Hollow Stones, drawn naturally onto Brown Tongue and then into close company with Lingmell Gill.

For Seathwaite (6.5km): instead of veering left, go right, off the NW ridge, following the Corridor Route NE to Styhead Pass (**2**). From the stretcher box the old bridleway leads unerringly down to Stockley Bridge.

The return routes to Great Langdale (**1**) and Eskdale (**8**) are altogether rougher and longer. In bad weather either don't embark on these routes in the first place or if conditions unexpectedly close in turn down to Wasdale Head or Borrowdale.

Ridge routes

Great End →*2.5km/1½ miles* ↓*185m/605ft* ↑*100m/330ft* ⏲*40min*
Descend N via the narrow sorely eroded arête into the tight neck of Broadcrag Col. Traverse the ensuing bouldery shoulder into Illcrag Col, sweep up the gravel slope to a short boulder section over a crest and then down onto the broad saddle. Divert half-left, off the popular path to Esk Hause which leads down Calf Cove, and keep on the easy ground on the ridge heading N to a choice of two summit cairns.

Scafell →*2km/1¼ miles* ↓*290m/950ft* ↑*275m/900ft* ⏲*1hr 20min*
Aim SE to pick up a cairned path leading to the narrow connecting ridge of Mickledore and passing the stretcher box. The drama of Scafell wonderfully apparent, Broad Stand blocks off the ridge-end to walkers. Descend left into the combe beneath Scafell's East Buttress. Find the easy gully to the right (there is only one) and climb it to Foxes Tarn. Then tackle the partially restored zig-zag path climbing up onto the saddle and go left to the summit.

Lingmell →*1.6km/1 mile* ↓*255m/835ft* ↑*85m/280ft* ⏲*45min*
Walk NW across the boulder-field on the popular Wasdale path sprinkled with minor cairns. A larger cairn marks the scarp edge. From here wind down aiming for the depression, avoiding the natural urge to follow the stronger paths which veer left for Hollow Stones and right for the Corridor Route. Crossing the broken wall in the Lingmell Col depression rise NNW to the thrilling summit.

Typical summit throng at the memorial cairn

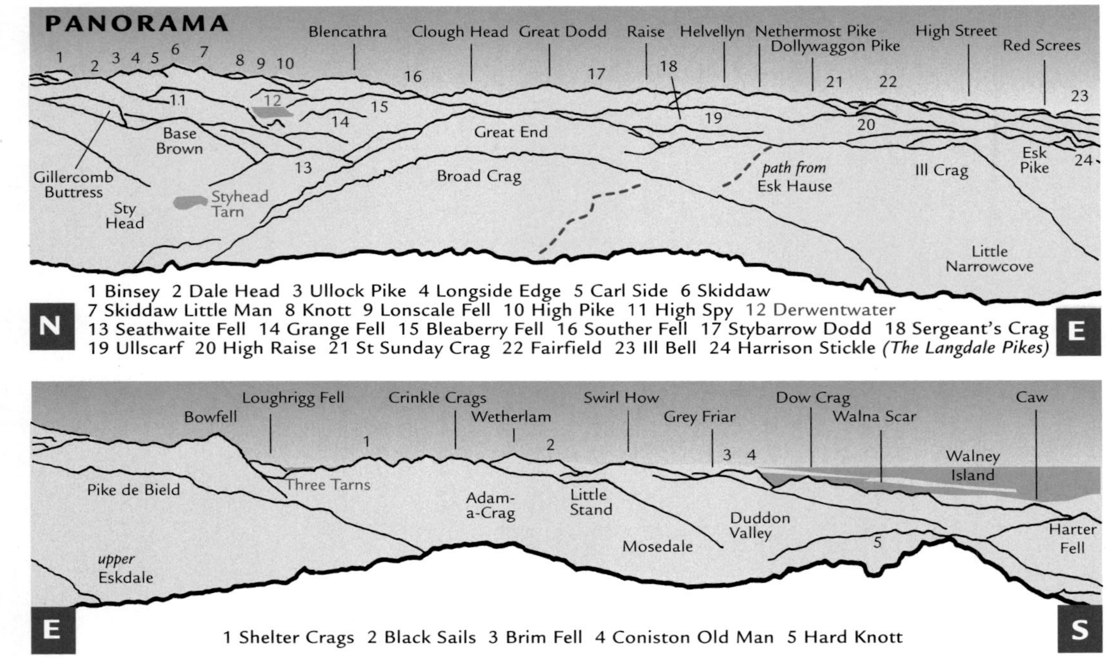
PANORAMA
Blencathra
Clough Head
Great Dodd
Raise
Helvellyn
Nethermost Pike
Dollywaggon Pike
High Street
Red Screes
1 2 3 4 5 6 7 8 9 10
11 12 13 14 15 16 17 18 19 20 21 22 23 24
Gillercomb Buttress
Sty Head
Base Brown
Styhead Tarn
Great End
Broad Crag
path from Esk Hause
Ill Crag
Esk Pike
Little Narrowcove
N
E
1 Binsey 2 Dale Head 3 Ullock Pike 4 Longside Edge 5 Carl Side 6 Skiddaw
7 Skiddaw Little Man 8 Knott 9 Lonscale Fell 10 High Pike 11 High Spy 12 Derwentwater
13 Seathwaite Fell 14 Grange Fell 15 Bleaberry Fell 16 Souther Fell 17 Stybarrow Dodd 18 Sergeant's Crag
19 Ullscarf 20 High Raise 21 St Sunday Crag 22 Fairfield 23 Ill Bell 24 Harrison Stickle (The Langdale Pikes)
Loughrigg Fell
Bowfell
Crinkle Crags
Wetherlam
Swirl How
Grey Friar
Dow Crag
Walna Scar
Caw
1 2 3 4 5
Pike de Bield
Three Tarns
Adam-a-Crag
Little Stand
Mosedale
Duddon Valley
Walney Island
Harter Fell
upper Eskdale
E
S
1 Shelter Crags 2 Black Sails 3 Brim Fell 4 Coniston Old Man 5 Hard Knott

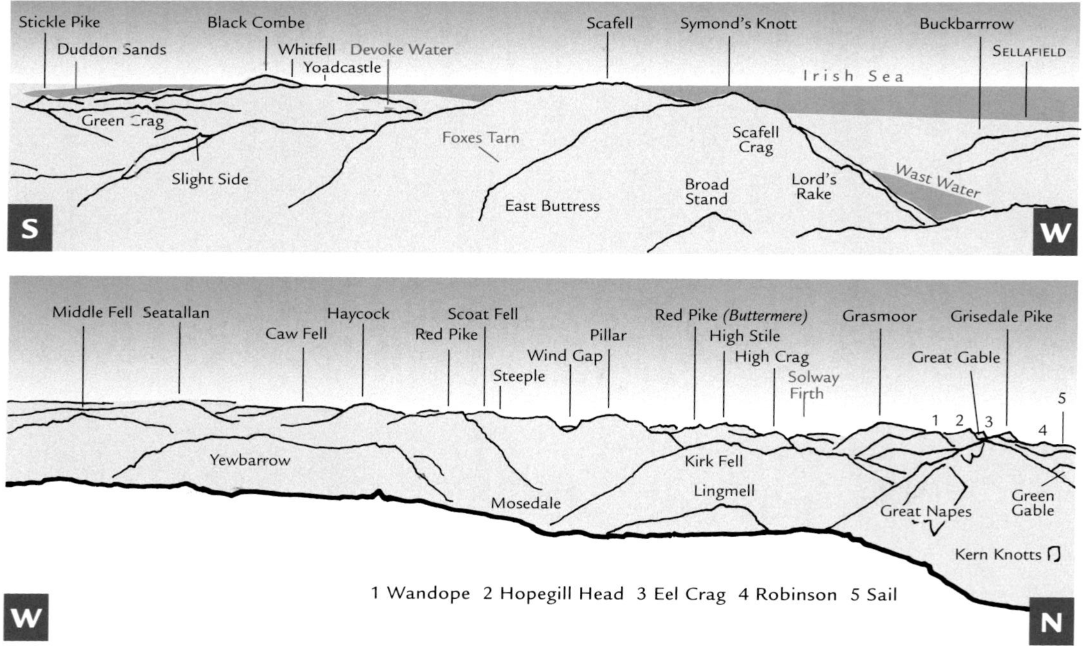

1 Wandope 2 Hopegill Head 3 Eel Crag 4 Robinson 5 Sail

20 SCOAT FELL 843M/2766FT

Climb it from	Bowness Knott **16**, Netherbeck Bridge **4** or Wasdale Green **1**
Character	A major summit west of Pillar, overlooking Steeple, grand surveyor of Ennerdale
Fell-friendly route	4
Summit grid ref	NY 159 114
Link it with	Haycock, Pillar, Red Pike or Steeple
Part of	The Nether Beck Horseshoe

Scoat Fell is something of a cornerstone, a mighty junction of ridges, with Black Crag the first subsidiary component. Steeple and Red Pike project to north and south, adding to the dramatic effect. To the north this mass of craggy fell cradles three great hanging valleys overhung by forbidding crags embodying the spirit of Wild Ennerdale. Between them rises a most imposing ridge, the final thrust of rock christened the Steeple by local shepherds. To the southeast Black'em Head is a further craggy haven of deep shadows. Even the grassy southern slopes are home to a tarn as hauntingly beautiful as any in the Lakes – Scoat Tarn.

The fell-top marks the eastern limit of the Ennerdale Fence, an aged ridge wall which stretches west over Haycock and Caw Fell before turning north over

↑ *Scoat Fell from Iron Crag*

Iron Crag. In Lakeland terms this is a remote fell, the quickest ascent by Black'em Head an uncommon occurrence. The long Nether Beck approach (4–5) provides the easiest gradient, while Ennerdale ascents (1–3) are hampered by the distant siting of the main valley car parks (unless you base yourself at High Gillerthwaite Youth Hostel or Black Sail Hut). Quite the majority of visitors simply step onto the top on their way round the Mosedale Round, but they can be forgiven... the rule with fellwalking is, there are no rules.

Ascent from Bowness Knott 16 *off map NW*

Two lines are up for grabs, sharing a common approach (1), and would make a good circuit.

1 Follow the main forest track leading by the lake to cross the concrete flood-relief bridge spanning the **River Liza**. The lane leads to a double-gate, where you enter the forestry. Bear left and cross a similar flood bridge over Woundell Beck.

Via Tewit How →*8.8km/5½ miles* ↑*730m/2395ft* ⏲*4hr 30min*

2 After a forest track enters from the right, watch for the broad forest break climbing steeply right. Follow this – it is cattle-poached at the bottom, but make your way as best you can up to a hand-gate in a light cross-fence.

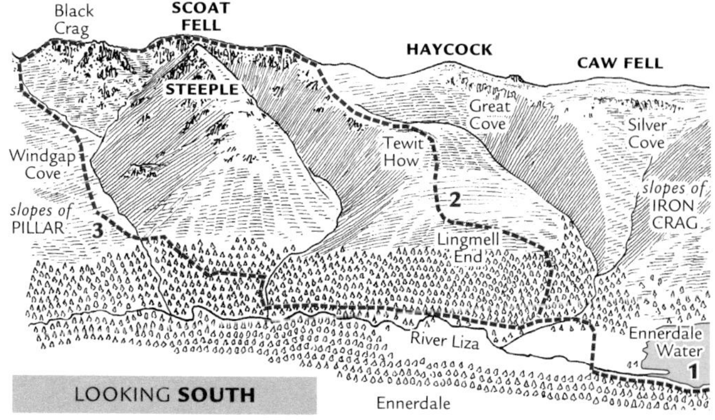

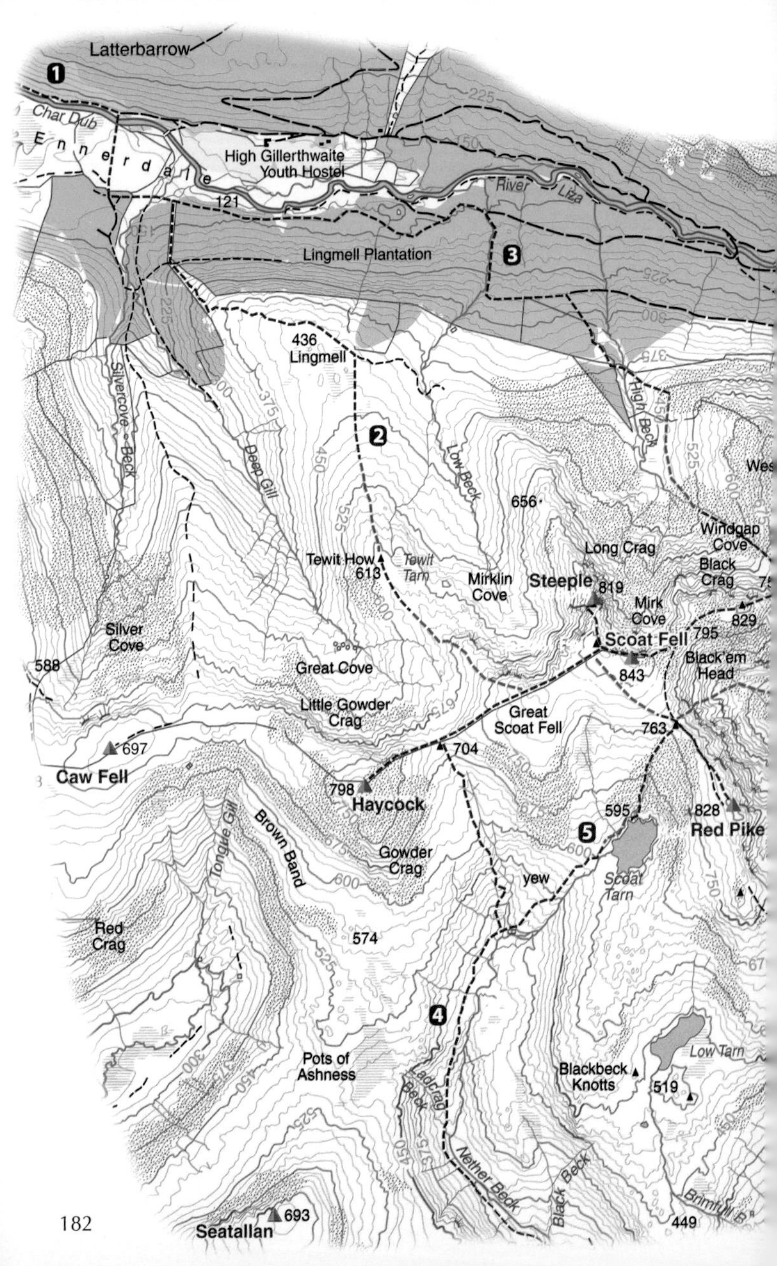
Latterbarrow
1
Char Dub
Ennerdale
High Gillerthwaite
Youth Hostel
121
River Liza
Lingmell Plantation
3
436
Lingmell
2
Silvercove Beck
Deep Gill
Low Beck
High Beck
656
Tewit How
613
Tewit Tarn
Mirklin Cove
Steeple
819
Long Crag
Windgap Cove
Black Crag
Mirk Cove
829
Scoat Fell
795
843
Black'em Head
Silver Cove
588
Great Cove
Little Gowder Crag
Great Scoat Fell
763
697
Caw Fell
704
798
Haycock
595
5
828
Red Pike
Tongue Gill
Brown Band
Gowder Crag
yew
Scoat Tarn
Red Crag
574
4
Pots of Ashness
Ladcrag Beck
Blackbeck Knotts
Low Tarn
519
Nether Beck
Black Beck
Brimfull B
449
693
Seatallan

Continue by a seat on firmer ground. The forest gangway steps onto rockier ground, with heather, and leads ultimately to a fence-stile onto the ridge of **Lingmell End**. Continue E beside the fell-top fence, and after a large boulder, as the ground shapes to descend towards **Low Beck**, veer right with only a hint of a path initially through the heather. A path soon becomes apparent leading up the broad ridge. It fades as the heather is left behind and it rises onto the crest of **Tewit How**. The cairn sits above the marshy hollow of **Tewit Tarn**, but there is now hardly enough open water to merit the description. Continue along the ridge, angling round the right-hand side of outcropping to enjoy fine views into Mirklin Cove towards Steeple. Climb onto the higher ridge by skirting right, then left, onto the high lip of Mirklin Cove to join the broken Ennerdale Fence and reach the summit.

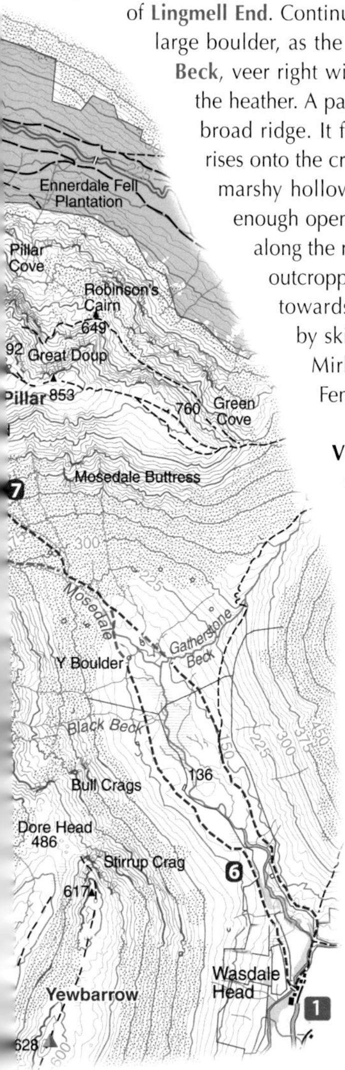

Via Windgap Cove → *10.8km/6¾ miles* ↑*740m/2428ft* ⏲*5hr*

3 Instead of turning right with Route **2**, pass through a gate, keeping to the dale-floor forest track. After 2km come to a second conventional bridge crossing. Immediately after this, turn up right (this is easy to miss), keeping close order with **Low Beck**. The path, sorely worn in places, leads up through a hand-gate beside the ravine to step up onto a forest track. Follow this track, left, for 400m, keeping a sharp eye out for a path stepping off the track into the trees on the right. This path then escapes the trees into rough cleared ground and follows an old wall up to cross a fence-stile. Turn left and gingerly ford **High Beck**, scrambling up the facing bank by the fence. Ascend

Looking down the scree path from Wind Gap into Mosedale

initially beside an old wall/fence-line, find a crossing sheep trod, and contour right to slip through the broken wall. The path becomes less certain from this point, as marshy ground predominates. Ahead is the impressive craggy shield of Black Crag and Mirk Cove. As height is gained in **Windgap Cove** ford the beck. Evidence of a path is resurrected only as stonier ground is encountered in the midst of the upper cove, and it leads to the saddle of **Wind Gap** itself. Bear right, following the ridge E over **Black Crag** to the ultimate summit, clambering up the boulders and by the Ennerdale Fence wall-end.

Ascent from Netherbeck Bridge 4 *off map S*

Another pair of routes rise up from the south, splitting at a waters-meet to go directly up to the summit ridge (4) or take in Scoat Tarn and a pathless boulder scramble to the top (5).

The path steps up from the layby and skirts the marsh, finding a brief weakness in the bracken to bear up left to join the bridleway. Turn right and accompany this age-old trail, sustaining a historical wild connection with Ennerdale. The path is prone to stoniness, and may cause a brisk stride to falter. The best 'water show' occurs early on as **Nether Beck** crashes down a notable fall amongst the last tree shelter. Wast Water is soon lost to view and attention taken by the lonely interior, with the

Mirklin Cove (photo: Maggie Allan)

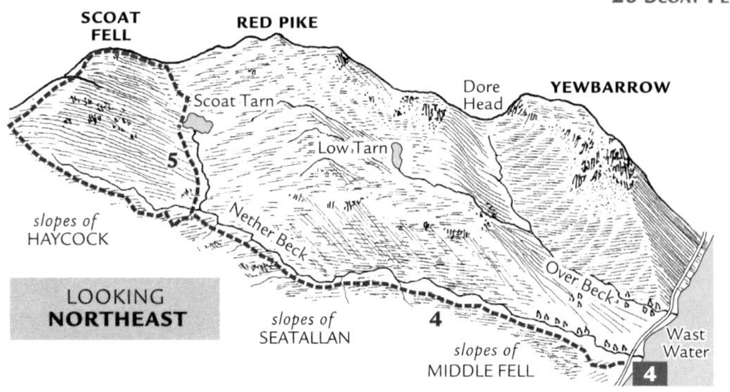

dale hemmed in, and the beck hidden where it runs in a ravine beyond Lad Crag. Keep company with the old bridle-path.

Via Great Scoat Fell →*6.4km/4 miles* ↑*780m/2560ft* ⏲*4hr 15min*

4 There is no mystery on the northward section of this ascent – just avoid being lured right at the major waters-meet, beside a large sheepfold. Keep N via early zig-zags, then continue over damp ground, rising assuredly to the depression in the main ridge, marked by a cairn short of the broken wall. Turn right (NE) following this, the Ennerdale Fence, over **Great Scoat Fell** to reach the summit.

Via Scoat Tarn →*6.8km/4¼ miles* ↑*780m/2560ft* ⏲*4hr 25min*

5 Alternatively at the waters-meet short of the 450m contour, beside a compound

Solitary yew tree above Nether Beck, on the ascent to Scoat Tarn

sheepfold, ford the beck and follow the rising path aiming NE. Notice the solitary yew tree stoically growing among lichened boulders over to the left. The path runs up close to the outflow of **Scoat Tarn**. The path falters as it leads along the western shore then resumes on the northerly rise beyond the tarn. Switch sides of the tiny tributary hollow and continue up to the high saddle. Bear left and pick your way across the part-boulder slope to gain the broken wall and the ridge (Route **4**), the slope easing close to the summit.

Ascent from Wasdale Green 1

Via Black'em Head →*4.8km/3 miles* ↑*790m/2600ft* ◷*3hr 30min*

Traditionally, walkers approaching from this valley base stick to the ridges. But the inquisitive explorer will relish venturing by the seldom-visited Black'em Head. There is precious little evidence on the ground of walkers choosing to come this way in any number, but the wild surroundings make this a rewarding undertaking. However, keep well clear in hill fog which would make navigation tricky.

6 Begin by crossing the lovely single-arched stone bridge directly after the stile behind the Wasdale Head Inn. Follow the walled drove-way leading N, and soon come above the pines shrouding Ritson's Force. From the succeeding gate the path contours through the bracken. Keep to the lower path, advancing to a ladder-stile after fording **Black Beck**. Continue to a tall, fractured rock – known as the **Y Boulder**. Skirt left to evade the marsh and ford **Mosedale Beck**. A path is followed early on, but as this veers up the ridge keep harmony with Mosedale Beck, climbing pathless into **Black'em Head** and getting close to a sequence of entertaining waterfalls. Where three gills converge to form a single beck, turn your attention to the one and only escape to the skyline ridge. To the right, screes spill from **Black Crag**, and to the left all seems conclusively rock girth. However, it is a simple matter to spot a narrow gully left of the headwall. Weave up to surprise yourself with the ease of its discovery and your prompt delivery upon the saddle above. From the ridge-top saddle take a bearing half-left (NW) over the shoulder to the wall-bend and cairn above **Steeple**, thereby avoiding the greater mass of boulders shrouding the summit wall.

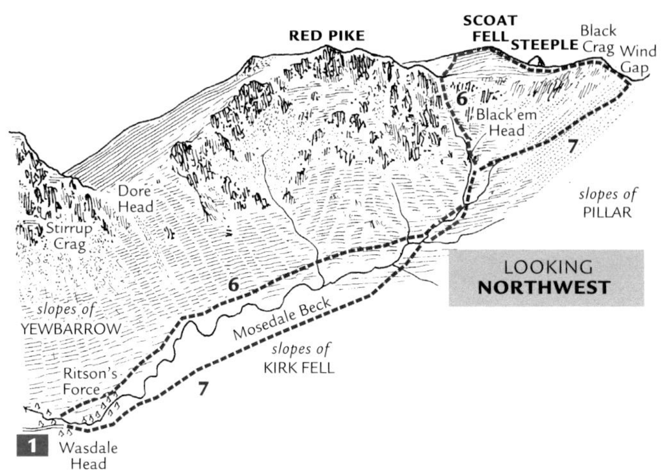

Via Wind Gap →*4.8km/3 miles* ↑*795m/2610ft* ⌚*4hr*

The skyline nick of Wind Gap provides the most obvious direct ascent of the fell from Wasdale Head. However, it has been spoilt by thoughtless walkers racing off the ridge creating an unsightly and uncomfortable scree run.

7 Start from behind the Wasdale Head Inn, pass the beautiful single-arched stone bridge via hand-gates and swing left into Mosedale. Watch for the large cairn at NY 183 103, where a path bears left off the main trail. Keep below the bracken in traversing the valley floor by an area of possible ancient cairns and go through a fenced pen and gate in the wall. Mosedale lives up to its name, being very wet and mossy. Ford **Gatherstone Beck** and angle half-left by an old sheepfold. The path is intermittent and less evident than may be expected, keeping close to **Mosedale Beck**. Advance up the grass ridge, aiming for the extended ribbon of scree. With the screes gained, the going gets even less appealing with every stride – find the firmer footing predominantly on the left-hand side. Reach the **Wind Gap** saddle up the boulders, half-left, avoiding the final fellside insult of scree, and turn left again to join Route **3** to the summit.

Summit cairn atop the Ennerdale Fence wall (photo: Anne Bowskill)

The summit

The wall of the Ennerdale Fence was solidly built across the top of Scoat Fell. In fact visitors have chosen to place a few stones on top of the wall to mark where it actually runs over the highest ground. The more casual majority of visitors are content to stand beside the cairn at the wall angle a little further to the west.

Safe descents

For Wasdale, the safest routes lead into the Nether Beck valley, either from the depression west of Great Scoat Fell (**4**) or the saddle short of Red Pike (**5**). The ridge over Red Pike is fine in most conditions, and aims for Dore Head and the Over Beck valley. For Ennerdale, you can safely return off Great Scoat Fell by Tewit How for Lingmell End (**2**).

Ridge routes

Haycock →*1.6km/1 mile* ↓*135m/445ft* ↑*90m/295ft* ⌚*30min*
Follow the ridge wall unwaveringly SW.

Pillar →*2km/1¼ miles* ↓*90m/295ft* ↑*140m/460ft* ⌚*40min*
Head E, slipping through the great boulders at the end of the Ennerdale Fence. Boulder-hop NE down to the grassy plateau connecting to Black Crag. Barring high winds, keep E, taking every opportunity to view the craggy scenery about Mirk Cove, with Steeple seen as a mighty cliff-top peak, and to look down into Mosedale grandly towards the Scafells. From the cairn on Black Crag descend through the boulders into the narrow saddle of Wind Gap and climb the loose, scrambly facing ridge onto Pillar. The summit plateau comes as a blessed relief. Head NE to the wind-shelter and stone-built Ordnance Survey column.

Red Pike →*1.2km/¾ mile* ↓*80m/260ft* ↑*70m/230ft* 🕒*20min*

From the angle in the wall slip through the wall-gap and traverse the stony slope SE easily down to the saddle. From here ascend the sensational escarpment edge. Be careful not to be lured by the heavily used path – the tame pasture on the west side of the fell-top causes walkers to miss the summit by mistake.

Steeple →*negligible* ↓*45m/150ft* ↑*20m/65ft* 🕒*10min*

From the cairn at the wall angle, follow the cairns N, avoiding the edge, to walk down the tapering ridge with its dragon's-back arête into a nick, then easily work up to the summit from the west.

Scoat Fell from the summit of Steeple (photo: Maggie Allan)

21 SEATALLAN 693M/2274FT

Climb it from	Harrow Head **9**, Greendale **6** or Netherbeck Bridge **4**
Character	Sentinel summit above lonely Blengdale
Fell-friendly route	4
Summit grid ref	NY 139 084
Link it with	Buckbarrow, Haycock or Middle Fell
Part of	The Nether Beck Horseshoe

Standing elegantly well back from Wasdale's renowned showcase, this sleek-lined height dominates a forgotten quarter, the roaming pleasure of the connoisseur. A southern off-shoot of Haycock, flanked by the wild upland pastures that form the source of the Bleng and Nether Beck, it cradles Greendale Tarn and boasts two sub-lieutenant ridge summits, Middle Fell and Buckbarrow.

Frequently and naturally, Seatallan, Middle Fell and Buckbarrow are climbed together as they make a compact fell-round, best begun from Nether Wasdale. The Bronze Age tumulus on the summit is far earlier evidence that this was long considered a fine resting place and a commanding view-station – and the view is no less uplifting today!

 ↑ *Seatallan from Coldfell Gate*

Routes 1 and 4 lead directly up the southern slopes whereas Routes 2 and 3 lead up from the walled-in headwaters of the River Bleng, providing a fascinating back-door approach to the fell and Route 5 explores Nether Beck straight up from the shores of Wast Water.

Ascent from Harrow Head 9

Via Buckbarrow →*4.5km/2¾ miles* ↑*600m/1970ft* ⌚*3hr 30min*

The common first-thought route on clear paths.

1 Leave the road above the lane from Gill Farm, with **Gill Beck** left and a wall right, and soon meet the remnants of a small sheepfold. The stony path fends off the bracken beside the beck and then drifts easily right. Gain ground to ford a tiny gill and follow the obvious rib onto the ridge. The path forks with the prospect of a great wall of rock ahead (don't try clambering up the steep ramp, unless you are a competent climber). Keep left, easing round the left-hand end of the rock band. The regular path to the summit heads on up to the notch, and passes a marsh before gaining the summit of **Buckbarrow** up to the left. A continuing path leads NW via the little cairned knoll of **Glade How**. The path winds over the odd damp patch and rises to the skyline, where there is a further distinctive cairn at **Cat Bields**. From here turn NE and pass unhindered along the grassy ridge-top direct to the summit.

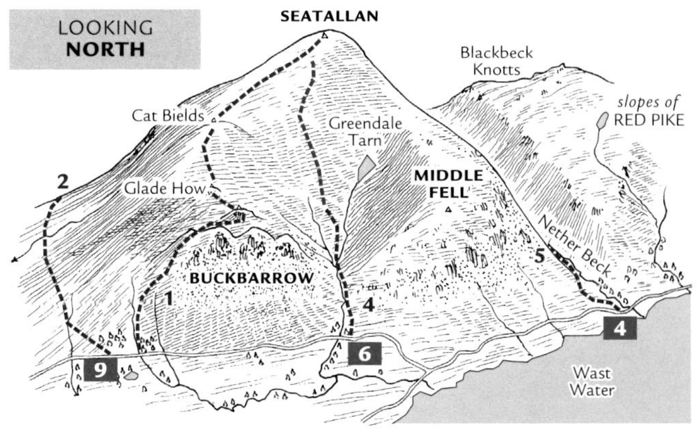

Via Ill Gill →*6.4km/4 miles* ↑*610m/2000ft* 🕒*3hr 45min*

Route 3 takes walkers all the way to the atmospheric source of the River Bleng or you can cut up, pathlessly, before Stockdale Head along Ill Gill for a more direct route to the summit (Route 2).

2 Follow the concrete roadway rising towards **Windsor Farm**. Bear off right, as indicated by the bridleway sign up the green track. Coming beside a wall, ford the gill and move on between the fenced fold and the trench of the washed-out gill. A green-way marches on free across the level moor. Gradually the path moves round the base of Seatallan, with Haycock coming into view on the skyline ahead, to the right of the bulky mass of Caw Fell. After fording Stare Beck, and just before **Swinsty Beck**, pass through a giant ring of stones, the remnants of a **Viking ring garth**. Pass under **Birk Crag** via a stone drove and come to the ford of **Ill Gill** below **Raven Crag**. Turn up the slope, left, of Ill Gill, quickly escaping the bracken. The twin headstreams soon open onto the bare slopes, and you angle E to progress to the summit unhindered.

Via Rossy Gill →*7.2km/4½ miles* ↑*610m/2000ft* 🕒*4hr*

3 Where Route **2** turns up **Ill Gill**, continue along the path, which is largely coherent as it runs on towards the steep slopes walling up the wild head of the Bleng valley, **Stockdale Head**. Climb up the left-hand side of **Rossy Gill** to find the ridge path in the grass, and climb right (S) to the summit.

Ascent from Greendale 6

Via Greendale Gill →*3.2km/2 miles* ↑*625m/2050ft* 🕒*3hr 45min*

A straightforward climb, at times pathless, tracks a course directly northwards to the summit.

4 A clear path heads up from the verge parking through the bracken to the portals of the **Greendale Gill** ravine. Coming by the gorse, ford the beck and ascend the ramped path, climbing

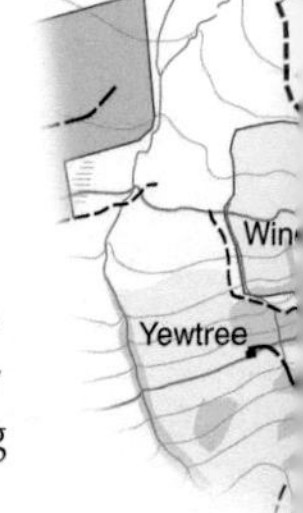

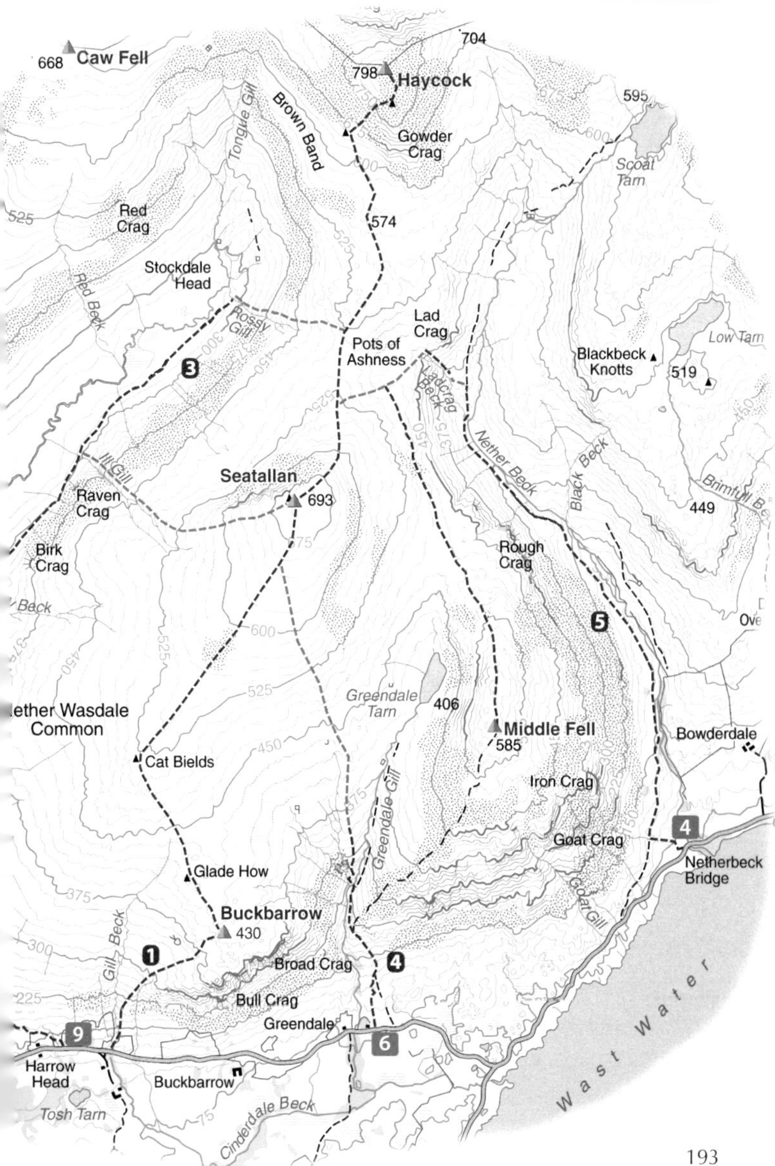

Caw Fell
668
Haycock
798
704
Gowder Crag
595
Scoat Tarn
Red Crag
Tongue Gill
Brown Band
574
Stockdale Head
Red Beck
Rossy Gill
Lad Crag
Pots of Ashness
Blackbeck Knotts
Low Tarn
519
Ladcrag Beck
Nether Beck
Black Beck
Brimfull Beck
Ill Gill
Seatallan
693
Raven Crag
449
Birk Crag
Rough Crag
Beck
Greendale Tarn
406
Nether Wasdale Common
Middle Fell
585
Bowderdale
Cat Bields
Iron Crag
Greendale Gill
Goat Crag
Netherbeck Bridge
Glade How
Goat Gill
Buckbarrow
430
Gill Beck
Broad Crag
Bull Crag
Greendale
Harrow Head
Buckbarrow
Tosh Tarn
Cinderdale Beck
Wast Water

the mid-ridge due N. Follow the natural lie of the slope onto the high pasture and the summit.

Ascent from Netherbeck Bridge 4

Via Nether Beck →*4.8km/3 miles* ↑*640m/2100ft* ⌚*3hr 30min*

A stony path up the deep sinuous valley of Nether Beck.

5 Step up from the parking space and skirt the marsh, following the bracken-free passage, left, to join the lateral bridleway into the long valley of the beck. Upon fording **Ladcrag Beck**, travel some 30m further up the path before breaking into the bracken, short of the fence enclosure on the right-hand ridge. A path exists, although the bracken can obscure it early on. This mounts under **Lad Crag** and close to the east bank of the beck. Upon reaching the brow bear left to avoid the marshy hollow of the **Pots of Ashness**. Head SW, without a hint of a path, to discover the ridge path, then follow this assiduously S up the plain northern slope of the fell to gain the summit plateau.

Drove-way to Stockdale Head

The summit

On the summit's broad, gently domed pasture, find a stone-built Ordnance Survey column and a wind-shelter. This latter structure was requisitioned from the underlying tumulus. It is interesting

Looking towards Great Gable from the barren southern slopes

how every generation makes its mark. The Bronze Age cairn is believed to have been created from stones carried to this high spot as a mark of respect for dead kin. Contemporary visitors have chosen to use the stones to fashion a crude shelter from the strong westerly winds to which this summit is inevitably exposed.

Safe descents

Dangers are few. In poor weather think 'S' for sanctuary. Either follow the ridge path SW to Cat Bields for Buckbarrow (**1**) or, simplest of all, go dead S (**4**) into the Greendale Gill valley.

Ridge routes

Buckbarrow →*3.2km/2 miles* ↓*280m/920ft* ↑*25m/80ft* ◷*45min*
Follow the pasture path SW for about 1.8km (about a mile) to reach the lone cairn on Cat Bields. This cairn is now often stained with the pale droppings of buzzard, whose lonely domain this is. Turn SE with a clear path, dipping through a damp hollow to pass the old shepherds' cairn on Glade How. Continue on to reach the summit-knoll cairn.

Haycock →*3.2km/2 miles* ↓*205m/670ft* ↑*310m/1020ft* 🕒*1hr 50min*
Aim NE to find the marker cairn guiding off the summit plateau. The path runs down the plain north slope onto the undulating plateau that forms the connection with Haycock. Inevitably marshy ground is found in abundance, and is none too effectively evaded by the ridge path. Getting to Haycock is not completely straightforward – it involves navigational strategy in the ascent, and requires particular attention in mist. The ridge path angles to the left-hand side of the rising ridge to avoid the mass of rock and unwelcome scree spilling from Gowder Crag. Find a boulder with a small cairn on top (NY 142 104). This is the keystone for the climb. Ascend the steep rake, a grassy gangway with the odd supportive cairn guiding to the high saddle behind the crest of Gowder Crag. Turn left and follow the easier ground to the ridge-wall summit.

Middle Fell →*2km/1¼ miles* ↓*220m/720ft* ↑*110m/360ft* 🕒*40min*
From the wind-shelter aim initially ESE, bending SE steeply down on an intermittent path towards the col above Greendale Tarn from where a distinct ridge path becomes quickly apparent. Join this as it bends S and leads easily up to the summit cairn.

Seatallan from Scafell Pike

22 SLIGHT SIDE 762M/2500FT

Climb it from	Dalegarth Station **25**, Woolpack Inn **24**, Wha House **23** or Brotherilkheld **22**
Character	Southernmost peaked flourish to the Scafell ridge
Fell-friendly route	4
Summit grid ref	NY 209 051
Link it with	Scafell

The summit of Slight Side, resting atop a natural fortress, brings the main Scafell massif to an end, its rocky spine making a perfect final flourish. It is both a remarkable place from which to survey the southern fells and a real peak in its own right.

The fortress is worth the storming, as the summit view is special, spanning the southern Lakeland fells from Bowfell to the east round to Coniston to the southeast and down to Black Combe on the coast. Reach it when evening sun lights up the wide stretch of the Irish Sea to the west and it is breathtaking.

Unlike most fells, Slight Side has only one natural final ascent line, but two approaches accessible from three starting points in Eskdale. Whichever way you choose to do it, the long lead-in gives the walker time to adjust to the wild setting and the pull to the top, largely on grass, is achieved in remarkably quick time.

↑ *Slight Side from Catcove Gill*

Ascent from Dalegarth Station 25

Via Eel Tarn →*6.5km/4 miles* ↑*710m/2330ft* ◷*3hr 45min*

Anyone contemplating climbing Slight Side from Boot is likely to have Scafell in their sights. If so a natural circuit is conjured by returning off the higher summit via Hard Rigg (just off map to the west). The walk in, via Eel Tarn and the curiously named Peelplace Noddle, has much the same feel as the approach to a remote Munro so it will strike a happy chord with hillwalkers familiar with Scotland.

The lane from Boot en route to Eel Tarn

1 From the short village street, passing the Burnmoor Inn, bear right, signed 'Eel Tarn'. A roadway winds up behind the tree-shaded mill, the thunderous thrashings of **Whillan Beck** making an early impression. As the tarmac ends leave the farm-track leading to **Gill Bank**, with its two monkey puzzle trees. Take the gate right, go left at the three-way footpath sign, again directing to 'Eel Tarn'. The green track threads through a walled passage, the immediate surroundings reminiscent of Yorkshire limestone country. The path curves up right. Do not be lured left onto the path to Lambford Bridge, but keep right to reach **Eel Tarn**. The boggy ground on this northern side has to be traversed before skirting to the east of the tarn, from where a path weaves on up through a confusing terrain leading by **Peelplace Noddle**. In mist you certainly do have to use your noddle and a compass would not come amiss. The path mounts onto a more definite ridge above **Stony Tarn**, and generally contours across marshy ground due northeast, fording several minor gills, latterly a grassy trod that meets up with the **Terrace Route**, as the slope steepens... now gird your loins for a final push for the top.

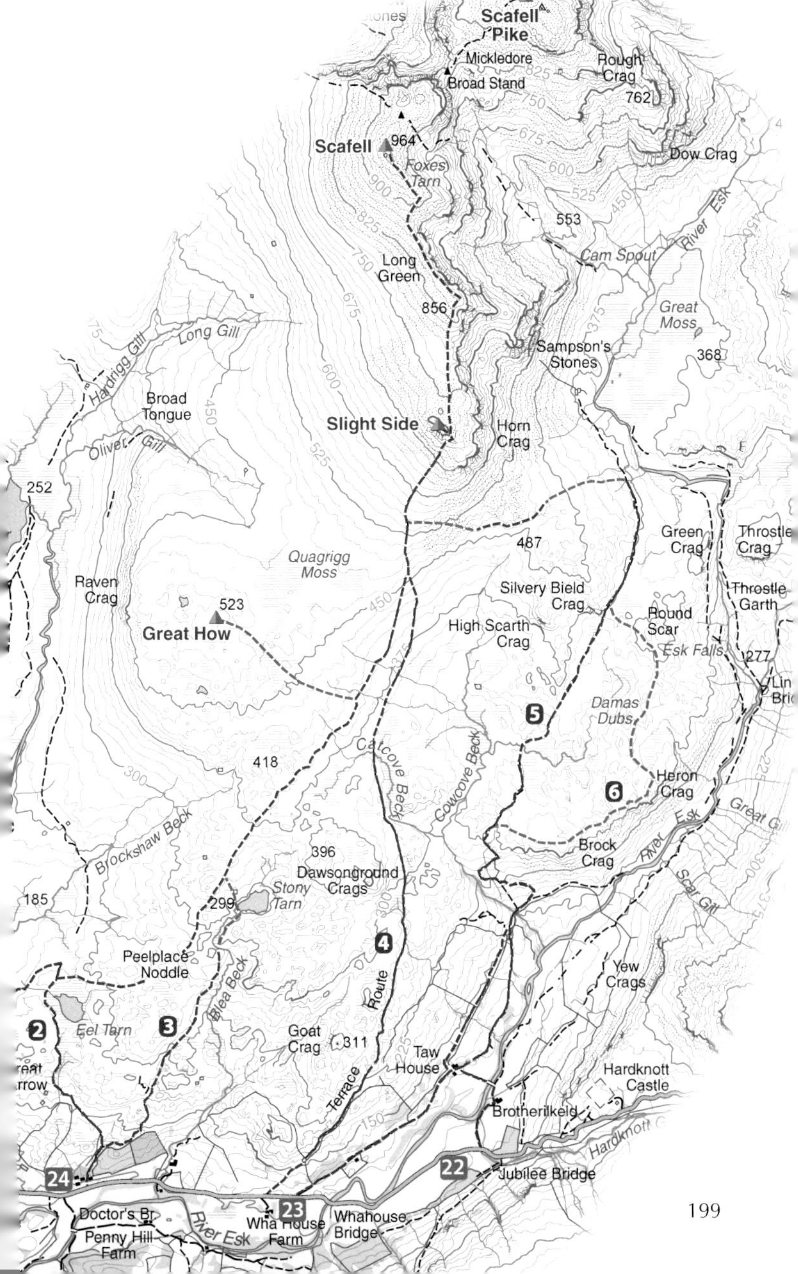
Scafell Pike
Mickledore
Broad Stand
Rough Crag
762
Scafell
964
Foxes Tarn
Dow Crag
553
Cam Spout
River Esk
Long Green
856
Great Moss
Long Gill
Hardrigg Gill
Sampson's Stones
368
Broad Tongue
Slight Side
Horn Crag
Oliver Gill
252
Green Crag
Throstle Crag
487
Quagrigg Moss
Raven Crag
Silvery Bield Crag
Throstle Garth
523
Great How
Round Scar
High Scarth Crag
Esk Falls
277
Damas Dubs
5
Catcove Beck
Cowcove Beck
418
Heron Crag
6
Great Gill
Brockshaw Beck
396
Brock Crag
River Esk
Dawsonground Crags
Stony Tarn
Scar Gill
185
299
4
Peelplace Noddle
Blea Beck
Yew Crags
Route
2
Eel Tarn
3
Goat Crag
311
Taw House
Terrace
Hardknott Castle
Brotherilkeld
Hardknott Gill
24
22
Jubilee Bridge
23
Doctor's Br.
Wha House Farm
Whahouse Bridge
Penny Hill Farm
River Esk

The final climb has the occasional gravel passage, but nothing of note. The summit can be reached either from a breach up to the left or by skirting round to climb from the north. The key word is climb, as the summit is naked rock, although there is nothing perilous.

Ascent from the Woolpack Inn 24

Two more standard approaches for Slight Side head off from the inn to visit Eel Tarn (2) and Stony Tarn (3) on their way to the top.

Via Eel Tarn →*6km/3¾ miles* ↑*670m/2200ft* 🕒*3hr 30min*

2 Follow the lane signed from the road left of the pub 'Burnmoor and Wasdale Head'. This leads up behind the inn to a gate, rising to an obvious path divide with bracken looming. Go left with the enclosure wall. This path rises close by a roofless stone bothy over the brow to encounter **Eel Tarn**. The path skirts the blanket bog to the left, keeping to firmer ground. Join the branch right that effectively swings on round the tarn to head east into the irregular area of craggy knolls known by the surreal name **Peelplace Noddle** to follow Route **1** to the top.

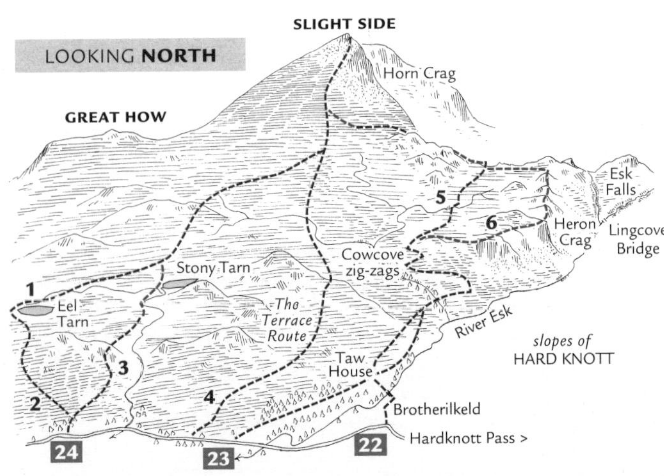

Cat Cove (photo: Maggie Allan)

Via Stony Tarn →*6km/3¾ miles* ↑*670m/2200ft* ⌚*3hr 50min*

3 The second approach from the Woolpack also eventually joins Route **1** but starts by branching right above the inn. This path rises naturally, in secretive spongy terrain, to come above the open marshy bowl of **Blea Beck**. Keep just to the left of the beck, into its upper amphitheatre. Ford the beck with small falls to the left. Climb a steeper bracken bank, with no evidence of a path, keep to the firmer ground in contouring to the natural dam rigg and drop to the outflow of **Stony Tarn**. Cross the outflow heading north by the sheepfold and climb onto the flat ridge to meet up with the path from Eel Tarn (**1**).

Ascent from Wha House 23 or Brotherilkeld 22

Via the Terrace Route →*4.7km/3 miles* ↑*670m/2200ft* ⌚*3hr 25min*

Take advantage of a dedicated car park and a clear and popular route to Scafell – the Terrace Route – on this northerly climb or, if more convenient, pick up the route from Brotherilkeld at Taw House.

4 The small Wha House car park has been made specifically for walkers embarking on this popular route to Scafell. Cross the fence-stile and mount

The Esk gorge from Heron Crag

the slope diagonally right to go through a cluster of stone sheepfolds via four hand-gates. The path continues, initially with the intake wall close right, then gradually rises above it and beneath the rough slopes of the **Goat Crag** ridge. A succession of rock-steps are taken in stride, with every good reason to pause from time to time to admire this truly handsome aspect of the heather-clad Harter Fell and Hard Knott with its Roman fort and craggy front to south and east. Fording a gill the path moves through irregular terrain in a natural manner, the sense of a terrace-cum-corridor evident to the point where the path comes above the **Catcove Beck** gorge and Slight Side comes strikingly into view.

The path steps over a shallow stony ford, continuing north in lower Cat Cove, and fords the beck, now no more than a minor gill. It works steadily across the slope with the great bowl of Cow Cove to the right, meeting up with the path from Boot (Route **1**) at a small cairn above a large erratic.

Via Cowcove zig-zags →*3.2km/2 miles* ↑*685m/2250ft* 🕒*3hr 10min*

Two intriguing variant routes explore Slight Side's craggy sub-scarp ridges west of the Esk Gorge.

5 A matter of 150 metres further east along the valley road a farm-track leads off. There are two recessed car-parking spots just beyond (with a signposted track linking up). Either follow the permissive path signed left just prior to the farmyard at **Taw House**, or go through the farmyard and along the gated lane. Follow an open track up pasture, via gates, to a fold where the two routes come together. Proceed to Scale Bridge to admire the sheltered falls upstream. Keep faith with the proper green path which leads on at a fork, curving up left through the bracken. There are some pitched sections on this, the **Cowcove zig-zags**. Keep with the regular path, ultimate destination the upper Esk and Cam Spout beneath the mighty Scafells.

Having skirted the marshy hollow of **Damas Dubs**, cross a plank bridge at the outflow in the combe's midst. Follow the main path, as to the upper Esk, but then, as the rough slope up to the left eases, branch off to climb the pathless grass fellside, with Slight Side's craggy upper face, **Horn Crag**, glowering from on high. Wander up to a notch, created by a large slab, to find a path in all probability established as much by contouring sheep as off-piste walkers. This path works across the rough slope on a southwesterly and then westerly line, fading in and out, until you reach the ascending **Terrace Route** path (**4**) on the steepening slope above the junction with the Boot path and turn right.

6 To visit Round Scar, take the fellwanderer's line by stepping off the regular path directly after the Cowcove zig-zags and just where it draws up onto the moor. Follow the scarp edge right above **Brock Crag**. There is no hint of a path, other than that created by cloven feet. Work your own instinctive way either over the highest ground, or find the top of **Heron Crag**, the more airy eyrie, and then angle west, skirting a tarn, to join the undulating ridge leading north via **Round Scar**, one of many classic remnant volcanic plugs hereabouts. The direct Cowcove path is rejoined beyond the buttress of **Silvery Bield Crag** at the threshold of the great amphitheatre of the upper Esk.

The summit

The summit cairn rests on top of a rocky massif with the same strikingly white-flecked surface as the summit rock on Esk Pike. There is nothing to impede the magnificent view of the southern fells and also the long horizon of the Irish Sea to the west, golden-hued in evening sunshine.

Safe descents

The eastern edge is precipitous. Keep it simple: the one way up is the one way down. Leave the summit, rounding the eastern end of the main outcrop, taking an initial SW line – the path is clear. The scree soon relents and the path descends uneventfully. A small cairn marks the point where the Boot path (**1**) veers half-right, traversing on a consistent SW line to Eel Tarn. The main path (**4**) runs S down the W side of Cow Cove to briefly accompany Catcove Beck, thereafter keeping to the natural terrace of the Terrace Route to reach the Wha House car park.

Ridge route

Scafell →*2km/1¼ miles* ↓*30m/100ft* ↑*210m/690ft* ⏲*45min*
This ridge just could not be simpler. There is nothing to impede your smooth progress to the top of the Long Green ridge but the occasional gravel patch. The ridge dips then climbs again, with moderate toil, to the skyward crest of Scafell – now you're talking!

Slight Side from Crinkle Crags

23 STEEPLE 819M/2687FT

Climb it from	Bowness Knott **16**
Character	A chunky hunk of rock culminating in a steepling ridge
Fell-friendly route	1
Summit grid ref	NY 156 117
Link it with	Scoat Fell

Steeple forms the northern spur of Scoat Fell. The Long Crag ridge on which it sits forms a well-defined division between Mirk and Mirklin Coves, two hanging valleys rarely visited by walkers or climbers. The quintessential elements of Wild Ennerdale (the first Lake District re-wilding scheme) lurk here, there being no sane route to the skyline within these mountain fastnesses.

Long Crag makes a superb route to the watershed and most visitors come and go from the summit of Steeple quite quickly – but there are plenty of reasons to linger long on this lovely fell! In addition to the stunning rock scenery the view from the top includes a wide sweep of empty Ennerdale, too, and a clear circuit can be followed from the head of the valley to make a fine day out.

Routes 1 and 2 both lead up from the River Liza. For a bit of variety, choose Route 2 for your ascent and enjoy the full sweep of the spur, and long views of Ennerdale, on your descent with Route 1.

↑ *Steeple from the saddle linking to Scoat Fell*

Ascent from Bowness Knott 16

Routes 1 and 2 start together, split at the plantation and later rejoin on the fellside, giving you the option of breaking a little new ground on your descent.

Follow the main forest track leading by the lake to cross the concrete Irish Bridge spanning the **River Liza**. The lane leads to a double gate, where it enters the forestry. Bear left and cross a second flood-bridge over Woundell Beck. Rounding the bend, after a forest track enters from the right, watch for the broad forest break, a sheep drove to the hill pasture, climbing steeply right.

Via Lingmell End →*8.4km/5¼ miles* ↑*725m/2380ft* ⏱*4hr 15min*

1 Take this right-hand path, cattle-poached at the bottom, and make your way as best you can up to a hand-gate in a light cross-fence. Continue, past a seat, on firmer ground. The forest gangway

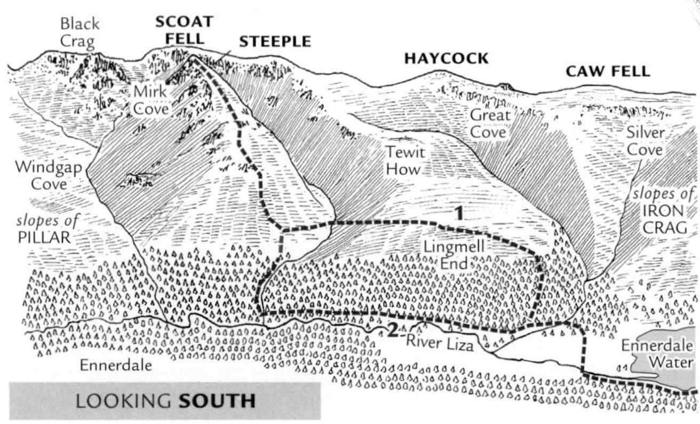

steps onto rockier ground, with heather leading ultimately to a fence-stile onto the ridge of **Lingmell End**. Continue E beside the fell-top fence, well above the present growth of conifers. Pass a large boulder amid the heather, and follow on with the clear path down the slope to ford **Low Beck**. (Route **2** joins from the left but there is no path on the ground.) The path winds on up the rough heather slope, guided by cairns as it climbs the ridge, with several handsome steps, including a brief, easily overcome rock band. Enjoy the cove scenery, with inviting views onto the floor of **Windgap Cove** and the beginnings of **Mirk Cove**. The ridge begins to taper, and exciting views up the steepling ridge urge you on for the final push to the top.

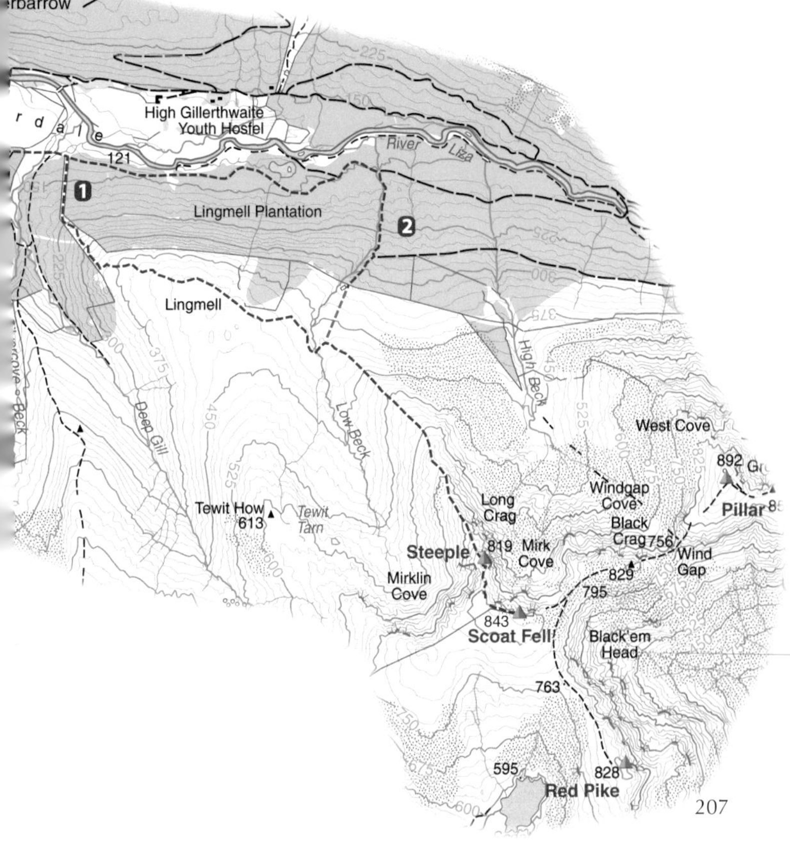

Pillar and the beginnings of the Steeple ridge from Lingmell End

Via Low Beck →*8km/5 miles* ↑*700m/2300ft* ◷*4hr*

2 Spurning the forest break rising to the right, keep along the dale-floor forest track. Some 2km from the foot of the sheep drove, cross the conventional bridge spanning **Low Beck**. Turn immediately right, keeping close to Low Beck, and pass up by a hand-gate. The path, sorely worn in places, leads up beside the ravine to step up onto a forest track. Ignore the track, keep on with the continuing path in harmony with Low Beck to escape the conifers and cross the stile in the forest-bounding fence. Passing an old sheepfold climb on, pathless, to unite with the cairned path of Route **1**, climbing SE onto the ridge.

The summit

As on Red Pike, the cairn is carefully positioned at the only point where you'll find a real all-round peak. The best of the view is towards Mirk Cove and the buttressed faces of Black Crag and Scoat Fell. There is also an airy outlook north over Ennerdale to admire at your leisure.

Safe descents

For all its apparent steepness the north ridge has few, if any, daunting moments. However, in severe weather it might be wisest to follow the Low Beck route (**2**) to gain the valley as quickly as possible.

Ridge route

Black Crag from the summit (photo: Anne Bowskill)

Scoat Fell →*negligible*
↓*20m/65ft* ↑*45m/150ft*
⏲*12min*

Can there be any doubt of the route? Perhaps in swirling mist, but have no fear – there is only one path. Dipping initially SW, this swings left into the nick and beside the dragon's-back connecting ridge to the parent fell. Climb quickly S onto the plateau, from where you are soon standing by the large cairn beside the angle of the Ennerdale Fence (wall).

Looking up the north ridge of Steeple (photo: Maggie Allan)

24 WHIN RIGG 536M/1759FT

Climb it from	Nether Wasdale **7**, Santon Bridge **28** or Eskdale Green **26**
Character	Westernmost end of the famous Wasdale Screes ridge
Fell-friendly route	3
Summit grid ref	NY 151 035
Link it with	Illgill Head

The most ferocious sequence of crags and gullies dominates the lower reaches of Wast Water forming a majestic northern frontage to an otherwise lacklustre ridge. Illgill Head may be the highest point on the ridge, but Whin Rigg is certainly the dominant one of the Wast Water Screes massif. Its summit marks the western end of this famous mountain facade. The huge fans of scree hold Wasdale-bound travellers' spellbound attention, courting colourful light and shadow effects above the dark waters of this, the deepest lake in the National Park.

Without question, the first thought on fellwalkers' minds will be to combine the Screes Footpath with a high-level traverse of the two fell-tops from Nether Wasdale, but there are routes to various points along the summit ridge from almost all directions, confined by crags, scree and forestry. When the weather is iffy and cloud shrouds the tops you can still enjoy the eight-mile circuit of this magnificent stretch of water.

↑ *Looking east along the ridge to Whin Rigg from Irton Pike*

The principal ascent (1) climbs Greathall Gill, with the bridleway linking Eskdale Green with Nether Wasdale a solid alternative approach (via Route 2 from the north or Route 5 from the south) and the full ridge, off the Santon Bridge road beneath Irton Pike, a further natural choice (Routes 3–4).

Ascent from Nether Wasdale 7

Two routes brave the steep northwestern flank of Whin Rigg, Route 1 being more direct and a little steeper. Choose Route 2 to relish the views from the ridge for a little longer.

Via Greathall Gill →*3km/2 miles* ↑*480m/1570ft* ⌚*2hr*

Whin Rigg and the track to Easthwaite

1 Park on the verge near Forest Bridge. From the signpost 'Wast Water' stride out along the lane leading to **Easthwaite Farm** with Whin Rigg firmly in view. Pass on by the barns and farmhouse,

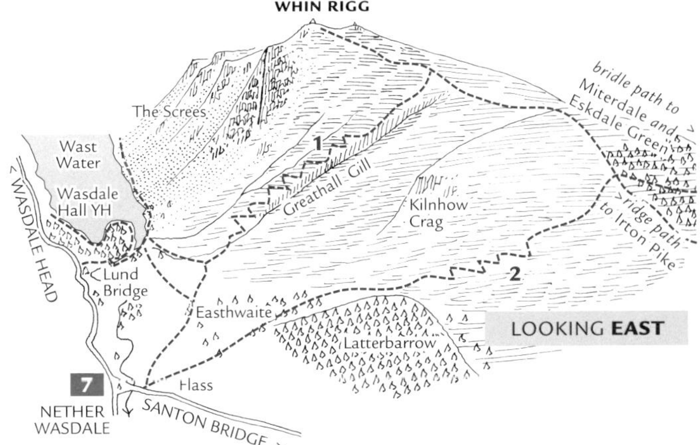

via a gate on the continuing track. As the track bears left through a gateway go straight on via a stile/gate, entering a narrow walled path. At the end, being greeted by 'no path' on the gatepost, turn up right, keeping the

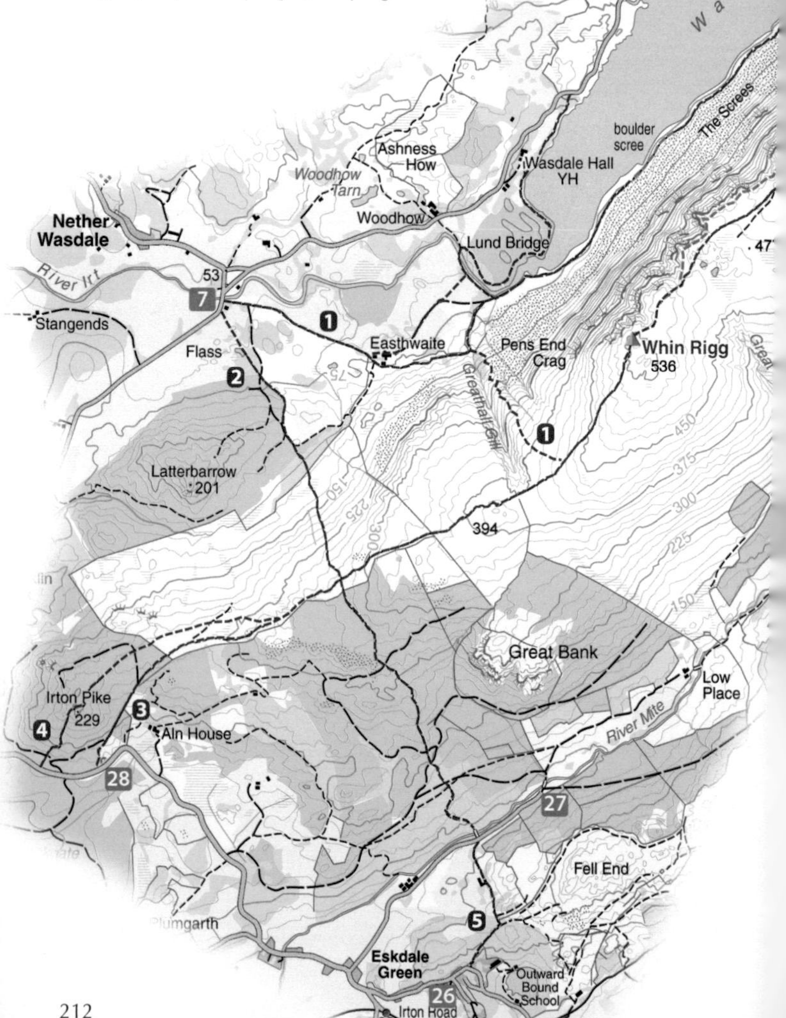

wall to the left to reach a kissing-gate. Go right to a stile and ford the gill to embark on a firm path mounting the really steep rigg on the east side of the deepening **Greathall Gill** ravine. Zig-zag up on a path sufficiently well used to beat back the bracken. The bracken relents and, in time, the grass slope follows suit. A large cairn heralds the junction with the ridge path. Go left, northeast on a steady plod to the summit.

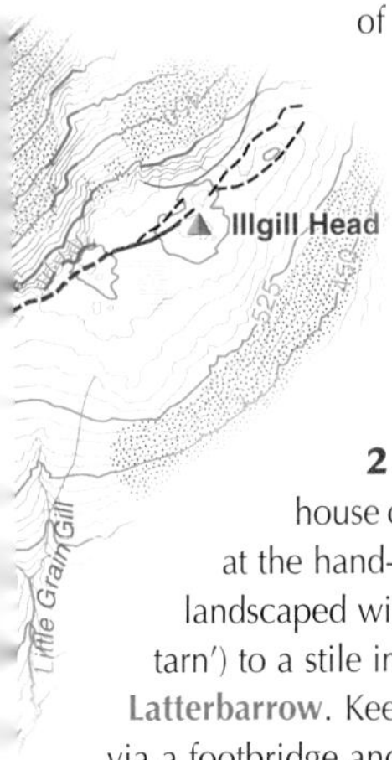

Illgill Head

525

450

Little Grain Gill

Via Latterbarrow →*4km/2½ miles* ↑*480m/1570ft* ⏱*2hr 20min*

2 To the right of the Easthwaite lane-end stands a white house called '**Flass**' and to its right is a bridleway signed 'Eskdale' at the hand-gate. Head straight ahead, traversing a parkland liberally landscaped with Scots pine. Pass the seasonal Flass Tarn (meaning 'tarn tarn') to a stile in the corner entering woodland at the northeastern tip of **Latterbarrow**. Keep the wall left, on an oft-muddy track, leading through via a footbridge and on to a railed path to exit the fenced copse at a hand-gate. The path negotiates marshy ground before heading up the steep fellside, bracken and a stony roughness putting a brake on progress. At the brow a path short-cuts half-left off the formal bridleway, leading, via a hand-gate, into a plantation of Miterdale Forest, the plantation currently reaching maturity. The ridge path winds steadily up following the wall. At a ladder-stile crossing a lateral ridge wall, continue up the damp moorland and slip over a broken wall onto the final open mass of fell to stride on with Route **1** to the summit.

Ascent from Santon Bridge 28

Via Irton Pike →*4.7km/3 miles* ↑*440m/1440ft* ⏱*2hr 45min*

The Irton Fell ridge leads up from above the former deer enclosure of afforested Mecklin and Irton Parks. Choose Route 4 to include the summit of Irton Pike.

3 Follow the easily graded track from the gate by the road, signposted 'Wasdale Head'. This reaches a fork in the track. Either go left to the ridge-top or right, closer to the forestry wall, to a gate in the fence. The two paths

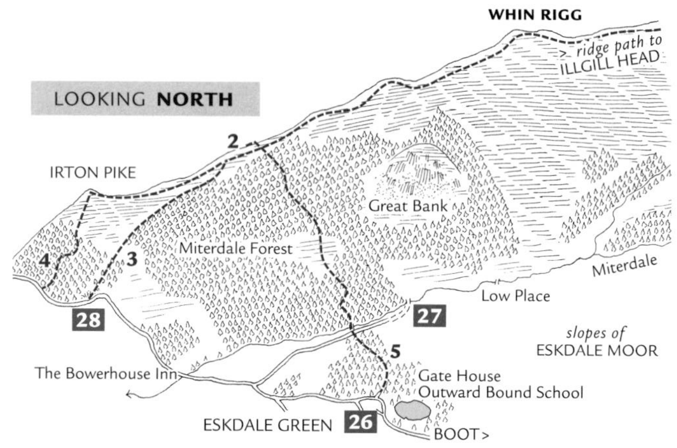

remain separate for quite some distance, re-uniting at a damp patch close to the wall, short of the final rise to meet the cross-ridge bridleway (**2**).

4 Alternatively, and this is recommended, climb Irton Pike. Walk west along the road some 220m to an opening into the woodland, four short paces after the roadside Malkinson memorial stone. This path makes a steep assault on the hill. Crossing a forest track, it runs up a slope, curves right, then climbs out of the trees onto the heather-capped hilltop. In late summer when the heather is out this is a delightful place to rest and soak up a wonderful view. Thankfully, Irton Pike's ridge-top conifers have been felled. The ridge path goes down to meet the forestry track and advances to step over a cross-ridge fence at a stile. Notice the fine view of Latterbarrow down to the left, then shortly after the pile of stones over to the right which are the remnants of a Bronze Age burial mound. Cross a rake dyke (former mining excavation) before walking up to join the ridge wall and meet the bridleway as it enters the forestry at the ridge wall. Join Route **2** and continue along the ridge.

Ascent from Eskdale Green 26

Via Miterdale Forest →*5.2km/3¼ miles* ↑*490m/1610ft* ◷*3hr*

A woodland approach to the southwest ridge path.

5 From the village car park turn up Giggle Alley, passing Low Holme via a gate. Descend to cross the by-road into Miterdale. Enter Miterdale Forest, crossing the stone bridge over the **River Mite**. A clearly marked path winds up, initially among deciduous woodland, then crossing various tracks and felled areas before being consumed in the higher, mature plantation to reach the hand-gate and the open ridge. Go right, following Route **2**.

The Screes Footpath – Wasdale Hall to Wasdale Head

→7.5km/4¾ miles ↑negligible ⏲2hr 30min

By and large, a walk around a Cumbrian lake is a gentle alternative to climbing a fell – a lazy Lakeland day. The Screes Footpath, part of a full seven-mile circuit of Wast Water, is, however, no such thing. The western approach leads in either by **Easthwaite Farm** from Nether Wasdale (**7**, Route **1**), giving a lovely view of Whin Rigg itself, or from the valley road at **Woodhow** (no parking in the vicinity of this former trekking centre, please note) where the mighty wall of crags and screes are softened by an under-mantel of trees.

The most attractive start uses the shoreline path from the ladder-stile off the open road north of **Wasdale Hall YH**. Sugaring the pill, this delightful woodland passage is in stark contrast to the rigours of the Screes Footpath itself. From in front of the handsome youth hostel the serried ranks of crags, gullies and near vertical screes can be studied with some perspective – and the whole notion of following the Screes Footpath considered… or re-considered!

Uniting with the Woodhow path at **Lund Bridge**, the path runs along the tree-shaded banks of the River Irt, via gates and along a track as the lake emerges from the river. Reach the pumping house, emitting its steady hum.

Here the path starts to dwindle to a narrow trod. Weave through an area of light tree growth to face, as face you must, the most awful tilt of boulders nature ever

Encountering boulder scree on the infamous Screes Footpath

bequeathed to a Lakeland path. Not even Broad Crag can match the sheer mind-boggling maze of boulder problems. There is no visible path and there never has been, only what looks like the result of a massive rockfall. Your natural tendency will be to climb gradually up but if you do you will only have to work your way back down at some point which is much harder. When the stones are wet they are slick and the whole process becomes painfully slow with little certainty of a firm footing.

The best line is between the central twin masses of large boulders but the time taken over this first scree fan can vary from 20 to 40 minutes. What follows, while intermittently troublesome, is never again quite as consistently bad, which is solace of sorts. Wast Water was never more imminent nor ominous. The rock framing the dark waters lapping at your feet runs down below the surface at the same angle as the screes, reaching some 18m below sea-level – a Cumbrian fjord. Back at the shoreline, the scree recedes and bracken takes over as your view of Wasdale Head fills the senses with anticipation of greater things to come. A field-gate heralds the advent of pasture passing Wasdale Head Hall farm. Cross a stile and join the access lane leading to the valley road beyond the tree-screened National Trust car park and camping ground below Brackenclose.

The summit

A small shelter-cairn sits on top of the knoll a few paces north of the ridge path. A second cairn rests on the south top, looking towards Eskdale. The main top is a wonderful spot, and if you have admired it from the shores of Wast Water then you will know you are on a significant summit, culminating in a mighty craggy fortress. Gingerly visit the top of Great Gully, a matter of a few paces north.

Safe descents

Clearly there is no way N and extensive bracken and forestry blanket the S slopes into Miterdale. Follow the ridge SW to Greathall Gill (**1**), a steep grassy path, or continue to the cross-ridge bridleway (**5**) linking Eskdale Green S, through the forestry, aiming for the footbridge over the River Mite, or N down the scarp, passing through the plantation fringe of Latterbarrow for Nether Wasdale **2**.

The main summit cairn

Ridge route

Illgill Head →*2.2km/1½ miles* ↓*75m/245ft* ↑*135m/440ft* ⌚*45min*
How you undertake this walk probably depends as much on whether you are alone or have company. If the latter you'll stride E with the well-defined ridge path, or should that be paths, passing either side of the brace of attractive tarns in the broad saddle.

If you have your liberty and find the escarpment compelling, then you'll be irresistibly drawn to follow the ragged, jagged edge. There are places where you can teeter out on arêtes – great fun in calm conditions. The W top cairn of Illgill Head stands only 30m in from the awesome N edge. The E top wind-shelter-cairn is better placed for relaxing and considering the impressive circle of fells around Wasdale Head, one of the natural homes of British mountaineering and an iconic landscape for fellwalkers.

25 YEWBARROW 628M/2060FT

Climb it from	Overbeck Bridge **3** or Wasdale Green **1**
Character	A great wedged pyramid overshadowing Wasdale Head, a tough nut to climb
Fell-friendly route	2 or 4
Summit grid ref	NY 173 084
Link it with	Red Pike
Part of	The Nether Beck Horseshoe and the Mosedale Round

Visitors to Wasdale Head relish the grand scenes that greet them. High ranking among the fells is the distinctive pyramid of Yewbarrow, admired from the road in above Wast Water, packing a punch well above its modest height. In visual terms, Yewbarrow resembles the hull of an upturned yacht, covered with craggy barnacles – how you long to climb it!

From the top of Stirrup Crag to Great Door the spine of Yewbarrow is a fellwalking treat. It takes a particular kind of fellwalker to get here, and they are well rewarded. The view takes some matching, too – an all-round view of great mountains.

There are no casual ways up. Walkers involved in the Mosedale Horseshoe might have it in their mind as they come off Red Pike, but even from here it

↑ *Yewbarrow from the road approaching Netherbeck Bridge*

makes a strenuous addition. Routes 1–3 here tackle the task from the shores of Wast Water while Route 4 makes a short but extremely sharp assault, starting from Wasdale Head and then turning southwest to battle up steep scree to Dore Head.

Ascent from Overbeck Bridge 3

A tough scree climb (1), a sneaky side approach (2) and a serious but do-able scramble (3) are all options for reaching the top of this rocky ridge.

Via Great Door →*2.4km/1½ miles* ↑*580m/1900ft* ⏲*2hr*

Unless you are an accomplished rock climber, Bell Rib, the peaked culmination of the south ridge, is definitely a rock barrier to Great Door. However, this route exploits a weakness in the armour by running up a rough gully beside Dropping Crag.

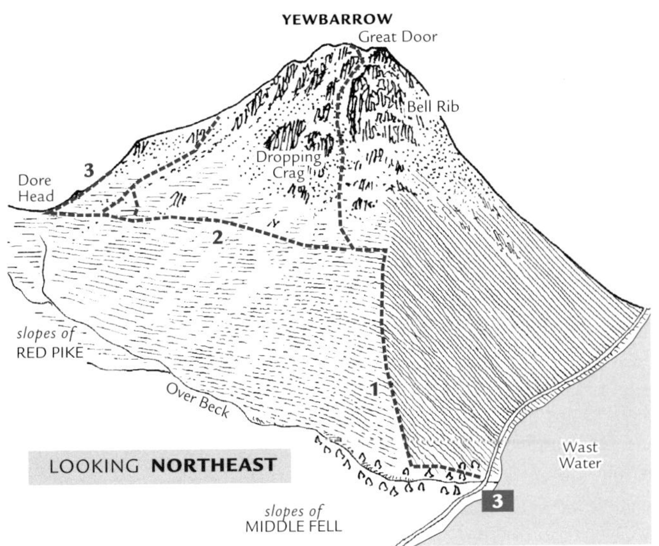

1 There is no acceptable way to the summit from the eastern side – except for members of the Bob Graham 24 Hour Club! Head up the valley from the car park and cross the fence-stile amid the gorse. The path now bends to its task, climbing the south ridge beside the rising fence. A ladder-stile, as the first rocks intervene, places the path on the west side of the ridge. As it contours you quickly come upon a definite fork. Turn up right. Bracken gives way to shards of scree as you make determined progress up the torn trail between rock walls. It's tough going, but on reaching **Great Door** the sense of achievement makes it all worthwhile. From this striking notch, set foot on the rising ridge, taking every opportunity to glance back over Wast Water and, in advance, survey the huge views to the Scafells, as you step up the grass ridge to the summit. (If you have a head for heights and the day is not too windy, the summit of Bell Rib itself is a fabulously airy spot from which to take it all in.)

Via Over Beck →*4.1km/2½ miles* ↑*580m/1900ft* ◷*2hr 30min*

2 Having crossed the ladder-stile on Route **1**, stay on the contouring path. This leads to a hand-gate in a wall directly beneath the characterful face of **Dropping Crag**. Go through, continuing N as towards **Dore Head**. Find a sneaky side-approach to the summit ridge higher up the valley, before a cluster of large boulders. Either step right up the rash of scree or follow the sheep trod from above the boulders tracking back S. Either way head up to the base of a short rock-wall and veer right, on a clear path which climbs naturally to the peaty ground in the fell-ridge depression. Turn right to reach the summit.

Via Stirrup Crag →*4.1km/2½ miles* ↑*590m/1936ft* ◷*2hr 45min*

3 Alternatively continue past the base of the scree scramble on Route **2** and complete the journey up the **Over Beck** valley to arrive at the brink of **Dore Head**, from where you can spot the jagged-tooth pinnacle on the lower side of Stirrup Crag. Turn right and climb up to the base of **Stirrup Crag** and scramble up the early cleft. Other gullies follow, making this a close-run thing to proper scrambling – certainly harder than normal ridge-path terrain. But it is nothing for the average fellwanderer to fear. The north top, at 617m, feels as though it must be the fell summit after all that rigour. But in fact you will find a slightly higher one if you wander S along the grassy ridge – two for the price of one, now that can't be bad!

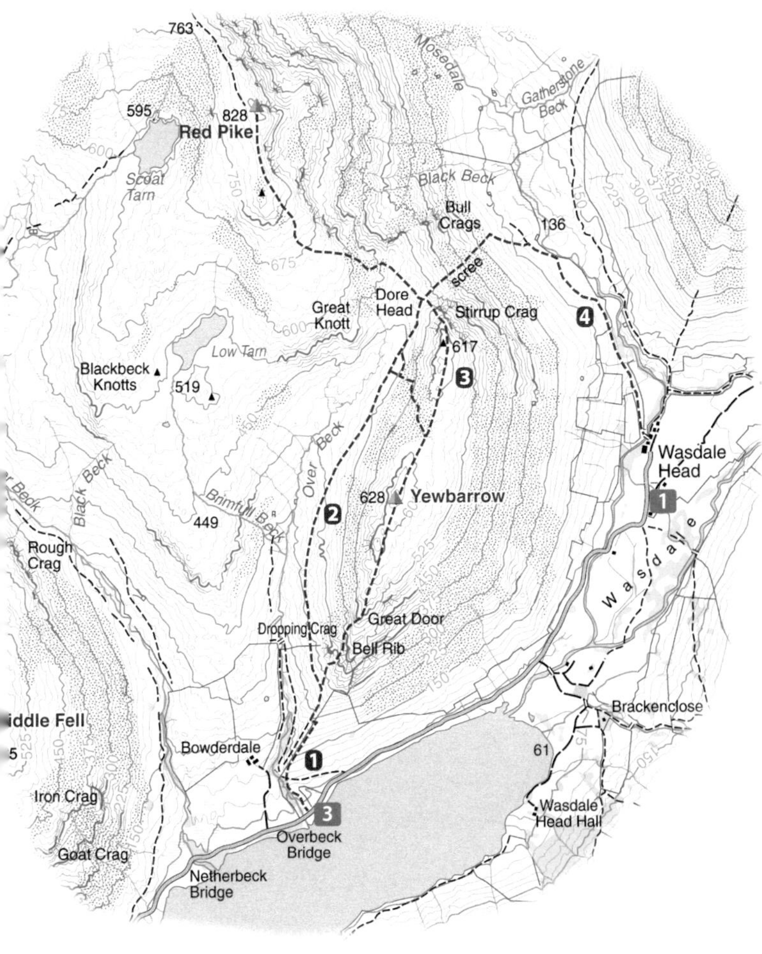

763
595
828
Red Pike
Scoat Tarn
Mosedale
Gatherstone Beck
Black Beck
Bull Crags
136
scree
Dore Head
Great Knott
Stirrup Crag
617
Low Tarn
Blackbeck Knotts
519
Over Beck
Wasdale Head
628
Yewbarrow
Brimfull Beck
449
Black Beck
Rough Crag
Wasdale
Great Door
Dropping Crag
Bell Rib
Brackenclose
Bowderdale
61
Iron Crag
Wasdale Head Hall
Overbeck Bridge
Goat Crag
Netherbeck Bridge

Ascent from Wasdale Green 1

Via Dore Head →*4.1km/2½ miles* ↑*580m/1900ft* ⌚*2hr 30min*

Forbidding as Yewbarrow may look from Wasdale Green, walkers have every right to give it a go from the common.

4 Follow the lane to the Wasdale Head Inn and, after passing the Barn Door Shop and Ritson's Bar (both logged for later attention!), cross the single-arched stone bridge and advance along the walled drove-way to go through a gate. Coming by a wall, the thunderous sounds of **Mosedale Beck** will entice you to a brief diversion through the access gap to visit the embowered Ritson's Falls. Regaining the green drove, pass through the next hand-gate and advance beyond the trees into Mosedale, flanked by an abundance of bracken and with the wall bounding the beck to the right. At a sheepfold the path pitches left and climbs towards the foot of the obvious ribbon of scree, the remnant of an old and now infamous scree-run worn almost to oblivion. The path picks it way across the river of stones and begins a far more stately climb on the grassy bank to the right of the scree scar. The slope is steep, and progress commensurately slow. Duly you arrive at the saddle of **Dore Head** and set to work on the rocky headland of **Stirrup Crag** to the left (**3**). It may look unpromising but it's worth getting to grips with.

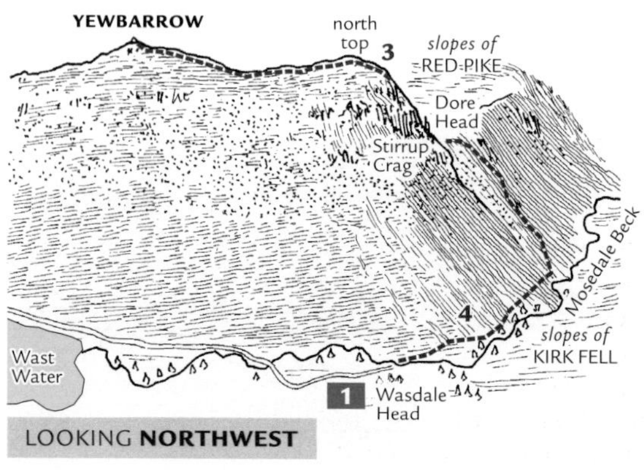

Looking up Bell Rib (photo: Anne Bowskill)

The summit

The steely impression of this fell from afar makes the broad, grassy summit ridge an unexpected treat. Whichever way you stride along it the easy terrain gives you licence to enjoy the spectacular views. From here you can enjoy the Scafells in all their magnificence and, in the opposite direction, Red Pike rises like a colossus with Great Gable set peerlessly in the midst.

Safe descents

Comfortable options are limited. The most secure route is the path least travelled. From the marshy depression, north of the summit, a path (**2**) innocently forks and leads niftily down and under the shield of rocks to gain the free-running path in the upper part of the Over Beck valley. Turn left onto this to reach the shores of the lake.

The Scafells from the north top

The ridge S to Great Door (**1**) promises hope, but on the way down to the right passes the remnants of a sheep-deflecting crag-top wall and, down the loose gully beside Dropping Crag, is not a nice affair, although it does put you quickly onto firm ground and an honest path, again bound for Overbeck Bridge.

Ridge route

Red Pike →*2.8km/1¾ miles* ↓*160m/525ft* ↑*365m/1200ft* ⏲*1hr 30min*
Scrupulous ridge-followers will head N, passing the cairn on top of Stirrup Crag and, taking their time, will shuffle and squeeze, stretch and grapple their way down the clefts to Dore Head, dusting themselves down to follow on naturally up the regular scarp-edge trail NW onto Red Pike. It's a big climb, but hugely rewarding. Less strict fell-folk will take heed of the opportunity to avoid Stirrup Crag, as described in the safe descents above, to reach Dore Head unruffled, except by any gusts of wind from the west!

Yewbarrow from the lakeside road

1 THE ROOF OF ENGLAND

Start/Finish	Wasdale Head **2**
Distance	13km (8 miles)
Ascent/Descent	1510m (4955ft)
Time	9hr
Terrain	Requires good weather as the route diverges from regular paths at times. Competence in a challenging mountain environment is a pre-requisite.
Summits	Lingmell, Great End, Scafell Pike and Scafell

An energetic, engrossing and hugely rewarding fell day by a little-followed route in a popular area, taking in the highest peak in England.

Exit the car park to join the track by a cattle grid and kissing-gate. Keep left and do not cross the bridge spanning **Lingmell Gill**. The initially gorse-lined path narrows and leads via a kissing-gate onto a beckside pasture.

Angle half-left up to a kissing-gate. A steady, oft Galloway-grazed slope ensues, crossing the regular path from Wasdale Green (as it swings into the Lingmell Gill valley). Keep on up the grassy slope, sparsely dotted with thorn,

↑ *The round from Lingmell on the left to Scafell on the right seen across Wast Water*

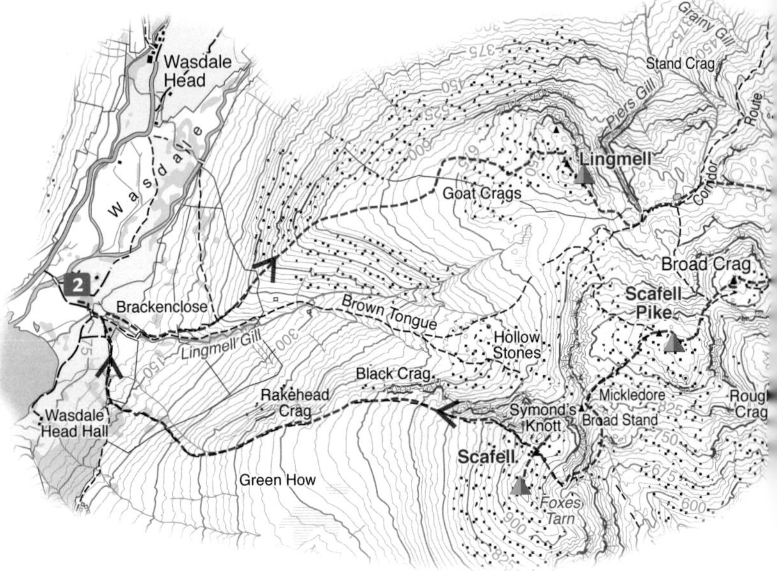

climbing to a ladder-stile spanning a ridge-straddling wall. The slope, now the domain of the Herdwick, steepens a tad up the nose of the ridge. Only latterly do you reach any hint of rock, aided by a stretch of stepped pitching, and crest the brow onto an almost level expanse of moor.

The views down on Wast Water, the field mazzle of walls at Wasdale Head below and the grand fells bounding Mosedale are a constant delight. Stride easily on from the cairn. The grassy pasture path angles up gently and, well short of the rocky ground of **Goat Crag**, comes to a fork.

Fork left on the less-trammelled grass path to step over a broken wall. The path swings right and makes a swift ascent to the top of **Lingmell**. (In fine weather you might be tempted to wander half-left onto the rocky ridge (no path) to find a slender cairn perched on a sumptuous brink from where you can admire Great Gable's unforgettable southern facade.) The summit is marked by a large cairn set in rocks above a breathtaking craggy abyss. Watch your step and enjoy your solitary airy station above the endless trail of people winding up the Hollow Stones path to the south.

Descend SE and when you come to a broken wall step over and follow it down into the hollow. Here bear right (faint path) to join the popular trail known as the **Corridor Route**. Follow this path left fording the feeder gill running into the awesome ravine of **Piers Gill**, smartly skipping over a ledge to meet the stepped start of the path to Broadcrag Col. Stick with the Corridor Route a little further below the impressive looming cliffs of Broad Crag. When you reach a tiny watercourse trickling down an open combe with the impressive rock shield of Round How up to your left bear off right (E) here beside Greta Gill and find a simple way up into the nameless hanging valley behind Round How, setting your sights on the natural breach in the scarp above from where the stream issues from the saddle above. There is a trace of a path only as you start the pull up to the breach but minimal loose gravel to inhibit progress.

The plateau is reached with more ease than you might expect. Bear left avoiding a small outcrop to reach the summit of **Great End**. Once there make sure to take advantage of the cliff-edge view north which is quite stunning. Backtrack to join the thoroughfare path rising out of Calf Cove from the left keeping SW. The ridge path, liberally sprinkled with cairns, tackles an area of boulders. Detour left (S) to revel in the scenic rocky sentinel summit of **Ill Crag** and a fabulous view down over Little Narrowcove onto Pen and Great Moss and W to Scafell Pike. Cut back onto the regular trail and seek out the

Deep Gill – well worth stepping away from the main route to admire (photo: Brian Gotts)

awkward top of **Broad Crag**, the cairn locked in among a tangle of igneous blocks close right beside the main thoroughfare. Once you've pitched down the loose trail to Broadcrag Col the final clamber onto the main summit of the district, and therefore England, is akin to scrabbling up a quarry, the ground so ill at ease with the endless flow of boots! Keep forward (SW) to the sturdy summit structure on **Scafell Pike**.

The final summit – Scafell – is not won easily. The intervening ridge has a serious life-threatening hazard (Broad Stand), that renders it off limits to non-climbers. And the gully route to Foxes Tarn (described below) can run a torrent in very wet conditions and be impossible to climb. (In this case, the smart choice is to skip Scafell altogether and take the popular path down from the summit of Scafell Pike via Lingmell Col down **Hollow Stones** and Brown Tongue.)

If conditions are reasonable, follow on W to bend SW off the more common heavily cairned trail and descend towards **Mickledore**. You have to lose height from the pass, descending SE either directly from the Rescue Post (easier underfoot) or advancing to the base of **Broad Stand** and slithering down the loose scree beneath the overbearing East Buttress. Either way the objective is an obvious square-cut gully. In mist you could miss it from the path direct from the stretcher box and you need to sidle over the boulders to enter. The rake when you reach it is great fun, hands-on rock in a confined and comparatively safe environment, jostling with the gill which at times hides beneath boulders and other times splashes you with abandon.

The climb ends in a deeply set hollow cradling **Foxes Tarn**, an L-shaped pool set around a large boulder. A steep scrappy path ensues, with some fragmentary evidence of pitching up to the ridge-top saddle. Turn right to visit the top of Symond's Knott from where Pulpit Rock and Great Gable are seen to fabulous effect and you can test your vertigo by peering down Deep Gill on your right. Or turn left (S) with the ridge path to reach the summit of **Scafell**. The cairn and wind-shelter sit bleak to the wild sky on a low rocky crest.

Backtrack to the low saddle with its stone cross laid in the grass. Turn W and begin the long descent, the craggy edge always of interest. The descending, mainly grassy path is much less boot-torn than any of those on Scafell Pike. Keep to the edge, skirting **Rakehead Crag**, finally accepting the lure of a shallow gill drawing into bracken and down to a wall-stile to come down to meet a farm track beside a gate. Go right by gates through the **Brackenclose** wooded enclosure and cross the Lingmell Gill bridge with the farm-access track to return to the car park.

2 THE MOSEDALE ROUND

Start/Finish	Wasdale Green **1**
Distance	17.5km (11 miles)
Ascent/Descent	1350m (4430ft)
Time	8hr
Terrain	A unambiguous walk that reserves all its issues for the final summit, Yewbarrow, which can honourably be skipped if you doubt you have the time, or it is wreathed in cloud. On the other hand, you could easily add in Scoat Fell if you have extra time and energy.
Summits	Pillar, Red Pike and Yewbarrow

A mighty round forging ever upward from Looking Stead onto the high plateau of Pillar, visiting Black Crag, with its impressive view over Mirk Cove and the fierce scarp of Red Pike and then descending to claim Yewbarrow, one of Lakeland's most distinctive smaller fells.

From behind the Wasdale Head Inn pass the beautiful single-arch stone bridge via hand-gates swinging left into Mosedale. Yewbarrow and Red Pike are the more impressive components of this short dale. Rising through the

↑ *Black'em Head between Red Pike and Pillar from Black Sail Pass*

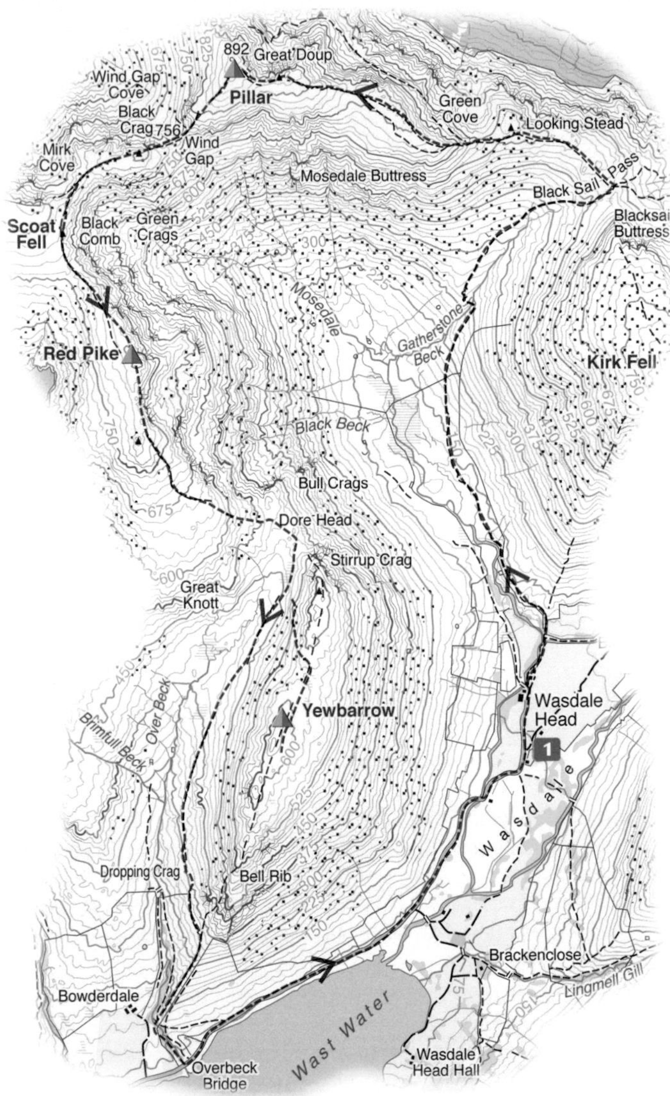
892
Great Doup
Pillar
Wind Gap Cove
Black Crag 756
Wind Gap
Mirk Cove
Green Cove
Looking Stead
Black Sail Pass
Mosedale Buttress
Blacksail Buttress
Scoat Fell
Black Comb
Green Crags
Mosedale
Gatherstone Beck
Red Pike
Kirk Fell
Black Beck
Bull Crags
Dore Head
Stirrup Crag
Great Knott
Yewbarrow
Wasdale Head
1
Over Beck
Brimfull Beck
Wasdale
Dropping Crag
Bell Rib
Brackenclose
Lingmell Gill
Bowderdale
West Water
Overbeck Bridge
Wasdale Head Hall

Scoat Tarn and Seatallan from Red Pike (photo: Anne Bowskill)

bracken the path comes onto pitching and addresses the handsome cascades of **Gatherstone Beck**. The path fords, hairpins left and right and heads reliably towards the pass, with good pitching ending just short of the **Black Sail Pass** saddle. Advance beyond the large cairn to the iron stakes where the ridge path crosses from Kirk Fell and turn up left.

Just a little to the right of the main ridge path (marked on the map) is the course of the old fence, marked by iron stakes and following the natural ridge-top. Follow either as far as **Looking Stead**, but the old, higher line offers a couple of tiny tarns and better views. Looking Stead (just above the main path on the right) lives up to its name, peering down upon Black Sail Hut and the wild head of Ennerdale and along the craggy northern flank of Pillar to the high-perched Robinson's Cairn. The ridge path turns upward tackling an easily overcome rocky sequence above **Green Cove**. A second pull brings you above Pillar Cove, the pinnacle scenery quite thrilling, eventually arriving upon the plateau where you head W and latterly NW to the wind-shelter and OS column on **Pillar**.

Continue SW. The descent to **Wind Gap** is uncomfortably loose in places towards the bottom. Cross the gap and walk up through the boulders to the cairn on **Black Crag**. Again it is worth detouring a little to the right of the ridge path here, further W, to visit the top of the NW spur which faces into **Mirk**

Cove, also a wonderful place to stand and study Steeple. The ridge path drifts naturally SW and forks. Keep left to spurn **Scoat Fell** and climb the sensational escarpment edge. Beware being lured too far right by the heavily used path. You need to angle slightly left (SE) off the path to find the summit of **Red Pike** (as marked on the map).

As you leave Red Pike, keep rigidly to the descending ridge path heading S to **Dore Head**. Here you have two options. If you prefer to avoid a gentle scramble, follow the route marked on the map and described below. (Alternatively, head straight across the gap to tackle **Stirrup Crag**. There are weaknesses in its armour, a cleft squeeze for one and several gully scramble sections to wriggle up, but all do-able with normal fell endeavour. This leads over the north top and on along the ridge which dips before the summit.) Turn right and follow the dale path down past a cluster of boulders to find a path that heads up the stony slope and veers right under the outcropping, working up onto the ridge at the saddle and thereby to the summit cairn of **Yewbarrow**.

Backtrack to the upper **Over Beck** for the final descent. (Great Door may offer a fabulous view of Wast Water, but the way down by **Dropping Crag** is appallingly loose and to stay safe and also protect the fell it is better avoided.) The path is straightforward, coming down the western flank of the fell to meet the Dropping Crag path and running down by the wall to a hand-gate, then contouring to a ladder-stile onto the road. Here turn left for a scenic road walk back to Wasdale Green (a little more than 2km).

3 THE NETHER BECK HORSESHOE

Start/Finish	Goat Gill **5**
Distance	16km (10 miles)
Ascent/Descent	1325m (4345ft)
Time	7hr 30min
Terrain	An energetic skyline with a rough off-beat start. Those with unlimited energy could opt to add in Yewbarrow on the final strait.
Summits	Middle Fell, Seatallan, Haycock, Scoat Fell and Red Pike

The core ridge route of this round is exhilarating, increasingly so with each new summit gained, but it is surprisingly seldom undertaken.

Look up the hillside and see the great mass of **Goat Crag**. To the crag's left a grassy breach at the headwaters of **Goat Gill** is the clue to a direct and uncommon route of ascent. Bracken is easily beaten as you head up by glacial bedrock riggs and gorse patches keeping to the left-hand side of the rising gill with no hint of a path. The grassy upper portion of the fell leads easily to the ridge path. Turn right on this to reach the solitary cairn defining the

↑ *Looking across to the Nether Beck Horseshoe from Whin Rigg – Seatallan on the left and Yewbarrow on the right (photo: Maggie Allan)*

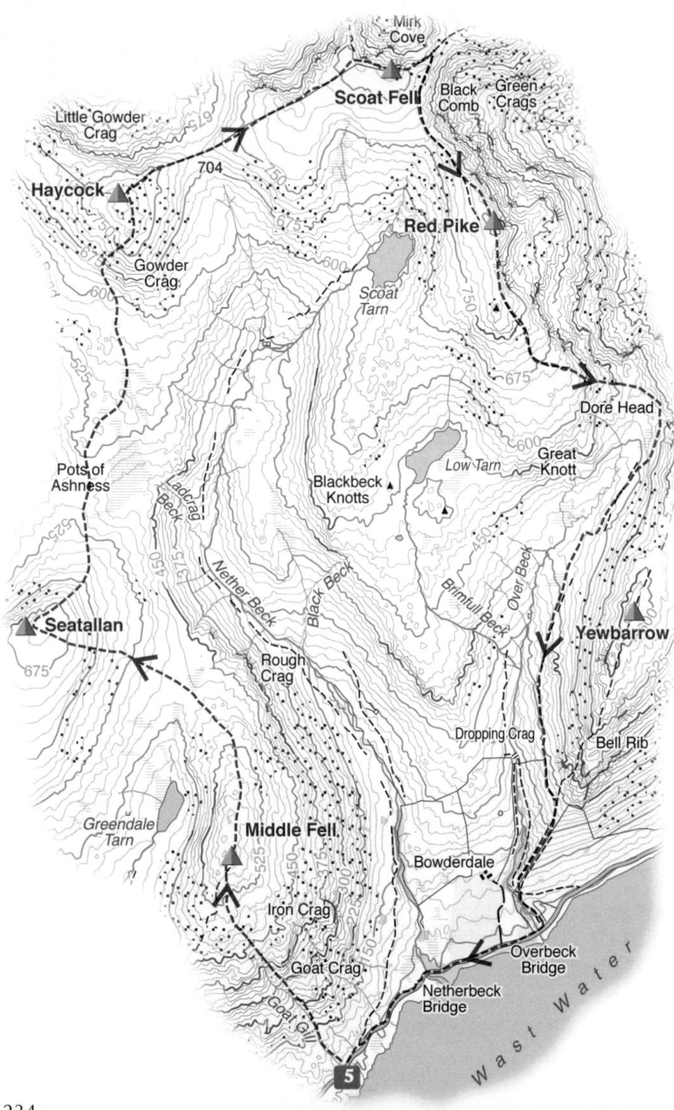
Mirk Cove
Scoat Fell
Black Comb
Green Crags
Little Gowder Crag
704
Haycock
Red Pike
Gowder Crag
Scoat Tarn
Dore Head
Low Tarn
Great Knott
Blackbeck Knotts
Pots of Ashness
Ladcrag Beck
Nether Beck
Black Beck
Brimfull Beck
Over Beck
Seatallan
Yewbarrow
Rough Crag
Dropping Crag
Bell Rib
Greendale Tarn
Middle Fell
Bowderdale
Iron Crag
Goat Crag
Overbeck Bridge
Netherbeck Bridge
Goat Gill
Wast Water
5

Aim for this breach on Middle Fell to find the ridge path

summit of **Middle Fell** and one of the best eastern panoramas available to the Lakeland fellwalker.

Attention now turns N to the bold fell 2.5km distant. Follow the ridge path as it descends to the marshy saddle at the head of the **Greendale Gill** valley. Trend half-left off the main path, which leads to the saddle to the north, to avoid the rushes and climb the steep pathless east slope unimpeded to the summit of **Seatallan**.

From here, aim NE to find the marker cairn guiding off the summit plateau. The path runs down the plain N slope onto the undulating plateau that forms the connection. Inevitably marshy ground is found in abundance, none-too effectively evaded by the ridge path. Haycock is not a 'gimme' – navigational strategy is required in the ascent, particularly in mist. The ridge path angles to the left-hand side of the rising ridge to avoid the mass of rock and unwelcome scree spilling from **Gowder Crag**. Find a boulder with a small cairn on top. This is the keystone marker for the climb where you turn right. Ascend the steep ramp/rake, a grassy gangway with the odd supportive cairn guiding to the high saddle behind the crest of Gowder Crag. Turn left and follow the easier ground to join the ridge wall to gain the summit of **Haycock**.

From here, keep E/NE with the wall (a section of the Ennerdale Fence), choosing the south side for underfoot comfort. After the grassy depression, choose the north side for the fine scarp-edge views into Mirk Cove and to Steeple. For all the ravages of time the ridge wall is a substantial feature and the perfect companion all the way to the top of **Scoat Fell**.

The next summit is even closer. Head E, slipping through the great boulders at the end of the Ennerdale Fence. Boulder-hop NE down to the grassy plateau connecting to Black Crag. Here turn back sharply right to follow the ridge path climbing the sensational escarpment edge. Beware being lured too far right by the heavily used path. You need to angle slightly left (SE) off the path to find the summit of **Red Pike** (as marked on the map).

From Red Pike, keep rigidly to the descending ridge path heading south to **Dore Head**. At the saddle, turn right in front of Yewbarrow to follow the dale path coming down the western flank of the fell to meet the path from **Dropping Crag**. It runs down by the wall to reach a hand-gate contouring to a ladder-stile onto the road. Follow the road right (W) back to the start, en route crossing **Overbeck** and **Netherbeck Bridges**, both with handsome views over Wast Water to the Screes.

Head of Mosedale from Kirk Fell

4 THE UPPER ENNERDALE ROUND

Start/Finish	Black Sail Hut **17**
Distance	13km (8 miles)
Ascent/Descent	1525m (5005ft)
Time	9hr
Terrain	Kirk Fell and Great Gable are seriously rocky obstacles and Haystacks can be confusing in mist if you stray from the popular path. There is a delightful lower horseshoe path that runs below the first four summits round the dale-head for those days when cloud might dissuade you from visiting the heights (see below).
Summits	Kirk Fell, Great Gable, Green Gable, Brandreth and Haystacks

A handsome ridge walk with two steep ascents and grand fell-top views, this is a fabulous expedition that concludes with the intimate fascination of Haystacks with all its rock outcropping, luxuriant heather and rock-cradled pools. The nature of the steep ascent of Kirk Fell from above Black Sail Pass means the Round is best undertaken anti-clockwise, as described.

↑ *The head of Ennerdale from Haystacks (photo: Anne Bowskill)*

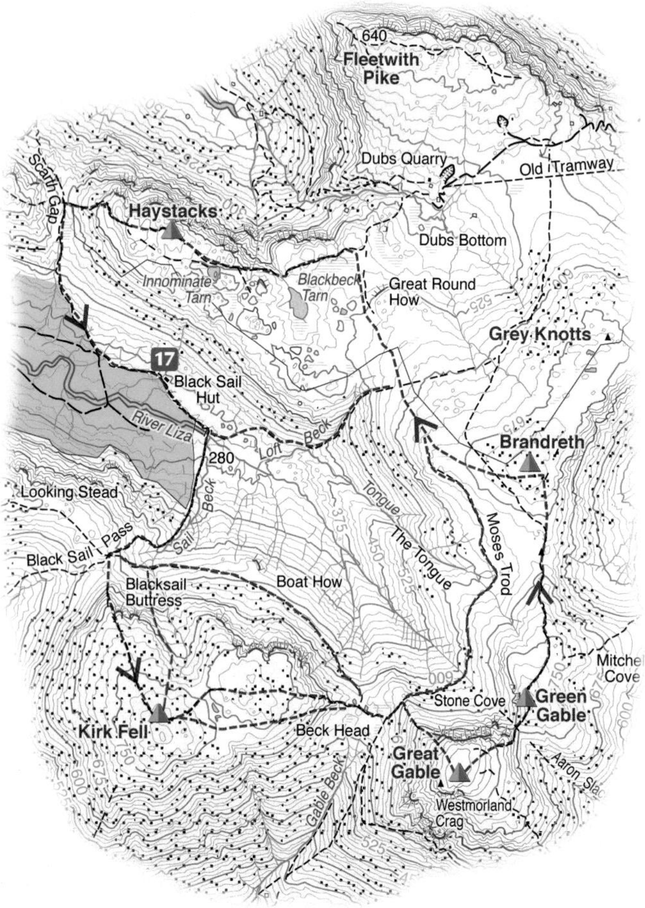

Follow the path which angles down to cross the footbridge spanning the youthful **River Liza**, above the re-wilding felled upper reaches of the plantations. Mount the notable slope on a palpable path with one small rock-step. Keep with the path onto grassy **Black Sail Pass**. The countenance of Kirk Fell from here is unwelcoming – a great bastion of rock appropriately called

Kirkfell Crags on OS maps (and **Blacksail Buttress** on this map) more daunting the higher you look. (It is possible to avoid it altogether by climbing up the right side of **Sail Beck**, pathlessly, to the combe of Baysoar Slack, if you fancy going off piste.) Bear left at the remnant metal gate in the pass. As the grass becomes scree the path appears to fork. Be sure to bear right on the less-travelled path here. This holds to the spine of the overbearing ridge, encountering the odd metal fence post by a series of rock-steps onto the plateau. Thereafter follow the fence-line to the summit wind-shelter on **Kirk Fell**.

You may go either side of the saddle pools to take in, or sidestep, the east top, then descend the loose path to **Beck Head**. Pass more pools as you wind up the stony west slope catching a glimpse of Gable Crag (usually in shade). Higher up the blocks become more sizable eventually breaking onto the rocky fell-top of **Great Gable** to reach the summit outcrop with its poignant memorial plaque.

Bear north following a line of cairns guiding down to the saddle (Windy Gap) then take the loose scree path to the top of **Green Gable**. The going eases on the descent. Beyond another cluster of tarns at Gillercomb Head, shallow outcropping leads to the stony summit of **Brandreth**. Bear left with the metal fence posts to join the wood and mesh fence declining gently westwards. There are several opportunities to cross to the north side of the fence but you might find it more comfortable to wait until you come to the gate where the Coast to Coast Walk crosses your path and then switch sides, continuing down and round a leftward bend. Some 150m after this, bear off right on an unmarked grass and mossy path leading under the impressive wall of **Great Round How** to meet the popular path from Warnscale.

Turn left and keep with the path along the head of the Black Beck ravine, just after a handsome view over **Blackbeck Tarn**. This path angles up round to pass **Innominate Tarn** and a small shelf tarn cradled in the heather to reach the N–S rock spine that forms the **Haystacks** summit. Descend carefully in a series of staggered rock-steps to **Scarth Gap Pass** and go left, descending to join the track emerging from the part-felled forest to reach the hostel... and no doubt welcome refreshment from their self-service (honesty box) kitchen.

Lower dale-head option

If the fell-tops are capped in cloud you can enjoy a great dale-head wander at a somewhat lower level. From Black Sail Pass a lateral trod has evolved fording **Sail Beck** to come above **Boat How** latterly rising to **Beck Head** from

Black Sail Hostel

where you can follow **Moses Trod**. This old trade route keeps to grass contouring, as much as possible, well below Great and Green Gable to encounter the fence descending from Brandreth linking sweetly with the ridge route for **Haystacks** or descending with the Coast to Coast Walk by **Loft Beck** directly to the hostel.

MORE TO EXPLORE

Circular

- from Bleach Green **15**: Crag Fell – Iron Crag – Caw Fell – Haycock
- from Greendale **6** or Nether Wasdale **8**: Buckbarrow – Seatallan – Middle Fell

Linear

- Bowness Knott **16** to Black Sail Hut **17**: Steeple – Scoat Fell – Pillar
- Nether Wasdale **8** to Wasdale Head **2**: Whin Rigg – Illgill Head
- Wha House **23** to Wasdale Head **2**: Slight Side – Scafell – Scafell Pike – Lingmell

Wast Water

USEFUL CONTACTS

Tourist information

There are no National Park information centres in the area covered by this guide but lots of information is available on the National Park website: www.lakedistrict.gov.uk.

If you want to talk to someone about what you need, the closest centres are in Keswick (National Park), Coniston (community-run) and Broughton (community-run).

Keswick
0845 901 0845
(calls cost 2p a minute on top of your phone company's access charge)
KeswickTIC@lakedistrict.gov.uk

Coniston
www.conistontic.org
015394 41533
mail@conistontic.org

Broughton
01229 716115
broughtontic@btconnect.com

Accommodation

In addition to the tourist information centres, and the search engines, the Visit Cumbria website has a good database of local accommodation options: www.visitcumbria.com.

Weather

It is well worth consulting either of these forecasts to gauge the best times to be on the tops.

Lake District Weatherline
0844 846 2444
www.lakedistrictweatherline.co.uk

Mountain Weather Information Service
Fully daily mountain forecasts for 3 days at a time (choose Lake District)
www.mwis.org.uk
(choose English and Welsh Forecast/ Lake District)
App: Mountain Forecast Viewer

Transport

Traveline
Bus, train and coach information – such as it is.
www.traveline.info

Stagecoach
Bus information
www.stagecoachbus.com
App: Stagecoach Bus

Ravenglass & Eskdale Railway
The timetable of La'al Ratty, a seasonal narrow-gauge tourist service from Ravenglass to Dalegarth (the only public transport option thereabouts)
https://ravenglass-railway.co.uk/

Organisations

The National Trust
The National Trust owns 90% of the farms in the national park, as well as historic sites and properties, camp sites and car parks.
www.nationaltrust.org.uk
App: National Trust – Days Out

Modern pitching on the bridleway crossing Sty Head

Fix the Fells

Fix the Fells repairs and maintains 330 upland paths in the national park. Read about their work, volunteer or donate on this website.

www.fixthefells.co.uk

Mountain Rescue

The Lake District Search and Mountain Rescue Association manages 12 teams of volunteers across the national park. The site has useful safety information. Downloading the free OS Locate app will enable you to tell the team your grid ref, whether you have phone signal or not, should you need to call them.

www.ldsamra.org.uk

A FELLRANGER'S GLOSSARY

Navigational features

word	explanation
arête	knife-edge ridge
band	binding strip of land
beck	main stream flowing into and through valleys to lakes and rivers
boiler-plates	non-technical term for exposed broad slabs of rock
cairn/man	small pile of loose stones indicating a path or path junction
comb/cove	hanging valley high in the fells
common	undivided land grazed by several farmers
crag	substantial outcrop of rock
dale	valley
dodd	rounded hilltop
drumlin	large mound accumulated beneath a melting glacier
dub	dark pool
fell	mountain pasture, frequently attributed to the whole hill
force	waterfall
garth	small enclosure close to farm-buildings
gate	dialect term for a track
ghyll/gill	steeply sloping watercourse
glen	from British term 'glyn', meaning valley
grain	lesser watercourse above confluence
hag	eroded section of peat-moor
hause, saddle, col, dore, scarth	high gap between fells
holm	dry riverside meadow
hope	secluded valley
howe	hill or mound
ill	treacherous
in-bye pastures	enclosed valley pastures below the rough common grazing
intake	upper limit of valley enclosure
keld	spring
knott	compact or rugged hilltop

ling	heather
lonnin	quiet lane
mell	bald hill
mere	pool or lake
mire	marshy ground
moraine	residual valley-head pillow mound debris left once a glacier melts away
nab	hill-spur or nose
ness	promontory
nether	lower
nook	secluded corner
outcrop	crag or obvious collection of rocks
raise	heap of stones
rake	grooved track
ridding	(the action of) clearing
rigg	ridge
park	enclosed hunting ground
pike	sharp or rocky summit
place	plot of ground
scale	summer pasture shieling (hut)
scarp/scar	steep hillside
scree	weathered rock debris beneath a crag
seat	summer pasture/high place
shaw	small wood
shelter-cairn	circular windbreak wall
sike	small stream
slack	small, shallow or stony valley
slump	sedimentary rock that has slipped creating dykes (intrusions), fractures or ridges
stang	pole
stead	site of farm
sty	steep path
swine	pigs
tarn	small mountain pool from the Norse 'tjorn', meaning tear
traverse	walking route across the fells

trod	path created by animals
trig point	Ordnance Survey triangulation column
thwaite	clearing
wick	inlet or bay or subsidiary farm
water	feeder lake to river
wath	ford
whin	gorse
wray	secluded corner
yeat	gate

Place names

name	**explanation**
Black Sail	a peaty mire that once blanketed the pass, first recorded in 1322 as 'Le Blackzol'
Black'em (Head)	black combe
(River) Bleng	the dark one
Boot	humble dwelling or bend in the river
Bowderdale	the valley with a hut
Cat Bields	wild cat hideout
Black Waugh	the dark stranger (Norse) – the native Celts were termed 'woffs' by Norse folk
Brat's Moss	brat = apron (dialect)
Brock (Crag)	badger (Celtic)
Cow Cove	summer grazing of suckler cattle
Eel Tarn	dangerous bog (Norse)
Ennerdale Fence	an aged ridge wall (only rarely patched with fencing) which stretches from west of Iron Crag to the summit of Scoat Fell
Gavel Neese	gable nose
Glade How	hill of red kite
(Little) Gowder Crag	gowder = echoing rocks
Heron Crag	from erne (Norse) = nesting place of sea eagles
Ill Gill	treacherous ravine
Latterbarrow	rocky lair of wild creatures

Mickledore	big (mickle) + gap (dore)
Moses' Trod	route named after Moses Rigg – a Honister quarryman who took slate by pony to the coast via Wasdale and Miterdale, also famous for his whisky which he concealed in the hefty pony panniers
Ritson's Force	named after the first publican of the Wasdale Head Inn, opened in 1860
Scalderskew	place of the shield-maker + wood (Norse)
Scoat/Scout	projecting rock
Styhead (Pass)	sty = steep path
Swarth Beck	dark stream

Fell names

Just the more intriguing ones…

name	**explanation**
Buckbarrow	he-goat crags
Caw Fell	lesser hill (to Haycock)
Grike	fissured hill
Haycock	stack of drying grass (Cumbrian)
Illgill Head	top of a treacherous ravine
Kirk Fell	mountain grazing owned by the church
Lingmell	heather-clad round hill
Scafell	originally Scawfell, meaning great sheltering height
Scoat Fell	hill with projecting rock
Seatallan	summer pasture belonging to Allein
Yewbarrow	sheep (yow) mountain
Whin Rigg	gorse-clad ridge

Fell name	Height	Volume
Allen Crags	784m/2572ft	Borrowdale
Angletarn Pikes	567m/1860ft	Mardale and the Far East
Ard Crags	581m/1906ft	Buttermere
Armboth Fell	479m/1572ft	Borrowdale
Arnison Crag	434m/1424ft	Patterdale
Arthur's Pike	533m/1749ft	Mardale and the Far East
Bakestall	673m/2208ft	Keswick and the North
Bannerdale Crags	683m/2241ft	Keswick and the North
Barf	468m/1535ft	Keswick and the North
Barrow	456m/1496ft	Buttermere
Base Brown	646m/2119ft	Borrowdale
Beda Fell	509m/1670ft	Mardale and the Far East
Bell Crags	558m/1831ft	Borrowdale
Binsey	447m/1467ft	Keswick and the North
Birkhouse Moor	718m/2356ft	Patterdale
Birks	622m/2241ft	Patterdale
Black Combe	600m/1969ft	Coniston
Black Fell	323m/1060ft	Coniston
Blake Fell	573m/1880ft	Buttermere
Bleaberry Fell	589m/1932ft	Borrowdale
Blea Rigg	556m/1824ft	Langdale
Blencathra	868m/2848ft	Keswick and the North
Bonscale Pike	529m/1736ft	Mardale and the Far East
Bowfell	903m/2963ft	Langdale
Bowscale Fell	702m/2303ft	Keswick and the North
Brae Fell	586m/1923ft	Keswick and the North
Brandreth	715m/2346ft	Borrowdale
Branstree	713m/2339ft	Mardale and the Far East
Brim Fell	795m/2608ft	Coniston

Fell name	Height	Volume
Brock Crags	561m/1841ft	Mardale and the Far East
Broom Fell	511m/1676ft	Keswick and the North
Buckbarrow (Corney Fell)	549m/1801ft	Coniston
Buckbarrow (Wast Water)	430m/1411ft	Wasdale
Calf Crag	537m/1762ft	Langdale
Carl Side	746m/2448ft	Keswick and the North
Carrock Fell	662m/2172ft	Keswick and the North
Castle Crag	290m/951ft	Borrowdale
Catbells	451m/1480ft	Borrowdale
Catstycam	890m/2920ft	Patterdale
Caudale Moor	764m/2507ft	Mardale and the Far East
Causey Pike	637m/2090ft	Buttermere
Caw	529m/1736ft	Coniston
Caw Fell	697m/2287ft	Wasdale
Clough Head	726m/2386ft	Patterdale
Cold Pike	701m/2300ft	Langdale
Coniston Old Man	803m/2635ft	Coniston
Crag Fell	523m/1716ft	Wasdale
Crag Hill	839m/2753ft	Buttermere
Crinkle Crags	840m/2756ft	Langdale
Dale Head	753m/2470ft	Buttermere
Dodd	502m/1647ft	Keswick and the North
Dollywaggon Pike	858m/2815ft	Patterdale
Dove Crag	792m/2599ft	Patterdale
Dow Crag	778m/2553ft	Coniston
Eagle Crag	520m/1706ft	Borrowdale
Eskdale Moor	337m/1105ft	Wasdale
Esk Pike	885m/2904ft	Langdale
Fairfield	873m/2864ft	Patterdale

Fell name	Height	Volume
Fellbarrow	416m/1365ft	Buttermere
Fleetwith Pike	648m/2126ft	Buttermere
Froswick	720m/2362ft	Mardale and the Far East
Gavel Fell	526m/1726ft	Buttermere
Gibson Knott	421m/1381ft	Langdale
Glaramara	783m/2569ft	Borrowdale
Glenridding Dodd	442m/1450ft	Patterdale
Gowbarrow Fell	481m/1578ft	Patterdale
Grange Fell	416m/1365ft	Borrowdale
Grasmoor	852m/2795ft	Buttermere
Gray Crag	697m/2287ft	Mardale and the Far East
Grayrigg Forest	494m/1621ft	Mardale and the Far East
Graystones	456m/1496ft	Keswick and the North
Great Borne	616m/2021ft	Buttermere
Great Calva	690m/2264ft	Keswick and the North
Great Carrs	788m/2585ft	Coniston
Great Cockup	526m/1726ft	Keswick and the North
Great Crag	452m/1483ft	Borrowdale
Great Dodd	857m/2812ft	Patterdale
Great End	907m/2976ft	Borrowdale, Langdale, Wasdale
Great Gable	899m/2949ft	Borrowdale, Wasdale
Great How	523m/1716ft	Wasdale
Great Mell Fell	537m/1762ft	Patterdale
Great Rigg	767m/2516ft	Patterdale
Great Sca Fell	651m/2136ft	Keswick and the North
Great Worm Crag	427m/1401ft	Coniston
Green Crag	489m/1604ft	Coniston
Green Gable	801m/2628ft	Borrowdale
Grey Crag	638m/2093ft	Mardale and the Far East

Fell name	Height	Volume
Grey Friar	772m/2533ft	Coniston
Grey Knotts	697m/2287ft	Borrowdale
Grike	488m/1601ft	Wasdale
Grisedale Pike	791m/2595ft	Buttermere
Hallin Fell	388m/1273ft	Mardale and the Far East
Hard Knott	552m/1811ft	Coniston
Harrison Stickle	736m/2415ft	Langdale
Hart Crag	822m/2697ft	Patterdale
Harter Fell (Eskdale)	653m/2142ft	Coniston
Harter Fell (Mardale)	778m/2553ft	Mardale and the Far East
Hart Side	758m/2487ft	Patterdale
Hartsop above How	586m/1923ft	Patterdale
Hartsop Dodd	618m/2028ft	Mardale and the Far East
Haycock	798m/2618ft	Wasdale
Haystacks	598m/1962ft	Buttermere
Helm Crag	405m/1329ft	Langdale
Helvellyn	950m/3116ft	Patterdale
Hen Comb	509m/1670ft	Buttermere
Heron Pike	621m/2037ft	Patterdale
Hesk Fell	476m/1562ft	Coniston
High Crag	744m/2441ft	Buttermere
High Hartsop Dodd	519m/1703ft	Patterdale
High Pike (Caldbeck)	658m/2159ft	Keswick and the North
High Pike (Scandale Fell)	656m/2152ft	Patterdale
High Raise (Central Fells)	762m/2500ft	Langdale
High Raise (Haweswater)	802m/2631ft	Mardale and the Far East
High Rigg	355m/1165ft	Borrowdale
High Seat	608m/1995ft	Borrowdale
High Spy	653m/2142ft	Borrowdale

Fell name	Height	Volume
High Stile	807m/2648ft	Buttermere
High Street	828m/2717ft	Mardale and the Far East
High Tove	515m/1690ft	Borrowdale
Hindscarth	727m/2385ft	Buttermere
Holme Fell	317m/1040ft	Coniston
Hopegill Head	770m/2526ft	Buttermere
Ill Bell	757m/2484ft	Mardale and the Far East
Illgill Head	609m/1998ft	Wasdale
Iron Crag	640m/2100ft	Wasdale
Kentmere Pike	730m/2395ft	Mardale and the Far East
Kidsty Pike	780m/2559ft	Mardale and the Far East
Kirk Fell	802m/2631ft	Wasdale
Knock Murton	447m/1467ft	Buttermere
Knott	710m/2329ft	Keswick and the North
Knott Rigg	556m/1824ft	Buttermere
Lank Rigg	541m/1775ft	Wasdale
Latrigg	368m/1207ft	Keswick and the North
Ling Fell	373m/1224ft	Keswick and the North
Lingmell	807m/2649ft	Wasdale
Lingmoor Fell	470m/1542ft	Langdale
Little Hart Crag	637m/2090ft	Patterdale
Little Mell Fell	505m/1657ft	Patterdale
Little Stand	739m/2426ft	Langdale
Loadpot Hill	671m/2201ft	Mardale and the Far East
Loft Crag	682m/2237ft	Langdale
Longlands Fell	483m/1585ft	Keswick and the North
Long Side	734m/2408ft	Keswick and the North
Lonscale Fell	715m/2346ft	Keswick and the North
Lord's Seat	552m/1811ft	Keswick and the North

Fell name	Height	Volume
Loughrigg Fell	335m/1099ft	Langdale
Low Fell	423m/1388ft	Buttermere
Low Pike	507m/1663ft	Patterdale
Maiden Moor	576m/1890ft	Borrowdale
Mardale Ill Bell	761m/2497ft	Mardale and the Far East
Meal Fell	550m/1804ft	Keswick and the North
Mellbreak	512m/1680ft	Buttermere
Middle Dodd	653m/2143ft	Patterdale
Middle Fell	585m/1919ft	Wasdale
Muncaster Fell	231m/758ft	Coniston
Nab Scar	450m/1476ft	Patterdale
Nethermost Pike	891m/2923ft	Patterdale
Outerside	568m/1863ft	Buttermere
Pavey Ark	697m/2287ft	Langdale
Pike o'Blisco	705m/2313ft	Langdale
Pike o'Stickle	708m/2323ft	Langdale
Pillar	892m/2926ft	Wasdale
Place Fell	657m/2155ft	Mardale and the Far East
Raise	884m/2900ft	Patterdale
Rampsgill Head	792m/2598ft	Mardale and the Far East
Rannerdale Knotts	355m/1165ft	Buttermere
Raven Crag	463m/1519ft	Borrowdale
Red Pike (Buttermere)	755m/2477ft	Buttermere
Red Pike (Wasdale)	828m/2717ft	Wasdale
Red Screes	777m/2549ft	Patterdale
Rest Dodd	697m/2287ft	Mardale and the Far East
Robinson	737m/2418ft	Buttermere
Rossett Pike	651m/2136ft	Langdale
Rosthwaite Fell	551m/1808ft	Borrowdale

Fell name	Height	Volume
Sail	771m/2529ft	Buttermere
Sale Fell	359m/1178ft	Keswick and the North
Sallows	516m/1693ft	Mardale and the Far East
Scafell	964m/3163ft	Wasdale
Scafell Pike	977m/3206ft	Borrowdale, Langdale, Wasdale
Scar Crags	672m/2205ft	Buttermere
Scoat Fell	843m/2766ft	Wasdale
Seatallan	693m/2274ft	Wasdale
Seathwaite Fell	631m/2070ft	Borrowdale
Seat Sandal	736m/2415ft	Patterdale
Selside Pike	655m/2149ft	Mardale and the Far East
Sergeant Man	736m/2414ft	Langdale
Sergeant's Crag	574m/1883ft	Borrowdale
Sheffield Pike	675m/2215ft	Patterdale
Shipman Knotts	587m/1926ft	Mardale and the Far East
Silver How	395m/1296ft	Langdale
Skiddaw	931m/3054ft	Keswick and the North
Skiddaw Little Man	865m/2838ft	Keswick and the North
Slight Side	762m/2500ft	Wasdale
Souther Fell	522m/1713ft	Keswick and the North
Stainton Pike	498m/1634ft	Coniston
Starling Dodd	635m/2083ft	Buttermere
Steel Fell	553m/1814ft	Langdale
Steel Knotts	433m/1421ft	Mardale and the Far East
Steeple	819m/2687ft	Wasdale
Stickle Pike	376m/1234ft	Coniston
Stone Arthur	503m/1650ft	Patterdale
St Sunday Crag	841m/2759ft	Patterdale
Stybarrow Dodd	846m/2776ft	Patterdale

Fell name	Height	Volume
Swirl How	804m/2638ft	Coniston
Tarn Crag (Easedale)	485m/1591ft	Langdale
Tarn Crag (Longsleddale)	664m/2179ft	Mardale and the Far East
Thornthwaite Crag	784m/2572ft	Mardale and the Far East
Thunacar Knott	723m/2372ft	Langdale
Troutbeck Tongue	363m/1191ft	Mardale and the Far East
Ullock Pike	690m/2264ft	Keswick and the North
Ullscarf	726m/2382ft	Borrowdale
Walla Crag	379m/1243ft	Borrowdale
Wallowbarrow Crag	292m/958ft	Coniston
Walna Scar	621m/2037ft	Coniston
Wandope	772m/2533ft	Buttermere
Wansfell	489m/1604ft	Mardale and the Far East
Watson's Dodd	789m/2589ft	Patterdale
Wether Hill	673m/2208ft	Mardale and the Far East
Wetherlam	762m/2500ft	Coniston
Whinfell Beacon	494m/1620ft	Mardale and the Far East
Whinlatter	517m/1696ft	Keswick and the North
Whin Rigg	536m/1759ft	Wasdale
Whiteless Pike	660m/2165ft	Buttermere
Whiteside	707m/2320ft	Buttermere
White Side	863m/2831ft	Patterdale
Whitfell	573m/1880ft	Coniston
Winterscleugh	471m/1545ft	Mardale and the Far East
Yewbarrow	628m/2060ft	Wasdale
Yoadcastle	494m/1621ft	Coniston
Yoke	706m/2316ft	Mardale and the Far East